Literacy Tutoring That Works: A Look at Successful In-School, After-School, and Summer Programs

Janet C. Richards and Cynthia A. Lassonde

Editors

INTERNATIONAL Reading Association
800 BARKSDALE ROAD, PO BOX 8139
NEWARK, DE 19714-8139, USA
www.reading.org

The International Reading Association attempts, through its publications, to provide a forum for a wide spectrum of opinions on reading. This policy permits divergent viewpoints without implying the endorsement of the Association.

Executive Editor, Books	Corinne M. Mooney
Developmental Editor	Charlene M. Nichols
Developmental Editor	Tori Mello Bachman
Developmental Editor	Stacey L. Reid
Editorial Production Manager	Shannon T. Fortner
Design and Composition Manager	Anette Schuetz

Project Editors   Tori M. Bachman and Rebecca A. Stewart

Cover   Design, Lise Holliker Dykes; Photographs, © 2008 Jupiterimages Corporation (second from top left), Shutterstock (all others)

Library of Congress Cataloging-in-Publication Data

Literacy tutoring that works : a look at successful in-school, after-school, and summer programs / Janet C. Richards and Cynthia A. Lassonde, editors.

  p. cm.

 Includes bibliographical references and index.

 ISBN 978-0-87207-694-5

 1. Reading—Remedial teaching—United States. 2. Literacy programs—United States. 3. Tutors and tutoring—United States.   I. Richards, Janet C.   II. Lassonde, Cynthia A.   III. International Reading Association.

 LB1050.5.L574 2009

 372.43—dc22

                                    2009003667

We dedicate this book to the educators and families who support struggling readers and writers.
—Janet and Cindy

CONTENTS

SECTION I
In-School Literacy Tutoring Programs
5

SECTION II
After-School Literacy Tutoring Programs
83

SECTION III
Summer Literacy Programs
157

ABOUT THE EDITORS

 **Janet C. Richards** is a professor in the Department of Childhood Education and Literacy Studies at the University of South Florida, Tampa, Florida, USA, where she teaches graduate courses in reading, writing, and qualitative research. She has published over 130 scholarly articles and book chapters as well as textbooks on topics such as multiple literacies, teaching cases, and university/public school field-based courses. Her book titled *Integrating Multiple Literacies in K–8 Classrooms: Cases, Commentaries, and Practical Applications* (Erlbaum, 2003), co-authored with Michael McKenna, was one of the top 10 volumes considered for the Edward Fry National Reading Conference Annual Book Award. In 2008 she was selected as the Lansdowne Visiting Scholar at the University of Victoria, British Columbia, Canada. Richards initiated and mentors the University of South Florida Round Table Writing Group for advanced graduate students and faculty. She also organized and supervises a Community of Practice Summer Literacy Camp for children at risk in which master's students collaborate with preservice teachers as they tutor small groups of children. Doctoral students serve as mentors to the program. Richards is editor-in-chief of the *Journal of Reading Education*.

 **Cynthia A. Lassonde** is an associate professor in the Elementary Education and Reading Department at the State University of New York College at Oneonta, New York, USA. Previously an elementary teacher for over 20 years, she now teaches undergraduate and graduate courses in language and literacy development, content literacy, and critical reading and writing to teacher candidates. She is the author of *Strategies and Practice Guide for the New York State Grade 6 English Language Arts Test* (Barrons, 2009), co-author with Susan Israel of *Teacher Collaboration for Professional Learning: Facilitating Study, Research, and Inquiry Communities* (Jossey-Bass, 2009), and co-editor with Susan Israel of *The Ethical Educator: Integrating Ethics Within the Context of Teaching and Teacher Research* (Peter Lang Publishers, 2008) and *Teachers Taking Action: A Comprehensive Guide to Teacher Research* (International Reading Association, 2008). Lassonde is the editor of the journal *Excelsior: Leadership in Teaching and Learning*.

FOREWORD

The question that guides this book and most books on literacy instruction is, How can we increase student reading achievement? Two basic principles for increasing student reading achievement are (1) increase the amount of authentic contextual reading by students, and (2) increase the amount of instruction in reading provided to students. It is clear that students are likely to become better readers if they read more and if they are given more instruction in reading, especially when that instruction is focused on the instructional needs of the students.

Although conceptually simple, the notion of increasing time spent reading and time spent in instruction is not necessarily easy to implement. Attempting to expand reading and reading instruction within the existing school curriculum is a challenge, to say the least. The curriculum is already filled, and schools and teachers seem to be under continual pressure to take on even more instructional responsibilities that go beyond literacy.

One answer to the problem of increasing instructional time and time spent reading is through tutoring programs—both in and out of school. Well-trained, motivated, and closely supervised and supported tutors can provide individual students and small groups of students with the kind of instructional reading experiences that can lead to significant growth in reading achievement.

On the surface, tutoring programs in reading seem ideally suited for helping those students who need the most help. Can it be that hard for adults to tutor students in an activity such as reading that the adults themselves are skilled at doing? And, can it be that hard for schools and teachers to set up such programs for students?

In reality, although clear in concept and seemingly easy to implement, tutoring programs in reading require thoughtful planning and implementation. If not, the tutoring program may not be worth the effort. *The Washington Post* (Glod, 2008) reported that a study of tutoring programs established in Maryland and Virginia as part of the federal Reading First program did not lead to improved student performance in reading. Researchers suggest that the tutoring programs were not well designed and were flawed in their implementation.

For tutoring to work, it must be thoughtfully and thoroughly conceived and planned, well implemented, and supported by schools. That is no small task, and that is where this volume comes in. This book is one of the first of its kind to present educators with principles for designing effective tutoring programs in reading and models of programs that have actually met with success in raising student performance. Readers of this volume will find a valuable resource for developing programs for tutoring in reading, whether in school or out, that work for students.

Well-planned and well-implemented programs can make a difference. I know; I am coauthor of a tutoring program for families called Fast Start for Early Readers (see Padak & Rasinski, 2005). We designed a program that was simple and quick for families to implement, yet based on fundamentally sound and developmentally appropriate principles of literacy instruction. It involves the reading of authentic texts, followed by simple word study. Key to the program is the support provided by teachers. Our research and the research of others has shown the program to be remarkably positive in improving young students' reading performance, and empowering and engaging for families searching for a way to help their children learn to read (e.g., Rasinski & Stevenson, 2005).

Teaching reading is not easy work. Neither is tutoring in reading. And developing, implementing, and supporting effective tutoring programs in reading are also challenges. This volume is a welcome and long-awaited first step in bringing tutoring in reading and writing into the fold of the literacy education profession. I commend editors Janet Richards and Cindy Lassonde and the various chapter contributors for developing this volume that has been needed for so long. And I commend you, the reader, for taking on the challenge of developing tutoring programs that work for students.

Timothy Rasinski
Kent State University
Kent, Ohio

REFERENCES

Glod, M. (2008, June 13). Mandated tutoring not helping MD and VA scores. *The Washington Post,* p. B01. Retrieved June 17, 2008, from www.washingtonpost.com/wp-dyn/content/article/2008/06/12/AR2008061203681.html

Padak, N., & Rasinski, T. (2005). *Fast start for early readers: A research-based send-home literacy program.* New York: Scholastic.

Rasinski, T., & Stevenson, B. (2005). The effects of Fast Start reading, a fluency-based home involvement reading program, on the reading achievement of beginning readers. *Reading Psychology: An International Quarterly, 26*(2), 109–125.

ACKNOWLEDGMENTS

We are pleased that the International Reading Association (IRA) published this book. From the onset of our ideas for this volume, we believed our purposes were strongly connected to IRA's overarching goal of enhancing children's and adolescents' literacy achievements.

We first must acknowledge Corinne M. Mooney, Executive Editor of Books, and Tori Bachman, Developmental Editor. Corinne and Tori were always available to answer our questions and assist us with small and large dilemmas related to the completion of this project.

We also want to thank the proposal reviewers, Mary DeKonty Applegate, Helen Hoffner, Gay Ivey, Charlene Nichols, and James Phillips. They took considerable time to thoughtfully and thoroughly offer specific comments that helped us make this book better.

As always, we thank our preservice teachers and graduate students and applaud all classroom teachers and literacy teacher educators. Their enthusiasm for the teaching and learning of literacy is infectious. We learn from them every day.

We also applaud the chapter contributors who enthusiastically responded to our call for manuscripts. We are impressed with their professional experiences, scholarliness, and dedication to enhancing literacy learning opportunities for elementary through high school students. They truly care about children's literacy development.

Finally, we are most grateful to our families, who always support our work. They have come to recognize that literacy is just another member of our families!

INTRODUCTION

Janet C. Richards and Cynthia A. Lassonde

We must do more—to make sure every child can read well.
—President Bill Clinton, State of the Union Address, February 4, 1997

*We must increase funds for students who struggle—and make sure
these children get the special help they need.*
—President George W. Bush, State of the Union Address, January 23, 2007

As the opening quotes from two presidencies' State of the Union Addresses express, the United States continues to search for ways to help struggling students. However, there is hope! Research shows that "students who are behind in reading can catch up to grade level with additional reading instruction and tutoring [in school], after school, and in the summer" (*Bringing Education to After-School Programs,* 1999, n.p.). Likewise "evidence indicates well designed tutoring programs utilizing trained volunteers and non-professionals can be effective in improving children's reading skills" (U.S. Department of Education, 2001, as cited in *Background Research: Tutoring Programs,* 2005, p. 2).

The idea for this edited volume evolved from our recognition of the need for a unified compilation of information about locally sponsored, evidence-based, quality literacy tutoring programs so educators would have a comprehensive resource to "make sure every child can read well" (Clinton, 1997) and "make sure these children get the special help they need" (Bush, 2007). As Allington and McGill-Franzen (2003) state, "If current education reform efforts are to be successful in narrowing the reading achievement gap, the intervention designs must reflect the scientific research available" (p. 69).

Despite recognition of the importance of evidence-based tutoring initiatives, there are few reports that examine the basic elements of new or established local tutoring programs honestly and objectively (Elbaum, Vaughn, Hughes, & Moody, 2000). In fact, only a small number of published articles and papers presented at scholarly conferences have highlighted local tutoring initiatives. Furthermore, a review of the literature shows that many of these reports were anecdotal and some of the research methodology was flawed (Elbaum et al., 2000; Wasik, 1998), and none have been compiled into a cohesive volume. Although large-scale tutoring programs, such as America Reads, Reading Recovery, and Success for All are well known (Miller, 2008), to date, no comprehensive resource exists that synthesizes what goes on in local university, school, and community-sponsored literacy programs (see Wimer & Gunther, 2006). Unless leaders of local tutoring programs explicitly document their work objectively and tie their work to research-based results, those who want to develop, coordinate, redesign, or participate in similar tutorial-based instruction have few

Literacy Tutoring That Works: A Look at Successful In-School, After-School, and Summer Programs, edited by Janet C. Richards
and Cynthia A. Lassonde. © 2009 International Reading Association.

exemplary models to emulate (Miller, 2008). The evidence within this book supplies this needed information.

We are pleased that this volume will serve as a research-based resource and also a practical source of information, a type of handbook, for those who want to begin a literacy tutoring program, enhance or redirect the focus of their current program, or conduct research that illuminates dimensions of their current tutoring initiatives. Thus, this book provides a helpful framework for education faculty, preservice teachers, and graduate students who want to coordinate a university/public school literacy tutoring collaboration; speaks to community volunteers and families engaged in literacy tutoring projects; and also offers information to classroom teachers, school administrators, reading coaches, and language arts supervisors who want to engage in tutoring projects that will foster the literacy achievement of children and youth with whom they work.

The chapters in this volume provide readers with an understanding of the following:

- How to structure and successfully operate in-school, after-school, and summer literacy tutoring programs
- The variety of tutoring initiatives that exist
- The theoretical perspectives that guide these programs
- Who tutors in these programs
- The children and adolescents who attend these programs
- The range of instruction offered in these initiatives
- The diverse learning contexts in which these quality programs take place

Most important, the chapters supply research evidence illuminating what makes these initiatives quality programs. The chapters also cast light on common themes and patterns as well as differences across programs.

This book does not tout specific commercial reading programs. Note also that contributors do not offer information about large-scale national and state literacy projects. Rather, the book highlights quality, local, university/school and community-sponsored literacy tutoring programs with diverse goals, objectives, and methods that are situated in various geographical regions of the United States. These quality programs may or may not be funded by school districts or nonprofit agencies. The majority of the programs are free of charge but a few do charge a fee for tutoring sessions. Tutors in the programs range from teacher educators, teachers, preservice teachers, and graduate students to family members, retirees, and other community volunteers.

Enhancing reading and writing abilities is a common goal of all of the tutoring programs portrayed in this volume. However, despite this shared purpose, the information presented offers a rich diversity of tutoring initiatives according to the following:

- The context in which tutoring takes place
- Whether tutoring is offered in small groups or through one-on-one interactions
- What program leaders believe about effective reading and writing instruction
- The philosophical stance undergirding tutoring programs' progress and direction
- How tutors are trained
- Whether instruction links text-based literacy with other symbol systems (e.g., the visual and communicative arts) or deliberately uses the arts as a pathway and

foundation for literacy (e.g., film-making or creative writing)

Of further interest is that a few chapters concentrate on the connection between tutoring initiatives and graduate education majors' professional development.

Regardless of differences in instructional approaches and particular focus of research, the majority of tutoring programs described in this volume take a broad view of literacy; that is, literacy is not simply the ability to read and write. Rather, literacy is the interpretation of a wide range of text based upon personal experiences, perceptions, and beliefs. Moreover literacy instruction encourages children and adolescents to read and think critically, embrace habits of wide reading for pleasure and information, and use "reading and writing for a variety of personally meaningful and socially valued purposes" (Spielberger & Halpern, 2002, p. 5). As Kathleen Blake Yancey, past president of the National Council of Teachers of English, explains in many of her recent essays and speeches, the 21st century is the century of literacies with new practices for multimodal communication—from books and paper to computer screens, web logs, and text messages (see for example, "Speakers at Annual Convention," retrieved December 19, 2008, from www.ncte.org/annual/speakers).

How This Book Is Organized

You will notice we have positioned the chapters in this book in three discrete sections. Section I supplies information about in-school literacy programs. Section II offers information about after-school literacy programs, and Section III provides descriptions of summer literacy programs. We hope that organizing the book into these discrete sections will allow you to easily locate information about program structures that connect to your interests and needs.

Each of the three sections in the book begins with an overview to alert you to the information that follows in the chapters in that section. All chapters adhere to a similar configuration to help you locate information easily. For example, each chapter begins with a brief, authentic vignette to help you personally connect with the participants and the instruction offered in the tutoring program discussed. (To protect the identities of the young participants all names of program participants throughout the book are pseudonyms, and many of the dialogue transcripts are composites.) Then, chapter contributors describe the context in which their initiatives take place and the framework undergirding their tutoring sessions. They also list the questions that guided their research, present the theoretical perspectives in which their inquiries are grounded, and describe their data collection methods. In addition, chapter contributors include the limitations of their inquiries, their data analysis procedures, results of the research, and implications of their findings. To close the chapters, contributors impart practical insights. They list key points they want you to glean from their work by supplying a Words of Advice paragraph that delineates what they have learned as supervisors of extended literacy learning programs.

> Use reading and writing for a variety of personally meaningful and socially valued purposes.

The book's appendix contains an extensive annotated bibliography of important research related to tutoring. The studies listed there cross age ranges and settings. We hope these studies will provide you with a solid foundation of research on which to build your own work.

All of the chapter contributors have included their e-mail addresses along with their biographical information at the end of their chapters. The contributors want to hear from you. They hope to answer your questions and offer any information you might need about the projects they describe in their chapters.

How to Use This Book

You can use this book in different ways. Perhaps you seek information about literacy tutoring programs with a particular emphasis, such as those with an imagery or mentor-based focus. Or, because each section of the book supplies information about program models offered either in school, after school, or in the summer, you might initially read the chapters in one of these sections because you want to learn more about tutoring initiatives that are offered during a particular time frame and in a specific context. Perhaps you want to acquire a comprehensive, broad overview of the literacy tutoring programs presented in the book before you focus on a particular section, so you might choose to read the volume in sequential order and then reread certain sections of the chapters, such as research methodologies or tutoring focus, or review particular chapters that capture your attention and relate to your needs. Regardless of how you choose to read this book, we hope you find it useful. And we'd like to hear from you.

Janet (JRichards@coedu.usf.edu)
Cindy (Lassonc@oneonta.edu)

REFERENCES

Allington, R.L., & McGill-Franzen, A. (2003). The impact of summer reading setback on the reading achievement gap. *Phi Delta Kappan, 85*(1), 68–75.

Background research: Tutoring programs. (2005). Center for Prevention Research and Development, Institute for Government and Public Affairs, University of Illinois, Urbana-Champaign. Retrieved December 19, 2008, from www.cprd.uiuc.edu/pubs/documents/ResearchSummary_Tutoring.pdf

Bringing education to after-school programs. (1999, Summer). Retrieved April 22, 2008, from www.ed.gov/pubs/After_School_Programs/index.html

Bush, G.W. (2007). *State of the Union address.* Retrieved May 21, 2008, from www.cbsnews.com/stories/2007/01/23/politics/main2391957.shtml

Clinton, W.J. (1997). *State of the Union address.* Retrieved May 21, 2008, from www.presidency.ucsb.edu/ws/index.php?pid=53358

Elbaum, B., Vaughn, S., Hughes, M.T., & Moody, S.W. (2000). How effective are one-to-one tutoring programs in reading for elementary students at-risk for reading failure? A meta-analysis of the intervention research. *Journal of Behavioral Psychology, 92*(4), 605–619.

Miller, C.P. (2008). *What reading research says about volunteer tutoring.* Retrieved April 22, 2008, from www.literacyconnections.com/ResearchCPM.html

Spielberger, J., & Halpern, R. (with Pitale, S., Nelson, E., Mello-Temple, S., Ticer-Wurr, L., et al.). (2002). *The role of after-school programs in children's literacy development.* Chicago: University of Chicago, Chapin Hall Center for Children.

Wasik, B.A. (1998). Volunteer tutoring programs in reading: A review. *Reading Research Quarterly, 33*(3), 266–291. doi:10.1598/RRQ.33.3.2

Wimer, C., & Gunther, R. (2006, October). *Summer success: Challenges and strategies in creating quality academically focused summer programs* (Issues and Opportunities in Out-of-School Time Evaluation, Brief No. 9). Cambridge, MA: Harvard Family Research Project.

SECTION I

In-School Literacy Tutoring Programs

We—educators, policymakers, families, and community members—are all accountable for students' literacy achievement. The in-school literacy interventions presented in Section I of this book aim to ensure that students who are at risk can achieve academic proficiency. We view the concept of being at risk not only through social or economic perspectives but also through the perspective of an academic achievement gap.

Chapter 1 in this section discusses STELLAR tutoring. Authored by James V. Hoffman, Melissa Mosley, Deborah A. Horan, Katie Russell, Heather K. Warren, and Audra K. Roach, this chapter describes the development and use of a Web-based video system to support preservice teachers in elementary tutoring experiences. The website they describe offers interactive capabilities for faculty and preservice teachers to discuss video cases with immediate applications to tutoring experiences.

One organization that works to enrich students' literacy success is Big Brothers and Big Sisters of the Sun Coast, Inc. This organization works with professors from the University of South Florida, Sarasota/Manatee, and with community members who volunteer their time in two counties in southern Florida. The Reading Bigs program builds mentor relationships around literacy events. In Chapter 2, Elizabeth Larkin and G. Pat Wilson describe how mentoring relationships and meaningful literacy events enriched the background knowledge and world view of students and motivated students to read.

In another tutoring initiative, Nancy Frey, Diane Lapp, and Douglas Fisher, all professors from San Diego State University, learned of a local school district's plan to raise student achievement through a retention program mandating that students significantly below grade level should repeat first grade. The professors offered their support and stepped in to become accountable for students' learning by developing an intervention program to augment students' classroom instruction. Chapter 3 shares the results of this study. The district anticipated first-grade retention rates before the booster-shot program would be higher in poor and urban elementary schools in the district than in more advantaged schools. However, statistically, results indicated that gains made during the intervention closed the achievement gap between the two schools studied.

In Chapter 4, Mellinee Lesley reports findings of her study of an in-school intervention program that involved struggling adolescent readers who were identified as at risk for academic failure. Through her work with the Communities in Schools program, she noted how students selected and responded to texts in a literacy study group setting. This setting was designed to motivate students to take interpretive authority over texts through the incorporation of performance strategies. Participants became accountable for closing the achievement gap.

Graduate students, elementary teachers, and university professors learn how they can help struggling readers in Chapter 5. Authors Kelly B. Cartwright, Donna S. Savage, Kathryn D.S. Morgan, and Brian J. Nichols share how students benefited from research-based, individualized instruction in a school–university partnership.

Chapter 6, authored by Eva Garin and W. Dorsey Hammond, explains how professional development school reading clinics open spaces for preservice teachers to be accountable for students' literacy learning. In addition, results indicate that participation in the professional development school reading clinics affected students' reading achievement and motivation.

The chapters in this section all serve to inform educators and community leaders about effective, scientifically researched, theoretically based in-school interventions that show us how we can situate ourselves in positions of accountability to intervene when students need our help in filling in literacy achievement gaps.

CHAPTER 1

STELLAR Tutoring in Preservice Teacher Preparation: Exploring Video Case Support for Learning to Teach

James V. Hoffman, Melissa Mosley, Deborah A. Horan, Katie Russell, Heather K. Warren, and Audra K. Roach

Katrina, a preservice teacher, after her first day of tutoring (January 31, 2008):

> This actually turned out to be really difficult for me. I am not sure if I can explain exactly what happened, but I didn't really know what to do. Maybe I was asking the wrong kind of questions to engage him. I would ask him things about the story that was illustrated on the pages, but he still didn't answer any questions correctly. I was really baffled and need some advice about what to do with this student. I felt really overwhelmed and baffled by my session with Todd. I really would like to get more background information on him. Before today, I felt pretty confident about my tutoring skills because I tutored a kindergartener, second grader, and fourth grader last semester in Spanish, mainly on reading skills. I also have always felt pretty "good with kids." However, today I felt pretty disheartened and awkward. I'm going to try very hard to make our future sessions better than today's but may need some help!

Katrina after the completion of the semester of tutoring (May 1, 2008):

> I really can't describe how much this experience helped me understand so many things about teaching that I hadn't personally experienced yet. I became much more aware of the way I spoke to Todd, trying to phrase things in ways that weren't direct questions but elicited meaningful responses from him to enable him to connect to text. I began to be able to see reading through his eyes.... I have been reading for such a long time that it's hard to imagine what it's like for a child.

Katrina is just beginning her learning-to-teach journey. Her reflections before and after a semester of intensive tutoring reveal the range of emotional, intellectual, and social challenges of this process. Through this semester-long experience, Katrina has developed practical knowledge, refined the skills of developing knowledge through experience, and developed stamina for the journey ahead. In this chapter, we focus on the qualities and impact of the tutoring program that is part of Katrina's teacher preparation experience.

We examine Katrina's and two other preservice teachers' participation in a tutoring practicum

---

Literacy Tutoring That Works: A Look at Successful In-School, After-School, and Summer Programs, edited by Janet C. Richards and Cynthia A. Lassonde. © 2009 International Reading Association.

and their interactions with the Supportive Technology for the Education of Literacy Learners and Reading (STELLAR) website at the University of Texas at Austin. We also draw on multiple data sources to describe the learning of the preservice teachers and conclude with implications and words of advice. We will begin by providing an overview of the tutoring practicum and the STELLAR website.

Within the STELLAR tutoring context, we partner university preservice teachers with first-grade children at a public school serving a low-income, predominantly Hispanic community. Preservice teachers engage in biweekly, one-on-one tutoring with one child who is in first or second grade for a total of 24 sessions. During these 45-minute sessions, we expect our preservice teachers (tutors) to offer instruction in response to students' needs, backgrounds, and interests. Course instructors and teaching assistants guide discussions with the preservice teacher tutors, including discussions of course readings, tutor-authored lesson plans, and subsequent reflective posting within the STELLAR website listserv.

Our tutorial program is organized around the following instructional components:

- *Read-Aloud* for comprehension and appreciation
- *Language Experience* for the creation of texts from shared experiences
- *Poetry Warm-Ups* for phonological/phonemic awareness and fluency
- *Sentence Work* for sentence structure, grammar, and self-monitoring
- *Guided Reading* for strategic reading in meaningful texts
- *Word Work* for decoding and word recognition
- *Build-Up Reading* for rereading to build fluency
- *Inquiry* for flexibility, comprehension, and content learning
- *Jokes and Riddles* for language play, motivation, and vocabulary

The semester begins with tutors focusing on four components: read-aloud, language experience, poetry warm-ups, and jokes and riddles. As we introduce other components throughout the semester, tutors increase their repertoire. For each tutoring session, our preservice teachers select components they determine most appropriate to the needs of their students.

The STELLAR website was created to further support our preservice teachers in their reading tutorials and in their practical knowledge of these instructional components. (You may access this site through the following link, after registering as a guest: www.edb.utexas.edu/visionawards/hoffman/.) This Web-based program provided preservice teachers with

- Multiple video introductions to and demonstrations of each tutorial component
- Transcripts of the video interactions
- "Expert" commentary on video clips offered in side notes
- Opportunities for reflective responses and interactions on STELLAR's message board by both tutors and members of the instructional team (Figure 1.1)

Our preservice teachers can access, view, review, and respond to videos at any time through the STELLAR website. However, we sequenced the viewings to intentionally complement class lectures and readings over the course of the semester.

Figure 1.1 STELLAR Tutorial Component

- Build-up Reading
- Guided Reading
- Inquiry
- Jokes & Riddles
- Language Experience
- Poetry Warm-up
- Read Alouds
- Sentence Study
- Word Work
- Viewing
- Guest Tour

Video Tutorial: Martin Luther King

Back to the Video List

Martin Luther King

Annotation

Crystal opens spaces for the student to respond in conversational ways about the book. Together they engage in the strategy of connecting this book with other books they have read. Notice that it's more than just, "this reminds me of...". These are specific connections to content and themes of different books.

PAUSED   0:00:59.097

We used to read them. Last year I read some. And they had some real pictures and a fake... fake pictures.

Add Your Message in the space below.

[Clear] [Post this Message »]

View All Messages »

The STELLAR program was not designed as a substitute for hands-on practicum experiences but rather as a critical aspect of an instructional cycle that included readings, viewings, postings, Web-based interactions, and face-to-face discussions. To prepare for class viewings and discussions, preservice teachers individually examined how these instructional components were realized within sample classrooms as well as actualized in their tutoring experiences. This cyclic process provided a cognitive apprenticeship model that supported teacher reflection (Figure 1.2).

Questions Guiding the Research

We designed the current study to better understand the support that video cases can provide in learning to teach. To critically examine and inform the tutorial experience of our preservice teachers, we designed a qualitative study (Mertens, 2005) that addressed the following questions:

- What are the sources that preservice teachers draw upon to guide their thinking and their practices when engaging in a reading tutorial?

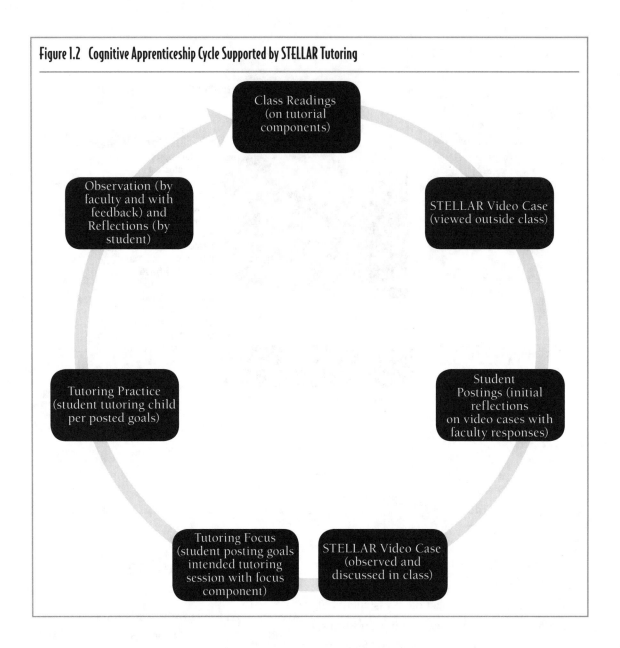

Figure 1.2 Cognitive Apprenticeship Cycle Supported by STELLAR Tutoring

Class Readings (on tutorial components)

STELLAR Video Case (viewed outside class)

Student Postings (initial reflections on video cases with faculty responses)

STELLAR Video Case (observed and discussed in class)

Tutoring Focus (student posting goals intended tutoring session with focus component)

Tutoring Practice (student tutoring child per posted goals)

Observation (by faculty and with feedback) and Reflections (by student)

• How do video case interactions support the development of participants' teaching practices?

For the longer term, we will use these data to continue to revise the video cases and the uses of them following a formative research design (Reinking & Bradley, 2008).

Theoretical Background and Perspectives

Hoffman and Roller (2001) document widespread beliefs concerning the significant need for preservice teachers to tutor local elementary students in reading, to work with students of diverse backgrounds, and to experience supervised field placements before student teaching.

The International Reading Association (2003) finds that tutoring was typically included as part of field experiences in the eight university programs they highlighted for excellence in reading teacher preparation.

However, research to date reveals very little about the qualities of these tutoring experiences (Fang & Ashley, 2004; Fitzgerald, 2001; Juel, 1996). This lack of research is all the more surprising given mounting evidence that beginning teachers highly value early field experiences (Sailors, Keehn, Harmon, & Martinez, 2005). Indeed, Fang and Ashley (2004) explain that preservice teachers cited tutoring as one of the most valuable aspects of their reading preparation courses. Given the opportunity to explore concepts and strategies inside of their field experiences, preservice teachers became more prepared and confident as future teachers of children with reading difficulties, and they developed more positive attitudes toward the teaching profession.

Hedrick, McGee, and Mittag (2000) report that tutoring influenced the attitudes, beliefs, and perceptions of preservice teachers, as they learned to flexibly apply and adjust strategies to the needs of individual students in particular socioeconomic and cultural contexts. Furthermore, these preservice teachers demonstrated new professional knowledge and insights on teaching and learning, including for the importance of flexible, individualized instruction based upon careful observation of children's reading and writing behaviors. In tutoring programs that involve careful planning, monitoring, and analyzing of tutorial experiences, tutors may be better prepared to adapt instruction for children of linguistically and culturally diverse populations (Harmon, Hedrick, Strecker, Martinez, & Perez, 2001). Given this increasingly widespread use of field-based tutorial experiences and the promise of programs that design and manage tutorials effectively, we identified a need for further research that closely examines tutoring and the ways in which tutorial programs support the development of knowledgeable, reflective reading teachers in diverse settings.

In addition to addressing the role of tutorials in diverse settings, we examined the increased interest and use of video case-based learning in preservice teacher education. Although no single model for programs adopts a video case-based approach, recent programs integrate high-quality videos to demonstrate particular aspects of teaching (e.g., comprehension strategy instruction), guided discussion of the content presented, and sometimes opportunities for learners to engage in Web-based interaction (Harrison, Pead, & Sheard, 2006). Similar to traditional methods of case-based study, video case-based learning provides opportunities for students to observe, discuss, and reflect on experts in authentic field-based settings (Teale, Leu, Labbo, & Kinzer, 2002).

In some models of video learning environments, a case consists of individual lessons demonstrating exemplary classroom instruction, such as the widely studied Reading Classroom Explorer (RCE) in which viewers can look broadly across instructional practices in a wide variety of contexts (Ferdig, Roehler, & Pearson, 2006). Other video-based models present individual classrooms as cases, such as in Case Technologies to Enhance Literacy Learning (CTELL; Kinzer, Cammack, Labbo, Teale, & Sanny, 2006). Video cases offer several immediate advantages over traditional print-based case studies, such as easy access for watching and revisiting particular scenes with differing focal points under consideration (Kinzer & Risko, 1998). Additionally, these Web-based hypermedia environments afford users opportunities to navigate related classroom artifacts, to explore links to related articles or websites, and to interact in online discussion forums.

Although technology expands options for preservice teacher education, studies of effectiveness concerning various approaches to video case-based learning across different contexts are yet to come. In a review of video technology usage in teacher education reforms, Wang and Hartley (2003) conclude, "the effects of video technology in supporting teacher education reform are more often assumed than carefully documented" (p. 129). Wang and Hartley point specifically to scarce research evidence for how video technology might change teachers' conceptualizations and knowledge of teaching and learning as well as how those changes might translate to teachers' instructional practices and work with children of diverse backgrounds. More research is needed concerning how preservice teachers learn from videos as well as how to better support their engagement with videos (Boling, 2007). Although researchers have given some attention to video case programs, few explorations exist of when, how, and for what purposes different types of video cases might be used successfully.

> The effects of video technology in supporting teacher education reform are more often assumed than carefully documented.

Methodology

Following Erickson (1986), we focused on uncovering the understandings of the participants as they engaged in tutorials during the process of learning to teach. We drew on multiple data sources using constant comparative methodology to construct individual case studies and cross-case analyses. The research team included three faculty members and three graduate students. All but one of the faculty members actively supported the tutoring through observation of sessions, feedback to lesson plans, responses to readings, and participation in class discussions.

Participants

Our participants included 19 preservice teachers (tutors) enrolled in a reading assessment course and participating in STELLAR, as described previously, and their first- and second-grade students. We focus our analysis on three participants and their first-grade students. The participants were purposely sampled based upon various criteria allowing for maximum variation within the sample. Such factors included participation in different tutor coaching groups as well as a range of participant experiences and background contrasts as students entered our teacher education program.

Typical of many teacher education programs, variation among our preservice teachers was not reflective of the cultural and linguistic diversity of the elementary school population, which was 98% Hispanic. Although Katrina, Emily, and Colleen reflect the trend in which the majority of preservice teachers in the United States identify as white, they do reflect maximum variation in background among their peers.

Katrina, who previously held an undergraduate degree in Spanish, was a 23-year-old student pursuing a post-baccalaureate degree in education. She came from a small town in Texas and a family of teachers. Katrina hoped to teach elementary as well as English as a Second Language (ESL) students. Katrina tutored Todd, a white student. A second participant, Emily, was an undergraduate student from Texas, pursuing an elementary certification. She came from a family of avid readers and she tutored Jonathan, a Hispanic male student. The final participant, Colleen, was a 27-year-old student who entered the teacher preparation program in 2008 when she returned to college to complete an undergraduate degree. Colleen had pursued a career as an artist for seven years before entering our teacher preparation program. She moved to Austin, Texas, where she found that she could be herself and in her words "take my time, and develop an appreciation for reading, thought, and community, while creating the family and home I cherish today" (personal correspondence, May 2, 2008). Colleen tutored Isabella, a Hispanic student.

The semester before our course, all three of these preservice teachers had participated in a different university–school partnership. Katrina, Emily, and Colleen described this previous reading tutorial program in our pretutoring survey as "low" in terms of preparation work (i.e., less than one hour of preparation for each session) and low (Colleen) to high (Katrina) on impact in terms of the knowledge developed.

Data Sources

We drew from a variety of learning artifacts collected during the semester. These included various interactions and reflections posted to the STELLAR website, such as responses to course readings and video cases; biweekly lesson plans and reflections of subsequent tutoring sessions in which these plans were implemented; and case study reports written by each participant concerning her student. Other data sources included instructional and observational notes taken during class sessions, tutoring sessions, and the final oral examination. Pre- and posttutoring surveys further added to our analysis.

Data Analysis

We analyzed case files for each participant for evidence of influential sources on the preservice

teachers' thinking and instructional practices. We created codes using a constant comparative methodology, focusing special attention on the influence of the STELLAR program. We looked across cases as well. Finally, we drew on our observational notes to triangulate the findings from the analysis of the collected artifacts.

Limitations

This study is limited to a focus on preservice teachers' reflections on tutoring practices with the support of video cases. Although there was direct observation of the preservice teachers in tutoring, there was no attempt made to systematically document changes in practice as a result of participation in the program nor was there any attempt to measure student outcomes (or growth) through participation in the study.

Results

We coded between 30 and 50 instances in the data of influences on tutoring. In our analysis of the three cases of preservice teacher learning, as previously stated, we found a total of four major influences on tutoring: reflections on practice, STELLAR videos, course readings, and interactions with instructors. We identified various examples across these four influences for each of the participants; however, we draw selectively from their examples due to the length constraints of this chapter.

Influences of Reflections on Practice: Examples From Colleen and Katrina

We saw evidence of the participants reflecting on practice as a means to build practical knowledge for their tutoring sessions and to construct beginning expertise in the teaching of reading. Participants drew from their increasing repertoire of instructional strategies to design tutoring sessions.

Both Katrina and Colleen expressed cause-and-effect relationships between their actions and their students' successes within any literacy activity. For example, Katrina noted that Todd did not comprehend a poem that contained the idiom "wear many hats." She wrote, "I needed to be really explicit throughout the duration of our session about what 'wearing many hats' means so that hopefully, at the end, he would get it" (Tutoring reflection, February 12, 2008).

> I also hope to continue to deepen our conversations about read-aloud books in the hopes that his reading comprehension skills strengthen even more.

Similarly, Colleen worked on extending text length for read-alouds to scaffold Isabella's engagement with stories. Colleen wrote in a reflection,

> I found a Dr. Seuss bookmark for us to use at the halfway point today, and she was very thrilled. When I saw her attention waning, I pushed her through a few more pages and then we put the marker in. (Tutoring reflection, April 1, 2008)

Neither Katrina nor Colleen lowered their expectations for their students based on what they assessed. Instead, they saw their roles as scaffolds between what their students might do alone and with assistance. In that way, Katrina and Colleen built practices that supported their students through their reflection on practice.

Colleen and Katrina both valued collaboration as necessary for effective instruction, based on reflections on their practice. The practical knowledge they gained allowed them to engage their students as equal partners in the literacy activity. When using the instructional component called sentence work, these preservice teachers and their students cut apart words from a sentence and built new sentences to explore

language structure. Colleen developed a belief about learning from her student that she called "teamwork." Teamwork entailed working side-by-side with her student to build new sentences, and Colleen and Isabella enacted the role of "word acrobats" together. In this practice, Colleen interacted as a teammate with Isabella. In read-alouds, however, Colleen focused on finding the just-right scaffold and was less likely to use language of teamwork.

In Katrina's case, she used the tutoring component of read-aloud to engage in teamwork with Todd. Katrina saw the read-aloud as a place where Todd wanted to become more active, as he would often read along with her. She wrote, "I also hope to continue to deepen our conversations about read-aloud books in the hopes that his reading comprehension skills strengthen even more" (Tutoring reflection, March 31, 2008).

Katrina reflected that she might let Todd know the theme of the day before reading a children's literature text aloud. Her purpose was to provide Todd with a job during the read-aloud. She wrote,

> In explicitly framing our lesson before it begins through connecting the lesson's theme to Todd as an individual, I give him something to search for in all the texts we will explore throughout the session. This gives him a basis for discussion to which he is more than capable of contributing. (Tutoring reflection, March 31, 2008)

Katrina constructed this belief through her observations of Todd's reading behaviors during read-alouds.

Influences of STELLAR Videos on Tutoring Lessons: Examples From Colleen and Emily

In addition to personal reflection, the building of practical knowledge was enhanced through the STELLAR video cases. Emily relied on STELLAR descriptions and demonstrations of instructional components, often writing enthusiastically about new strategies to implement with Jonathan, especially if she perceived the strategy as a means to target a necessary skill for Jonathan. For instance, when she viewed the segment on sentence work, she commented,

> My student Jonathan was so quick to create sentences when we created our book. I think that he is going to love this activity! His sentences tended to have the structure (I am at the library..., I am at the cafeteria). I think that this activity could encourage him to add some wonderful details into his sentences. (STELLAR online posting, February 11, 2008)

Similarly, Colleen reacted positively to the mystery word component by stating, "I think this will become my favorite part of tutoring—better than stories, better than glitter-glue, and better than jokes. I'm serious. We will be word acrobats" (STELLAR online posting, February 2, 2008).

These preservice teachers reacted to STELLAR videos as sources of inspiration that encouraged new instructional strategies not otherwise attempted. On describing the initial book that Emily and Jonathan created together, Emily noted,

> It's so important to be able to build a relationship with the student. My student really opened up when we began to take pictures around the school. I think this video really inspired me to do some really creative activities with my student. (STELLAR online posting, February 4, 2008)

The STELLAR videos supported Emily in reflecting on practice and considering how she might approach certain strategies differently. For example, Emily refined her read-aloud practice after watching an example of a read-aloud in a tutoring video on the STELLAR website. Emily observed the teacher engaging the student. She explained,

> I love how the teacher set it up as if she was the student and the student was teaching her. I sometimes feel as though he [Jonathan] may not be paying attention during the book, but maybe I need to improve my comments on the book. (STELLAR online posting, February 18, 2008)

Emily reflected on her own performance through STELLAR as well as how she used the online discussion board to reflect on practice.

In the same vein, Colleen reflected on building upon prior knowledge and the colearner relationship that she observed in the video. To this she added what she imagined as possible future engagements with Isabella during a second viewing:

> First of all, what a great little girl [the student in the video]. She is very interactive with the book and knowledgeable about the topic, which makes the experience seem very conversational (and lets it build upon prior knowledge) while sharing the story.... I love nonfiction books (especially with good art) and would love to move into place where we [Isabella and I] could do some history digging into a topic that we both have prior knowledge to contribute. I think it would be a nice arena in which to idea build and swap thoughts on life. (STELLAR online posting, February 16, 2008)

Colleen linked her observations of the STELLAR video with her own practice. She used the online posting to consider what kinds of books would allow her to scaffold her student into discoveries.

Influences of Course Readings: Examples From Colleen and Emily

A third influence on the construction of practical knowledge that surfaced in the cross-case analysis was course readings. The course readings were a source of tutoring ideas that allowed participants to raise questions about their practice. Emily responded to one reading

(Johnston, 1997), "Recently I have become so lost in my role during guided reading. It was motivating to read the various different strategies" (Reading response, March 18, 2008). The importance of continually learning about her practice came through in many of Emily's reflections. She often wrote about her changing views of assessment. She was improving through practice but also drew on course readings for support.

Similarly, Colleen drew on course readings to enhance her work with Isabella. Colleen's reading of Kuhn's (2003) chapter on fluency inspired her to consider how children's peers can support fluency. She wrote, "I noticed in my own one-on-one tutoring sessions with [Isabella] that when we had a second student join our session, she was thrilled with the competition, and I was thrilled with the peer scaffolding" (Reading response, April 1, 2008). Colleen expanded these thoughts in her tutoring response,

> Both [Isabella and another student] were peeking around the pages to see what was going to happen next.... There was a lot of page-flipping at the end, finding favorite parts, discussing the differences in the pages and illustrations, and defining of new terms such as charioteer and raja. Awesome. (Tutoring plans, March 18, 2008)

Both responses suggest how Colleen connects course readings to inform Isabella's tutoring.

Toward the end of the semester after reading an article titled *Improving the Assessment of Literacy* (Winograd, Paris, & Bridge, 1991), Colleen commented that readings from her Guiding Young Children in Groups class reinforced a key element of assessment. She mused in a reading response,

> We are really being trained to notice the little things about a learner—their miscues, how they self-correct, what they say in "their own words," their backgrounds and personalities—to really

tailor the assessment and thus, instruction (and vice versa), to the learner. It is becoming more tangible as a set of ideas we can really implement. (Reading response, April 22, 2008)

The course readings about reading assessment and instruction were not always assumed to be true. We were excited that Emily critically considered Kuhn's (2003) chapter as she struggled to support Jonathan's fluency. Jonathan was reading with frequent pauses even though his accuracy rate was very high. Emily drew on her experiences with Jonathan to interpret the reading:

> According to the article, it isn't until third or fourth grade that teachers focus on student's reading fluency.... I think that they should begin to work on fluency difficulties [in the earlier grades] because these problems can be really discouraging for students. If a student struggles with automatic recognition then they are concentrating on so many things as they read. (Reading response, March 30, 2008)

Emily questioned the article based upon her tutoring experiences, thereby suggesting a reciprocal influence between course readings and reflections on practice.

Influences of Feedback From Instructors

As course instructors, we were acutely aware of how feedback from instructors and peers influenced the tutoring sessions. We often saw references in lesson plans to a suggestion we made about language use, or we noticed key phrases surfacing in conversations between the preservice teachers and students. We did not see the influence of others stated explicitly in tutoring reflections except in Katrina's case.

Katrina noted that her instructors' comments led to reflections on how effective she was as a tutor. She mentioned three instances of influence. First, she noted that Jim (Hoffman, first author) modeled practices around read-aloud during her tutoring session with Todd. Through this modeling, Katrina noticed that good books that "grab Todd's attention and appeal to boys" were very important as an area of focus for her. She wrote, "I am very feminine, so this is an area of growth for me" (Tutoring reflection, February 25, 2008).

Second, as the read-aloud increasingly focused on both comprehension and engagement, Katrina pursued various resources for guidance and support. Jim reinforced that she focus on "think-alouds" versus direct questioning to model how readers comprehend a text. Katrina considered this idea as she compared the relative effectiveness of thinking aloud, direct questioning, and a third type of practice she had implemented, the "What do you think" question. In considering these three strategies, Katrina evoked Jim's voice:

> I feel like I can still improve modeling my think-aloud strategies I use while reading. I still catch myself asking him, "What do you think?" questions—though I don't necessarily think these are the same type of questions that Jim wants us to avoid. (Tutoring reflection, February 19, 2008)

Katrina drew on course instructor feedback that came through responses to lesson plans and during the small-group debriefing sessions each week. On one particular occasion, she used Jim's feedback to choose guided reading texts with particular phonetic patterns and to choose a theme that tied the lesson together. She pondered whether her lesson theme was "cutesy" or more meaningful, such as "the idea that the more you read, the more you learn and the smarter you can become/enjoying reading" (Tutoring reflection, February 12, 2008).

Interpretations:
The Assessment, Reflection, and Instruction Cycle

As presented, we identified four influences on three preservice teachers in this chapter. Through their tutoring reflections, STELLAR online postings, interactions with others, and reading responses, we saw how Katrina's, Colleen's, and Emily's reflections shaped their practices. For example, Emily questioned an article that suggested fluency not be a focus in a first-grade guided reading lesson, as her student's frustration grew during slow, drawn-out readings of a text. Colleen used the STELLAR videos along with her observations of Isabella's interests to contemplate how to choose a text that would engage her and Isabella in a search for new knowledge. Katrina bridged Jim's admonition of questioning during a read-aloud, the concept of think-aloud, and her practice to consider how to further engage Todd in building meaning around a text. These findings suggest a reciprocal relationship between the sources of influence and the ability of the preservice teacher to reflect on practice when planning new interventions for children.

The STELLAR website and course readings provided resources in a format that supported interacting around ideas about reading instruction. The online aspects of each component provided a way to initiate and continue interactions outside of the actual course session. Such interaction included the discussion board surrounding video on the STELLAR site, online reading responses, and instructor feedback on tutoring plans. This supported quiet reflection and thought after class, mid-week, or during lesson planning.

> "The idea [is] that the more you read, the more you learn and the smarter you can become/enjoying reading."

Implications

Drawing from data collected throughout the semester, these three cases suggest the complexity of preservice teachers' developing knowledge and expertise through the course of a one-semester tutorial experience. The growth in knowledge and teaching in these case participants is apparent. All participants drew on multiple sources to grow as tutors. The experience of tutoring appears both emotional and ideological in that each participant used the tutoring experience to construct her identity as a teacher, to recognize her agency as a literacy tutor, and to create a stance toward learning through experience.

> Tutorials can become an important source of learning in teacher preparation programs.

Reading teacher education has been chided in recent years for not attending to the "science of reading" (National Council on Teacher Quality [NCTQ], 2006). The NCTQ report suggests that course work in reading reflects low expectations, with little evidence of college-level work. It offers a simple solution: Teacher educators are urged to insert more scientific content into their courses and raise standards for learning this content. We take a different approach. We believe that teacher preparation programs need to spend more time engaging and supporting learners in the development of practical knowledge in contexts that are rich in complexity, challenge, and support.

Our research into tutoring suggests some of the ways practicum experiences, as in tutorials, can support the development of practical knowledge. These qualities include the importance of frequency of tutoring (at least twice a week for a full semester), a robust tutoring framework with supporting materials, and frequent, direct supervision by faculty. Furthermore, our research offers insight on how preservice teachers use tutoring experiences to construct beginning expertise in the teaching of reading. The processes of developing practical knowledge are complex and cannot be reduced to a set of discrete skills taught by course instructors and then put into practice. Rather, the tutorial context affords spaces for preservice teachers to learn through the experience of working with young learners.

Words of Advice

Tutorials can become an important source of learning in teacher preparation programs. For those incorporating tutorials into their teacher preparation programs, we offer the following words of advice:

- Schedule tutoring for at least two sessions per week with a minimum of 45-minute sessions. In our experience, this is the minimum level of intensity to realize the potential for tutoring for both preservice teachers and their students.

- Provide for different tutoring experiences across the preparation program that build toward classroom teaching. In their first semester, the preservice teachers in our program tutor adults in the local community in ESL and basic literacy. Each semester offers a slightly different context for them to explore teaching and literacy.

- Create structures for tutoring that provide opportunities for observation, reflection, and feedback. Provide a framework for the tutorial with expectations (e.g., read-alouds, word work, guided reading) but leave room for responsive planning (e.g., book selection, focus points, strategy teaching).

- Use video cases as a way of encouraging discussion and reflection on practice. The STELLAR framework is quite elaborate, but small clips of tutoring viewed and discussed can become a starting point and really push practices forward.

- Conduct research on your tutoring practices and share your findings. Our program changes every semester based on data that we gather through observations, postings, interviews, and other forms of evaluation. We learn from our experiences. Beyond our immediate context, there is also great potential for learning from each other as we share our work in conferences, informal networks, and publications such as this book.

REFERENCES

Boling, E.C. (2007). Linking technology, learning, and stories: Implications from research on hypermedia video cases. *Teaching and Teacher Education*, *23*(2), 189–200. doi:10.1016/j.tate.2006.04.015

Erickson, F. (1986). Qualitative methods in research in teaching. In M.C. Wittrock (Ed.), *Handbook of research on teaching* (3rd ed., pp. 119–161). New York: Macmillan.

Fang, Z., & Ashley, C. (2004). Preservice teachers' interpretations of a field-based reading block. *Journal of Teacher Education*, *55*(1), 39–54. doi:10.1177/0022487103259814

Ferdig, R.E., Roehler, L.R., & Pearson, P.D. (2006). Video- and database-driven web environments for preservice literacy teaching and learning. In D. Reinking, M.C. McKenna, L.D. Labbo, & R.D. Kieffer (Eds.), *International handbook of literacy and technology* (Vol. 2, pp. 235–256). Mahwah, NJ: Erlbaum.

Fitzgerald, J. (2001). Can minimally trained college student volunteers help young at-risk children to read better? *Reading Research Quarterly*, *36*(1), 28–46. doi:10.1598/RRQ.36.1.2

Harmon, J.M., Hedrick, W.B., Strecker, S.K., Martinez, M.G., & Perez, B. (2001). Field experiences in reading: Contextualizing and tailoring a reading specialization program. *The Reading Professor*, *23*(1), 49–77.

Harrison, C., Pead, D.A., & Sheard, M. (2006). "P, not -P, and Possibly Q": Literacy teachers learning from digital representations of the classroom. In D. Reinking, M.C. McKenna, L.D. Labbo, & R.D. Kieffer (Eds.), *International handbook of literacy and technology* (Vol. 2, pp. 257–272). Mahwah, NJ: Erlbaum.

Hedrick, W.B., McGee, P., & Mittag, K. (2000). Pre-service teacher learning through one-on-one tutoring: Reporting perceptions through e-mail. *Teaching and Teacher Education*, *16*(1), 47–63. doi:10.1016/S0742-051X(99)00033-5

Hoffman, J.V., & Roller, C.M. (2001). The IRA Excellence in Reading Teacher Preparation Commission's report: Current practices in reading teacher education at the undergraduate level in the United States. In C.M. Roller (Ed.), *Learning to teach reading: Setting the research agenda* (pp. 32–79). Newark, DE: International Reading Association.

International Reading Association. (2003). *Prepared to make a difference: An executive summary of the National Commission on Excellence in Elementary Teacher Preparation for Reading Instruction*. Newark, DE: International Reading Association.

Johnston, P.H. (1997). *Knowing literacy: Constructive literacy assessment*. Portland, ME: Stenhouse.

Juel, C. (1996). What makes literacy tutoring effective? *Reading Research Quarterly*, *31*(3), 268–289. doi:10.1598/RRQ.31.3.3

Kinzer, C.K., Cammack, D.W., Labbo, L.D., Teale, W.H., & Sanny, R. (2006). Using technology to (re)conceptualize preservice literacy teacher education: Considerations of design, pedagogy, and research. In D. Reinking, M.C. McKenna, L.D. Labbo, & R.D. Kieffer (Eds.), *International handbook of literacy and technology* (Vol. 2, pp. 211–233). Mahwah, NJ: Erlbaum.

Kinzer, C.K., & Risko, V.J. (1998). Multimedia and enhanced learning: Transforming preservice teacher education. In D. Reinking, M.C. McKenna, L.D. Labbo, & R.D. Kieffer (Eds.), *Handbook of literacy and technology: Transformations in a post-typographic world* (pp. 185–202). Mahwah, NJ: Erlbaum.

Kuhn, M. (2003). Fluency in the classroom: Strategies for whole-class and group work. In L.M. Morrow, L.B. Gambrell, & M. Pressley (Eds.), *Best practices in literacy instruction* (2nd ed., pp. 127–142). New York: Guilford.

Mertens, D.M. (2005). *Research and evaluation in education and psychology: Integrating diversity with quantitative, qualitative, and mixed methods* (2nd ed.). Thousand Oaks, CA: Sage.

National Council on Teacher Quality. (2006). *What education schools aren't teaching about reading, and what elementary teachers aren't learning*. Available at www.nctq.org/p/publications/docs/nctq_reading_study_app_20071202065019.pdf

Reinking, D., & Bradley, B. (2008). *On formative and design experiments: Approaches to language and literacy research*. New York: Teachers College Press.

Sailors, M., Keehn, S., Harmon, J., & Martinez, M. (2005). Early field experiences offered to and valued by preservice teaches at Sites of Excellence in Reading Teacher Education programs. *Teacher Education and Practice*, *18*(4), 458–470.

Teale, W.H., Leu, D.J., Jr., Labbo, L.D., & Kinzer, C. (2002). The CTELL project: New ways technology can help educate tomorrow's reading teachers. *The Reading Teacher*, *55*(7), 654–659.

Wang, J., & Hartley, K. (2003). Video technology as a support for teacher education reform. *Journal of Technology and Teacher Education*, *11*(1), 105–138.

Winograd, P., Paris, S., & Bridge, C. (1991). Improving the assessment of literacy. *The Reading Teacher*, *45*(2), 108–116.

ABOUT THE CONTRIBUTORS

James V. Hoffman is a professor of Language and Literacy Education at the University of Texas at Austin. He served as president of the National Reading Conference, a board member of the International Reading Association (IRA), and chair of IRA's National Commission on Teacher Preparation. He has served as editor of both Reading Research Quarterly and The Yearbook of the National Reading Conference. His research interests focus on classroom teaching, texts, and reading teacher preparation. E-mail: jhoffman@mail.utexas.edu

Melissa Mosley is an assistant professor of Language and Literacy at the University of Texas at Austin. Her research and teaching focuses on how preservice teachers integrate critical literacy and culturally relevant practices with their field-based literacy teaching experiences. She is also interested in critical literacy learning across the lifespan, particularly how teachers and students together use literacy practices toward social action in classrooms. E-mail: mmosley@mail.utexas.edu

Deborah A. Horan is an assistant professor of Language and Literacy at the University of Texas at Austin. As a former bilingual teacher, she holds a particular interest in K–5 language minority children. This includes children's development of both heritage and additional languages within varying educational contexts. Deborah's research focuses on writing pedagogy, literacy teacher preparation, and academic language. E-mail: Deborah_Horan@teachnet.edb.utexas.edu

Katie Russell has worked in public schools as a fourth-grade teacher, at the San Antonio Children's Museum as the Director of Education, and at Trinity University as the Certification, Accreditation, and Placement Officer in addition to teaching an undergraduate course titled Community and the School. Her research interests include children's literature, teacher retention, and preservice teacher education, specifically how we prepare teachers to be change agents in alleviating social inequalities in schools. E-mail: Katie_Russell@teachnet.edb.utexas.edu

Heather K. Warren has worked as a public school teacher for Houston Independent School District, a grant coordinator within the Language Education Department of Indiana University, and as an intensive English language instructor and adjunct faculty at the University of North Texas. Her interests include second-language acquisition and literacy in secondary students, preservice teacher preparation, and multicultural education. E-mail: Heather_Warren@teachnet.edb.utexas.edu

Audra K. Roach has been an educator in central Texas for the past 10 years, coteaching multiage elementary school classes and coordinating literacy programs in diverse communities. Her current research interests include preservice teacher education and the nature of children's understandings as they learn to read and write within literary genres. E-mail: Audra_Roach@teachnet.edb.utexas.edu

CHAPTER 2

Reading Bigs: An Intergenerational Literacy Mentoring Program

Elizabeth Larkin and G. Pat Wilson

Bea, a retired school teacher, is a volunteer in the Reading Bigs program of Big Brothers Big Sisters (BBBS) of the Sun Coast, Inc., in western Florida. She is an older adult mentor, called a Reading Big. The reluctant young reader she mentors is her Reading Little. To Bea, though, her Little is just Shelley, a delightful, somewhat sad, and often tired second grader.

Bea has been a Reading Big for several years; this year, she has volunteered to be part of a University of South Florida (USF) literacy mentoring research study. In this literacy mentoring project, Bigs are asked to be mentors, not reading tutors, and to build a relationship with their Littles through books. Together, they select from the recommended books in the bin of wonderful children's literature provided by BBBS and stored in the school's media center.

On their first day in the literacy mentoring project, Shelley pored over the book bin and chose *America the Beautiful* by Robert Sabuda (2004). She seemed entranced by the pop-up art in the book. Shelley asked Bea to read it to her, so Bea read aloud, stopping at words she knew Shelley would recognize. Bea explained "fruited plain" and told Shelley about her trip to New York City where she saw the sights that popped up on the last page—the Empire State Building and the Statue of Liberty.

Two months later, Shelley more often asks to read to Bea. Her current favorite book is *The Magic Finger* by Roald Dahl (1966), which they've been reading for several weeks. As she reads, Shelley imitates the role of her mentor and questions Bea about what she thinks will happen next. She talks about the characters and asks Bea, "How would you feel if…." In her mentoring log, Bea writes, "I love reading with her now!! She listens much more now and is much more interested in the stories. At the beginning, she didn't even want to read; last year we mostly just talked" (Mentor Log, 4/23/07).

Literacy Tutoring That Works: A Look at Successful In-School, After-School, and Summer Programs, edited by Janet C. Richards and Cynthia A. Lassonde. © 2009 International Reading Association.

Big Brothers Big Sisters of the Sun Coast, Inc. organizes a large program of volunteers working in the local school districts. Some of the volunteers are teachers or parents with children in the school; but most are recruited from retirement communities, where men and women search for meaningful opportunities to make a difference in the lives of children (Larkin, Mahler, & Sadler, 2005). Reading Bigs is a site-based program that requires a one-hour-per-week commitment. In most cases, children meet with the Reading Big in the school's media center during the day, but two mentors who are also teachers meet after school in one of the classrooms.

BBBS's Reading Bigs program has been in existence since 2004. Prior to the University of South Florida (USF) faculty involvement, the volunteers typically spent the hour reviewing worksheets sent by the classroom teachers. Following each session, the Reading Big completed a volunteer progress log to provide information about how social and academic goals were being met. The log included four categories: confidence, caring, competence, and accomplishment of specific tasks. These categories aligned with the program goals at the time.

The goal of the revised BBBS and USF collaborative mentoring program was to shift the focus of the existing program to complement classroom instruction by fostering trusting interpersonal relationships in which books served as a jumping-off point for heartfelt discussions evoked by a shared appreciation of reading. To this end, we created a bibliography of recommended books we believed to be exceptional literature—the kinds of stories that would capture children's interest even if they were beyond the child's skill level. We selected books that had what we considered to be outstanding literature that would build children's social/emotional growth as well as formats that would build skills (i.e., new vocabulary, repeating word patterns,

and meaningful word play). BBBS provided Anderson's (2007) book to all the Reading Bigs. We recommend the book as a resource for mentors because it provides a wealth of information, including briefs on 200 best-selling picture books that the author categorized by genre (e.g., animal fantasy, concept books) within clusters of ages for which the books hold appeal.

BBBS purchased sets of the recommended books and a storage bin for each of the participating schools to keep the collection available exclusively for the Reading Bigs program. The annotated bibliography is kept in the storage bins for easy reference in choosing appropriate books, and copies of the Mentor Log Form (see Figure 2.1) are also there for Reading Bigs to fill in after each session.

Questions Guiding the Research

The original purpose of studying the Reading Bigs program was to determine its effectiveness so BBBS could make improvements, recruit additional volunteers, and demonstrate to potential funders that the mentoring project is worthwhile. Our questions evolved as we progressed through the data collection and analysis of the study. Eventually, we refined our questions to the following:

- What relationships form among mentors, children, and literature as a result of the BBBS Reading Bigs program?
- How do these relationships influence literacy attitudes and perceptions?

Theoretical Background and Perspectives

We recommended four activities for the mentors that are considered effective in literacy growth as

Figure 2.1 Mentor Log Form

Activity	Book Title, Description of Activity, and Comments	Indicators Met
Book Read Aloud by Big		The goal of the project is to develop children's enjoyment of literature and to increase their understanding of the world around them. Your role is to create a bond with the child and to help the child connect with the story and the characters and find personal meaning in the events or facts described. • First and foremost, look for smiles!! It doesn't matter if the child seems happy about something in the story or seems just to be interacting with you.
Reread Familiar Book		• Look for indications that the child was anticipating your visit: for example, the child was ready and waiting when you arrived; the child told others about your visit; the child had already selected a book to show you. • Note if the child requests a particular book more than once, and then talk about its appeal. • Expand the child's vocabulary by explaining new words within the context of the story, and then note if the child begins to use that word or recognize the word in other contexts.
New Book Introduced		• Tell the child a story about yourself in relation to something in the book. Note if the child asks you questions or recounts a similar related story. • Ask the child to compare characters in the story to friends or family members. Note whether similarities or differences presented are superficial physical traits or more subtle personality characteristics. • Can the child recognize a range of emotions displayed by book characters? Ask what the child would do in the character's shoes. • Note if the child remembers previous conversations in relation to the current book you are reading together. Does the child see parallel situations or similar problems facing the characters?
Write, Draw		• Look for signs of disappointment if you will miss a week: for example, the child frowns; the child avoids eye contact; the child requests reassurance that you will be back when promised. • Note if the child initiates reading to you, asks for more books, or wants to write/draw something about the book.

established by research on programs such as Reading Recovery (Pikulski, 1994; Pinnell, Fried, & Estice, 1991; Shanahan & Barr, 1995; Taylor, Hanson, Justice-Swanson, & Watts, 1997):

1. Reading aloud to a child
2. Rereading familiar books
3. Introducing a new book
4. Writing or drawing responses to the books

Reading aloud offers the Little an opportunity to hear a book that might be too difficult for him or her to read independently. By listening and following along in the text, Littles can learn about the world and can build an understanding of how stories are structured. Sometimes read-alouds take the form of shared reading, with Bigs and Littles taking turns. Rereading provides "the sheer pleasure of reliving a book or of celebrating one's newly acquired reading expertise" (Hansen, 2001, p. 41) as well as practice. Reading and discussing a new book promote opportunities to learn about unfamiliar vocabulary as well as to compare books by the same author (e.g., Patricia Polacco, Kevin Henkes, Roald Dahl) or on the same topic (e.g., ladybugs, dinosaurs, wars). Bigs are encouraged to talk about key concepts before reading, to offer support while their Littles read, and to reflect on the book after reading. Writing or drawing is an additional avenue to extend thinking about the book or to share a personal story sparked by the reading. For each session, mentors maintain the Mentor Log, which outlines the literacy goals and provides a simplified structure for recording what took place. This log replaced the volunteer progress report that was used previously.

> Rereading provides "the sheer pleasure of reliving a book or of celebrating one's newly acquired reading expertise."

We designed the log as an activity guide and a ready reminder of the mentoring goals. It helps Bigs keep in mind the difference between literacy mentoring and trying to teach reading skills. Many Reading Bigs share a concern that they do not know how to teach a child to read (Faucy, 2005). In the past, volunteers, unless they were teachers, often did not feel equipped with the expertise to instruct children and, therefore, relied on work provided by teachers. Studies support the thinking that professional educator expertise is necessary in teaching reading skills whether through regular classroom instruction or tutorials. For example, Allington (2006) notes that effective tutoring is (a) designed around the specific needs of the individual child, (b) coordinated with the classroom teacher, and (c) best provided by reading specialists. When volunteers do not have teaching expertise, the responsibility to assess the child, design the instruction, teach the volunteer the literacy and pedagogical strategies needed, and assess the relative success falls on the classroom teacher. This places a burden on the classroom teacher and does not draw on the skills and expertise brought by the volunteer.

Volunteers do bring valuable attributes, including enjoyment of reading and the desire to build solid, positive relationships with children. The Reading Bigs literacy mentoring program uses mentors' capabilities to augment, complement, and support the larger literacy-building program provided by schools. The knowledge and skills volunteers bring are valuable in literacy education as supported by research into effective practices. For example, of the 18 principles behind best practices in reading identified by Zemelman, Daniels, and Hyde (as cited in Rosengarten, 2007, p. 1), at least five are within the expertise of volunteers:

- Reading means getting meaning from print.

- Reading is thinking.
- Hearing books read aloud is a key to learning to read.
- Reading is the best practice for learning to read.
- Children learn to read best in a low-risk environment.

Income and education are known to be variables in reading achievement. Research indicates positive motivation, which increases engagement in reading, "may substantially compensate for low family income and educational background" (Guthrie & Wigfield, 2000, p. 404). Caring and attentive mentors can create the kind of environment that motivates reluctant readers. Building "an interest in learning involves complex personal skills" such as "finding out what others value and empowering them to explore and build upon their dreams" (Bartholomew, 2008, p. 55). These are assets that mentors who are interested in reading and in children are likely to bring.

Methodology

Participants

The program director at BBBS identified possible school sites for the research project based on where Reading Bigs volunteers were already working and where USF had interns placed for their teacher preparation programs. We approached mentors that BBBS had recruited through presentations in the community to work as Reading Bigs in one-on-one relationships with struggling readers and asked if they would also be willing to participate in the research study. School personnel identified students for the mentoring program, and BBBS staff contacted those families individually to get the USF Institutional Review Board

Consent Forms signed to permit children to participate in the study.

Ultimately, there were two primary sites where clusters of Big/Little pairs were enrolled in the study, one in each of two counties. Most of the mentors were paired with students in a school where 94% of students are white, 5% are Hispanic, and 0.8% are black. Enrollment is 875 students. The school is categorized as rural and is situated in an area of the county where there are many gated communities with golf courses. According to their website, overall reading proficiency at this prekindergarten through fifth grade site is 80%. The second school, identified as urban fringe, serves 750 students in kindergarten through fifth grade. According to their website, the overall reading proficiency here is 65% with a 60% economically disadvantaged population. This school's racial mix is more diverse with 45% white, 27% black, and 28% Hispanic.

Twenty-five Reading Big/Reading Little pairs participated in the study, 11 in the first year and 14 in the second year. Three Reading Bigs were able to participate both years. All of the 3 male and 22 female mentors were white. Of the 25 Bigs enrolled in the study, 6 consistently completed their Mentor Logs, providing data for our analysis. Five of these mentors are older female adults and 1 is a teacher at the K–5 school.

Each literacy mentor attended an orientation session to learn how the Reading Bigs project was structured and to understand the purposes of the research study. We encouraged mentors to use the four recommended activities or alternative activities that had been requested by the classroom teachers or Little and to make decisions about how best to spend the time.

At the request of BBBS, we coauthors of this chapter, both instructors at USF, arranged seminar meetings periodically to support the mentors during the academic year. These seminars provided a forum for mentors to discuss what they were doing, what was successful for their Littles, and what seemed problematic. We organized the seminars to position the volunteers as knowledgeable experts. The mentors told us about the effectiveness of particular strategies they tried, and we discussed recommendations for book selections according to children's needs and interests.

Data Sources

We collected the Mentor Log Forms that Reading Bigs completed after each session from the BBBS staff at the end of each semester. The most useful logs were those that contained detailed descriptions of why children chose a particular book or had specific quotes capturing the Little's response to a book.

In addition to the logs, we had notes from the orientations and audiotaped transcripts of the seminar sessions. These sources captured insights on mentors' relationships with the children and what they found effective or problematic during their weekly encounters. Further, we interviewed the mentors to solicit input about where they felt most or least effective in supporting their Littles' literacy growth. The questions were open ended: How would you characterize your Little's attitude toward having a Reading Big? What does being a Big mean to you?

Data Analysis

Out of nine Big/Little matches in the spring of 2007, three contained enough detailed description in the Mentor Logs to examine the relationships closely. For the 2007–2008 academic year, another three matches yielded sufficient data for analysis. For each Big/Little match used, we organized the data chronologically. Using a constant comparative method (Mertler, 2006; Strauss, 1987) we triangulated all sources of data to look for recurring themes and trends that defined the program.

Limitations

There are a few limitations to this study. First, there was a smaller number of Big/Little pairs recruited for the study each year than we had hoped for. This was largely a consequence of difficulties in obtaining written consent from children's families, despite follow-up efforts by the BBBS staff such as phone calls and meetings with families. Finally, we had a smaller number of mentors than expected because some were not able to attend the required orientation session due to their busy schedules.

Several other complications emerged that were organizational in nature. Occasionally, a volunteer was unable to continue through the entire academic year, leaving the Little without a mentor. In February and March, the Florida Comprehensive Achievement Testing (FCAT) limited time for Bigs and Littles to meet, often suspending sessions for a month at a time.

Results

After reading and rereading the data, we organized recurring topics into coding categories, or overarching themes. Three broad themes that emerged in answer to our guiding questions are the role of the mentor, the choice factor, and challenges to mentoring.

Role of the Mentor

In the orientation sessions for the Reading Bigs, we explained the difference between trying to teach children to read and being a literacy mentor. We wanted the volunteers to build a relationship with their Little using books as the core of this relationship. During the study, we saw this goal realized when the Bigs enjoyed being with their Littles, made personal connections with the stories they read together, listened to what the Little wanted to read or discuss, and modeled being a lifelong learner.

In the role of mentor, the Big was a trusted adult. When children were given the opportunity to ask a person they trusted a confidential question, they opened to exploring life's puzzling questions. The Mentor Log Forms disclose that sibling rivalry, anger and forgiveness, saving money, Christianity and God, fiction versus reality, and other meaningful subjects cropped up in conversations about books. Such topics might be difficult to address in the public classroom arena, but in this confidential context, the Bigs could listen and share perspectives on social mores. Moreover, they could model positive, problem-solving behaviors. Such conversations have a positive impact on literacy, as noted by Henderson and May (2005): "Once their sense of social conscience begins to develop through the discoveries they make when reading and hearing good literature, they are on the road to being lifelong readers who are more aware of their world" (p. 118).

The informal exchanges about books enriched the background knowledge and world view of the Littles. In one example, when a Little read *The Ancient Cliff Dwellers of Mesa Verde* (Arnold, 2000), his mentor relayed experiences from her travels. She wrote, "I was able to describe the geography, the scale, and the emotions from my own trip" (Mentor Log, 2/26/07). A month later, the Little excitedly recognized Mesa Verde when they read Sabuda's (2004) *America the Beautiful.* Further, he summarized what it meant to him to learn, "The anthem and the pop-ups make me feel like I know the world" (Mentor Log, 4/9/07). Through these exchanges, his world view grew.

Most of the mentors were older adults, which may have contributed to the role being less didactic in tone compared with the role of tutors. This is consistent with another study of BBBS volunteers (Larkin et al., 2005). In our study, the older Reading Bigs had a relaxed perspective on the learning process; they did not have to assume the responsibilities that families and teachers do to correct behaviors or plan instruction for particular learning objectives. Nora, one of the Bigs in the research study, explained her role:

> At school, teachers take a positive interest in him [her Little]. He needs someone to take a *special* interest in him.... I allow him to be who he is. I'm not into "molding" him.... I am different than the school people who make demands.... I do enjoy his company and he sees that. (Interview, 2/25/08)

Nora saw her role as different from that of teacher or tutor.

The relationship built through the mentorship was not unilateral. As with any intergenerational program, the benefits are mutual, and older adult volunteers find satisfaction in being mentors to younger people who appreciate their caring attention. Nora felt a frustration during the early phase of her relationship with her Little. "Last year he didn't show up once because he wanted to eat lunch with his peers" (Interview, 2/25/08). Yet, this changed over time. "Now, he looks forward to our time together. He was excited about the possibility that I might come to the BBBS Christmas party" (Interview, 2/25/08).

"I was able to describe the geography, the scale, and the emotions from my own trip."

When Bigs and Littles established a bond of caring for one another, they built a foundation of trust to discuss all manner of topics. In the context of the one-on-one mentoring relationship, there were opportunities for Littles to ask questions without fear of embarrassment. They could find out what they wanted to know, and the books provided a springboard for their questions. Furthermore, they knew they would receive positive comments and support from their Bigs while they spent time together. Reading was associated with a pleasant relational experience.

The Choice Factor

The theme of choice as a critical issue emerged from the completed Mentor Log Forms. The Littles had control over how much to read and what to read. Over time, children chose to read more and more as the sessions continued. For example, Bea noted that Shelley "always asks to read *America the Beautiful* [Sabuda, 2004]—knows it by heart now" (Mentor Log, 4/4/07). Later in April, they were reading *The Magic Finger* (Dahl, 1966). Bea wrote, "[Shelley] loves this book—wants to hear it again even though she knows the plot," and "I usually read for awhile, but now Shelley asks if she can read it. She does this much more than before" (Mentor Log, 4/19/07).

A similar pattern occurred with Evelyn (Reading Big) and Robbie's (Little) partnership. On the last day of April Evelyn wrote, "Robbie did all the reading today." Robbie became more involved in reading over the course of their relationship, as supported by Evelyn's additional notation, "Robbie hasn't asked to finish [the session] with a game for several weeks" (Mentor Log, 4/30/07). Having choice in these cases led to more involvement, a concept supported by Routman (2000), who notes, "Students invest more in a task when they are given some say in how they will perform it" (p. 537).

> "Students invest more in a task when they are given some say in how they will perform it."

In some cases, children's choices revolved around characters with whom they could identify. One mentor wrote, "I've noticed that Denny picks books every time that have characters she can identify with—the characters are African American. I love that she has so many choices of books that interest her" (Mentor Log, 4/9/07). As McGlinn (2002) says, "Children want to see themselves and their everyday lives in the stories they read.... If the books they read don't feature people like them, doing things they do, children may lose interest in the story and give up" (p. 50).

The children frequently chose books that provided opportunities to talk about emotions and feelings. Robbie "compared *Verdi* [Cannon, 1997] to himself. He identified with some of the feelings and emotions" (Mentor Log, 4/9/07). Shelley talked about how Lilly felt in *Lilly's Purple Plastic Purse* (Henkes, 1996) and mentioned that similar incidents had happened in her own class at school. Through the stories, the Littles explored the social-affective world. Practitioners in the field of early childhood education have long recognized the importance of cultivating children's social cognition. Zeece (2000) notes that

> The development of an awareness and understanding of what people think, feel, and do is important for children's effective functioning in their social worlds.... Relations between social cognitive abilities and prosocial behavior may be mediated by situational variables, such as the provision of high quality, developmentally appropriate children's literature. (p. 239)

The books were a catalyst for talking about a whole range of social issues including saving money, being kind to others, being inspired by beauty, and sharing possessions.

The participants in our study have noted that the Littles especially enjoyed pop-up books, such as those by Robert Sabuda, and humorous books such as *The Three Little Wolves and the Big Bad Pig* (Trivizas & Oxenbury, 1993). It is easy to imagine why pop-up books were popular:

They hold visual appeal and have the tactile, interactive quality that most classroom books do not offer. Humor added a lighthearted quality to the interaction so that reading was a fun experience rather than an arduous chore. Sharing laughter created a bond between the Big and Little.

Often, Littles chose books that taught them something about the world. One Little chose two books about war (*Pink and Say* by Patricia Polacco, 1994, and *The Yellow Star* by Carmen Agra Deedy, 2000) and initiated a conversation about World War II, which he found "interesting because of his grandfather's participation" (Mentor Log, 11/14/07). One Little consistently chose information-laden texts, such as *Encyclopedia Prehistorica: Sharks and Other Sea Monsters* (Sabuda & Reinhart, 2006). The Littles had different reasons for the books they chose, and it was important to have a range of books that tapped whatever their interests and skill levels were.

The Bigs wanted to support the idea of choice, but they recognized a need to narrow down the number of choices based on topics of interest, favorite authors, or other information gleaned from the interviews that could guide them. The Bigs discussed how it was best at first to select just a few books from which the Little could choose. Otherwise, they reported the Littles ended up rifling through the entire bin and not knowing where to start.

Choice has been documented as important to literacy growth. After observing high school students who were given the opportunity to choose their books and discuss what they read with others, Hansen (2001) notes, "they appreciate talking with one another and making their own decisions about what to read. They started to label themselves as readers—for the first time in their lives" (p. 42). Hansen refers to a change in attitude toward reading and perception of self as a reader. Part of this change is that children will seek to become better readers. As children "become swept into the world of reading, they typically want to become better. They purposefully choose reading materials that will help them grow as readers" (p. 41). Because they had choices, the Littles made decisions and held some control over the mentoring session. The Mentor Logs document the Littles' growing confidence in themselves as learners. Once the Littles had established positive relationships with their Reading Bigs, they looked forward to the visits and initiated reading, asking questions, and learning new words. In other words, they were partners in this mutually rewarding relationship.

Challenges to Mentoring

Sometimes, a Little's choices presented a dilemma for the Big. The challenge arose from the Accelerated Reader (AR) program, published by Renaissance Learning and adopted by both counties as part of their curriculum. AR is a computer-based program that is designed to motivate children to read and to complement the classroom literacy program (Johnson, 2006). One Big reported that he did not use any of the books from the bin because his Little wanted to read AR books to earn points. Another Big, a kindergarten teacher working with two Littles, wrote that one of the girls delighted in the books from the bin. The other was "concerned about whether or not the books we read are AR books. They are earning points toward special field trips/activities" (Mentor Log, 3/12/07). About a month later, the Big writes again in her log, "Betsy doesn't seem enthused about reading. She seems to be focused on the number of AR points the book is worth" (Mentor Log, 4/16/07). In yet another case, Martha spoke of her Little's obsession to get a dog tag, one of the AR rewards. She said her Little was trying to take AR tests on Harry Potter books even though he was not able to read these chapter books independently. Martha helped her Little, usually by reading them aloud to him. She argued, "I need to have him feeling success" (notes from seminar, 2/11/08).

Our seminar discussion on February 11 centered on the tension in meeting a Little's AR objectives or honoring a Little's book choices in light of the BBBS literacy mentoring project's goals. Martha's Little had set an AR goal, and he met success in his own eyes. Martha stated, "We got his comprehension up to 69" (notes from seminar, 2/11/08). In the context of reading for AR points, the Little practiced skimming to find information in the story to answer questions. During AR tests Martha helped him read the questions but he answered them on his own. It became clear that the AR influence had subtly shifted several mentoring relationships away from the intended goal. The AR program motivated the Littles through extrinsic rewards, while the Reading Bigs program was predicated on intrinsic, social rewards. We advised the Bigs to use their own judgment about how to manage their time together and to encourage the Littles to explore the recommended books even if they did not carry AR points.

> "Readers are decision makers whose affect as well as their language and cognition play a role in their reading practices."

Discussion

The data show that Littles enjoyed reading with their Bigs and looked forward to the reading activities. Thus, we conclude that the Reading Bigs literacy mentoring program served to motivate Littles to read and to view books as exciting sources of information, at least during the mentoring sessions. Motivation was influenced through the positive relationship with a Big, and through having a choice about what to read and who would read. The Littles had some control over the reading experience, and could accomplish their own goals with the help of the Bigs. Guthrie and Wigfield (2000) note that "readers are decision makers whose affect as well as their language and cognition play a role in their reading practices" (pp. 403–404). In the Big/Little relationship, the agency of the Little was honored and respected, creating a stress-free social occasion for the shared enjoyment and practice of reading.

Over half of the Bigs in the study are older adults, bringing to light the value of intergenerational mentoring. DiPardo and Schnack (2004) studied an intergenerational relationship among eighth graders and elders that also centered on books. In their program, the students and adults read a book in common and communicated for five weeks through written correspondence. As in our study, the relationship within most of the partnerships grew from initial ice-breaking communication to a depth of personal exchanges that included sharing opinions, concerns, and life events. The eighth graders in the DiPardo and Schnack study articulated that they valued the first-hand experiences the elders shared regarding historical events. In our study, the Bigs shared experiences, such as trips to locations mentioned in books or informal exchanges about life (versus school-related) concepts such as sibling rivalry and saving money. DiPardo and Schnack found the establishment of interpersonal connections between the elders and students created a valuable space for learning that is not always part of in-school structures:

> This kind of reading and writing—enmeshed in emotionally warm relationships that promote...mutually negotiated participation—represents an important aspect of out-of-school literacy that is too often sadly neglected in classrooms.... Encouraged but not graded, these partners were intrinsically motivated to make meanings together. (p. 32)

Similarly, the Reading Bigs program promoted warm interpersonal relationships and negotiated participation in reading, despite the challenges.

More than once, we considered the merits of Littles selecting books from the media center collection for their point value in the AR program, which is part of the schools' curricula. In order for the mentors to generate enjoyment of reading and to help Littles find personal meaning in the books, the Bigs wanted to allow choice. They were reluctant to discourage the Littles from reading anything they wanted. Yet, there is a difference between reading for points and reading for pleasure. Nodelman and Reimer (2003) describe the difference this way:

> Ardent readers do not read texts just because someone else says they must; they choose what they want to read and when they want to read it.... They don't interrupt their pleasure in the development of a plot by looking up every unfamiliar word or preparing themselves to answer questions.... It's hard to imagine how being made to answer such a question might, as the Accelerated Reader Web site claims, "[get] kids excited about books." (p. 35)

At times, AR pulled Bigs and Littles back to "in-school" book choices. What seemed to help maintain the mentoring role, and literacy activities more typical of out-of-school experiences, was that many of the Reading Bigs were adults with a range of life experiences who did not wish to take on the role of teacher. Further, through support from seminars and the Mentor Log Forms with the list of behaviors that supported the program goals, the Bigs and Littles shared a relationship founded on an appreciation of books that was more aligned with out-of-school or family-type relationships.

Implications

The interpersonal relationship between Bigs and Littles was key in developing a positive sense of self as a reader and appreciating the value of books in life. The mentors were positive role models in terms of being lifelong learners themselves, and the adults offered wisdom and perspective from years of experience in discussing problems and questions that arise in the lives of children. Adult mentors in the BBBS programs were patient, caring, and steadfast in their commitment to children. They maintained their perspective on long-range goals in the face of children's immediate challenging behavior and negative attitudes (Larkin et al., 2005).

Words of Advice

We gained the following insights from this study of the Reading Bigs program, which may be helpful in replicating a similar intergenerational literacy mentoring program in other settings:

- Tutoring (instruction) and mentoring (overall support) differ, and each contributes to children's literacy growth in a different way. We recommend that children's needs be matched appropriately to the role or program.

- Recruit volunteers from the community, particularly those who have retired from professional roles; they are a valuable resource because the esteem in which they hold books, children, and their community is critical to mentoring.

- Support mentors with ways to guide children to make choices about what to read. Such support might include supplies of books, seminars, or other opportunities for ongoing discussion and access to expertise.

- We started with two sites and were spread too thin. We recommend starting the mentoring program in one school and, once it is well established, growing it to other sites.

- Work with community agencies to simplify the process of participating in research so that programs can be evaluated effectively.

NOTE

We would like to acknowledge BBBS of the Sun Coast Inc.'s Executive Director Joy Mahler for her leadership and commitment to the research study; the Reading Bigs for their dedication and willingness to try something new, to share their experiences, and to assist in data collection; and, of course, the Reading Littles, for being who they are and being willing to start on a journey with their Reading Bigs.

REFERENCES

Allington, R.L. (2006, April/May). Research and the three tier model. *Reading Today, 23*(5), 20.

Anderson, N.A. (2007). *What should I read aloud? A guide to 200 best-selling picture books.* Newark, DE: International Reading Association.

Bartholomew, B. (2008). Sustaining the fire. *Educational Leadership, 6*(65), 55–60.

DiPardo, A., & Schnack, P. (2004). Expanding the web of meaning: Thought and emotion in an intergenerational reading and writing program. *Reading Research Quarterly, 39*(1), 14–37. doi:10.1598/RRQ.39.1.3

Faucy, R. (2005). *Reading Rotarians unite for literacy: Program overview.* Unpublished report. Big Brothers Big Sisters of the Suncoast, Sarasota, FL.

Guthrie, J.T., & Wigfield, A. (2000). Engagement and motivation in reading. In M. Kamil, P.B. Mosenthal, P.D. Pearson, & R. Barr (Eds.), *Handbook of reading research* (Vol. III, pp. 403–422). Mahwah, NJ: Erlbaum.

Hansen, J. (2001). *When writers read* (2nd ed.). Portsmouth, NH: Heinemann.

Henderson, D.L., & May, J.P. (2005). *Exploring culturally diverse literature for children and adolescents.* Boston: Pearson Education.

Johnson, T. (2006). *Review of accelerated reader.* Tallahassee: Florida Center for Reading Research.

Larkin, E., Mahler, J., & Sadler, S.E. (2005). Benefits of volunteering for older adults working with at-risk youth. *Journal of Gerontological Social Work, 44*(3/4), 23–37. doi:10.1300/J083v44n03_03

McGlinn, J. (2002, January). Seeing themselves in what they read. *Book Links*, 50–54.

Mertler, C.A. (2006). *Action research: Teachers as researchers in the classroom.* Thousand Oaks, CA: Sage.

Nodelman, P., & Reimer, M. (2003). *The pleasures of children's literature* (3rd ed.). Boston: Allyn & Bacon.

Pikulski, J.J. (1994). Preventing reading failure: A review of five effective programs. *The Reading Teacher, 48*(1), 30–39.

Pinnell, G.S., Fried, M.D., & Estice, R.M. (1991). Reading Recovery: Learning how to make a difference. In D.E. DeFord, C.A. Lyons, & G.S. Pinnell (Eds.), *Bridges to literacy: Learning from reading recovery* (pp. 11–35). Portsmouth, NH: Heinemann.

Rosengarten, K.L. (2007). Implementing best practices of reading. *Focus on Elementary, 19*(3), 1–5.

Routman, R. (2000). *Conversations: Strategies for teaching, learning, and evaluating.* Portsmouth, NH: Heinemann.

Shanahan, T., & Barr, R. (1995). Reading recovery: An independent evaluation of the effects of an early instructional intervention for at-risk learners. *Reading Research Quarterly, 30*(4), 958–996. doi:10.2307/748206

Strauss, A. (1987). *Qualitative analysis for social scientists.* New York: Cambridge University Press.

Taylor, B.M., Hanson, B.E., Justice-Swanson, K., & Watts, S.M. (1997). Helping struggling readers: Linking small-group intervention with cross-age tutoring. *The Reading Teacher, 51*(3), 196–209. doi:10.1598/RT.51.3.4

Zeece, P.D. (2000). Supporting children's social cognitive development: Literature choices that make a difference. *Early Childhood Education Journal, 27*(4), 239–242. doi:10.1023/B:ECEJ.0000003688.56629.7f

LITERATURE CITED

Arnold, C. (2000). *The ancient cliff dwellers of Mesa Verde.* Boston: Houghton Mifflin.

Cannon, J. (1997). *Verdi.* San Diego, CA: Harcourt Brace.

Dahl, R. (1966). *The magic finger.* New York: Harper & Row.

Deedy, C.A. (2000). *The yellow star: The legend of King Christian X of Denmark.* Atlanta, GA: Peachtree.

Henkes, K. (1996). *Lilly's purple plastic purse.* New York: Greenwillow Books.

Polacco, P. (1994). *Pink and Say.* New York: Philomel Books.

Sabuda, R. (2004). *America the beautiful.* New York: Little Simon.

Sabuda, R., & Reinhart, M. (2006). *Encyclopedia prehistorica: Sharks and other sea monsters.* Cambridge, MA: Candlewick Press.

Trivizas, E., & Oxenbury, H. (1993). *The three little wolves and the big bad pig.* New York: Simon & Schuster.

ABOUT THE CONTRIBUTORS

Elizabeth Larkin *is an associate professor of Education at the University of South Florida, Sarasota/Manatee, Florida, USA. She teaches in the Early Childhood and Elementary teacher-preparation programs. Her research interests*

include looking at the professional development of educators, as well as studying intergenerational initiatives that bring older adults and younger populations together for their mutual benefit. She served on the BBBS Corporate Board from 2003 through 2007, and chaired the Program Committee. E-mail: llarkin@sar.usf.edu

G. Pat Wilson *is an assistant professor of Childhood Education and Literacy Studies at the University of South Florida, Sarasota/Manatee, Florida, USA. She studies the reading process of primary-grade children, using socio-psycholinguistic frames to explicate the relationships between text, instruction, readers, and meaning construction. E-mail: gpwilson@sar.usf.edu*

CHAPTER 3

The Academic Booster Shot:
In-School Tutoring to Prevent Grade-Level Retention

Nancy Frey, Diane Lapp, and Douglas Fisher

Freddie, a first grader at risk for retention, settled into a chair at a small table and immediately picked up a guided reading book. "I read this yesterday—should I read it again?" asked Freddie. His tutor Kerri said yes and recorded his oral reading performance on a running record form. Kerri's individual reading lesson plan stated that the objective was for Freddie to look at the words and use decoding strategies to figure them out. Freddie's classroom teacher had noted that he often used semantic cues to make guesses but paid less attention to the letters of the word. The objective of the tutoring session was to improve his directionality within words, particularly initial consonants.

After taking the running record, Kerri introduced a new book at the same level. She folded back each page so that only the picture could be seen and explained to Freddie that Dad has taken Nick, Kate, and James to ride on the merry-go-round. She drew his attention to the look on Nick's face when he wasn't able to sit on the ride's car or plane. She then opened the book and laid it flat on the desk so that Freddie could see both pages, saying, "Look at the names of the children—*James, Nick,* and *Kate* [pointing to each as she emphasized the words]." She then drew Freddie's attention to words that appeared repeatedly in this predictable text, especially the words *the* and *like.* Finally, she ended the book introduction by returning to the meaning of the story: "I think Nick looks mad because he has to ride the horse. Let's read the story to find out if he gets to ride something else." Because Kerri had not shown Freddie the last picture in the book, he would have to read the story to answer this question. While the focus of this particular lesson was on directionality within words, all of her lessons placed comprehension at the center of reading purpose.

Freddie then took the book into his hands and read the title, moving his finger under each word. At one point, the word *plane* stumped him. Freddie glanced at the picture and Kerri said, "I see you're looking at the picture to get an idea of what that word might be. Now look at the first letter. What is the name of that letter?" When Freddie answered correctly, she asked him to make the letter sound. She asked him to do the same for the next letter, *l*. Then she explained that in this word those letters would have a blended sound of /pl/.

After he finished reading the book, Kerri asked Freddie about the ending of the book. Freddie broke into a smile and said, "He did get to ride the plane!" She then shifted his focus to the next task: writing. She asked him to think of a sentence about the story. "I like the plane," he said immediately. Freddie opened his writing journal and began to write, receiving additional instruction from his tutor as he did so. Again, the lesson returned to meaning-making as the ultimate goal of reading.

With the scheduled 30 minutes of tutoring nearly finished, Kerri reminded Freddie that they would meet again the next day. "See you tomorrow!" Freddie called over his shoulder, then extended his arms like the wings of an airplane and returned to the independent reading center.

The lesson in the vignette is representative of some of the instruction delivered during a tutoring program designed to prevent grade-level retention, which is the policy and practice of repeating a grade in school due to academic failure or social immaturity. Some lessons end with a writing experience like the one in the vignette, but others focus on word work such as using magnetic letters to spell words, or playing flash card games like "My Pile, Your Pile" to practice sight words (words recognized and taught as a whole). The intent of every lesson is to increase comprehension through consolidation of the graphophonic, syntactic, and semantic cues of reading (Clay, 2001). We designed these lesson variations to meet the individual needs of learners. However, every lesson begins with a familiar reading and a running record, followed by a book introduction and an initial reading of the new book.

Our involvement in this research project began in the spring of 2001 when a large urban school district enacted a policy to end social promotion, the practice of advancing students to the next grade despite their lack of skills. The goal of the district was to raise student achievement through grade retention for students who were considered to be "significantly below grade level" (San Diego Unified School District, 2001, p. 1). These retention decisions, based on the Developmental Reading Assessment (DRA; 1999), were declared mandatory at grade 1 and influenced 2001–2002 placements. It is important to note that although the district reported that it expected an average first-grade retention rate of 4%, they also anticipated that poor and urban elementary schools would have much higher percentages.

We, the coauthors of this chapter, three professors from San Diego State University, designed this intervention program to augment students' classroom instruction. We worked with reading tutors who supplemented instruction through a short-term daily one-on-one intervention delivered at the end of the school year, and who collaborated with each child's classroom teachers. We hoped that this intervention, consisting of supplemental instruction provided during the school day, would be an alternative to grade-level retention or social promotion. Although prevention and intervention appear to be proactive responses to eliminate the need for retention, state and district policies continue to emphasize retention as the intervention itself, with access to remediation services available only after a student has been retained (Stuebing et al., 2002).

Questions Guiding the Research

The faculty at our partner school did not believe that retention was the solution to the achievement problem and asked the three of us to design a proactive intervention. We compared the results of the intervention we implemented to the retention of first-grade students from a demographically similar elementary school in the same neighborhood that implemented the district policy.

> Reading [is] "a message-getting, problem-solving activity, which increases in power and flexibility the more it is practiced."

Our research questions were as follows:

- Would reading scores improve if an intervention program was provided that supported students' literacy development?

- Would the tutoring program reduce the number of students retained in first grade?

- Would the academic progress made by tutored students be maintained in second grade?

The "academic booster shot" we provide for students requires between 10 and 12 tutors working daily over a period of 8 to 10 weeks. Each tutor provides 30 minutes of one-on-one instruction to approximately 12 students per day. We identify the students at risk of grade-level retention based on the classroom assessments that are administered during the school

year. Naturally, classroom teachers have already attempted to increase student achievement during the year before we initiate the intervention. Thus we only provide intervention services to students who have failed to respond to classroom support and who are not referred for special education services. Our intervention began in 2001, the year of the study reported in this chapter.

Theoretical Background and Perspectives

In this section, we will provide a brief review of the literature and the theoretical underpinnings that influenced the design of this intervention. Reading is the ability to decode and comprehend developmentally appropriate text. Clay (2001) describes reading as "a message-getting, problem-solving activity, which increases in power and flexibility the more it is practiced" (p. 1). In the first grade, reading is viewed as a strong predictor of who will be retained (Dauber, Alexander, & Entwisle, 1993). Juel (1988) reports that children identified as poor readers in first grade have a 90% likelihood of remaining poor readers in fourth grade. This is related to Stanovich's (1986) findings on reading volume. Stanovich argued that the "Matthew effect"—named for the biblical passage about the rich getting richer while the poor get poorer—indicates that depressed reading ability has an exponentially negative effect on the number of words a child reads over the course of a year when compared with more capable readers. Thus, stronger readers engage in more reading and acquire more content knowledge and literacy behaviors, while the students who read less continue to fall further behind in both areas.

One successful tutoring program is Early Steps (Santa & Hoein, 1999), which relies on certified teachers to implement daily instruction for first graders reading below grade level. In Early Steps, the tutor is also the child's classroom teacher, having been released from his or her classroom duties for 30 minutes a day. Leveled books with controlled, but not necessarily decodable, text are used for familiar and new readings. Word sorts and student-generated questions are prominently featured in the lessons, although vocabulary instruction is less formal (Invernizzi, 2001). Research studies suggest favorable results for this approach. For example, Morris, Tyner, and Perney (2000) followed the progress of 43 first graders who participated in a year of Early Steps tutoring. These students made more progress than a matched comparison group, with the lowest performing readers making the most growth.

We drew upon the knowledge base concerning early intervention and retention as described by Juel (1988) and Dauber and colleagues (1993) to determine the goals of this tutoring program: raise reading achievement among the most struggling readers while monitoring their progress and providing follow-up support the following school year. Programmatically, we drew upon some of the essential components of Early Steps, especially the length and purpose of the sessions, to develop a unique tutoring program for first-grade students at this school.

Methodology

We selected a quasi-experimental, mixed-methodology design for this study because random sampling of the children could not be employed, as we could not retain some children before offering them what we perceived as additional proactive instruction. We combined qualitative and quantitative approaches to answer various questions within this study (Johnson & Onwuegbuzie, 2004). Other researchers, such as Vellutino and Scanlon (2001), have also combined quantitative and qualitative methods to answer the complex questions related to literacy assessment and early intervention.

Participants

SCHOOLS. Two elementary schools from the same district are both located in the most ethnically diverse and lowest income community in the city. Thirty-nine languages are spoken by the 66,000 residents living in this five-square-mile community. The first school in the study, which is where we provided the intervention, we call Harriet Tubman (pseudonym). This school hosts 1,543 students at two campuses. Tubman is known for its student diversity—76.9% of the students are identified as Latino/Hispanic, 11.3% are Indochinese, 7.5% are African or African American, and 2.5% are Caucasian. Overall, 70.3% of the students are English-language learners. The entire school population qualifies for free or reduced-cost lunches. The school is staffed by 73 credentialed teachers.

The comparison school, which we call Benjamin Banneker (pseudonym), was identified by using the variable considered to be most salient, student demographics. Banneker is located only one mile away from Tubman in the same community. The demographics at Banneker are similar to Tubman. Latino students comprise 75.7% of the student population, 9.9% are Indochinese, 9.5% are African or African American, and 3.0% are Caucasian. Overall, 72.7% of the children are English-language learners. As at Tubman, 100% of the students attending Banneker qualify for free or reduced-cost lunches. There are 65 credentialed teachers on staff at Banneker.

FIRST-GRADE STUDENTS. At the initiation of the intervention efforts, Tubman had a population of 221 students enrolled in 12 first-grade classrooms, whereas Banneker had 250 first-grade students enrolled in 13 classrooms. We identified students at Tubman through analysis of their oral reading performance on the DRA (1999), which was administered to all first graders in March. At that time, 106 students at Tubman were identified because each scored an 8 or below on the DRA in either Spanish or English on the March administration. Although a score of 3 is the cut-point for mandatory retention in the district's retention plan, a score of 8 was chosen by the school in an effort to raise achievement. The governance committee of the school determined that because grade-level performance at the end of first grade is a level 16 on the DRA, setting a bar of 3 was too low. They believed other children at risk for future academic failure would be passed on to second grade without receiving early intervention. A student list was generated and classroom teachers provided input about student needs and instructional goals. Because 21 students had made progress during the period between the March DRA assessment and the start of the intervention, their teachers recommended that these students not be included. A total of 85 students participated in the intervention.

Proactive Intervention

We collaborated with the principal, the first-grade classroom teachers, and a site-based reading specialist to determine student scheduling and to select the reading tutors, who were enrolled in our university's credential program. Because the intervention was a daily event, it was important to rotate scheduled intervention times so that students would not miss 38 lessons in the same subject area. Each tutor met with each student for 30 minutes each day, delivering a total of 19 hours over 38 lessons during the 8-week intervention period.

During the first week, the tutors collected extensive formative assessment data about the current status of the identified students. They administered three of the five subtests on the Observation Survey of Early Literacy Achievement (1993)—the Ohio Word Test, Dictation Test, and the Written Vocabulary Test. The first is an assessment of 20 high-frequency words such as *and, the,* and *I,* arranged in a list. The second consists of a sentence dictated to the student. The student writes the sentence, which can be repeated word by word to facilitate his or her writing. The third, a test of written vocabulary, invites the student to write as many words as he or she can during a 10-minute period. The student is required to read the words as well. Two other subtests of the Observation Survey, Concepts About Print and Letter Recognition, were not formally administered, although similar information was gathered by the student's classroom teacher and recorded on a questionnaire. The use of these three subtests, as well as the results from the questionnaire, allowed the tutors to assemble basic literacy information about each student.

Another important component of the Observation Survey of Early Literacy Achievement (1993) is the running record that was used throughout the intervention. The running record is a tool for analysis of oral reading behavior. It is most commonly used with text that does not exceed 200 words and can provide information about a reader's ability to coordinate oral language with printed text. A running record is also useful for matching text to reader at the student's instructional level. The running record provides valuable and important information about the reader's ability to make meaning, not just to correctly identify words. In partnership with the school's reading specialist, we collected and reviewed weekly running records for every participating student.

The tutors had a broad range of materials available. They used small books of 20 to 40 words designed to support emergent reading instruction, called guided reading books (Fountas & Pinnell, 1996). These books were leveled, meaning that the publisher analyzed each text for readability. These levels correspond with the same system used to report DRA results (1999). Guided reading books were available in both Spanish and English; however, the participating first graders received instruction in only one language. Tutors of students enrolled in Spanish biliteracy classrooms used Spanish-language materials.

Tutors began teaching children at the beginning of the second week of the study. They used a lesson frame influenced by the Observation Survey of Early Literacy Achievement (1993; see Figure 3.1). Lessons began with the rereading of a familiar text, typically the one read during the previous lesson. This was done to support fluency of oral reading, a recognized indicator of reading development among emergent and early readers. Tutors collected a running record to document progress and to make decisions about subsequent instruction (Frey & Hiebert, 2003). After the familiar text rereading, tutors introduced a new book. They emphasized several primary teaching points depending on the

---

Figure 3.1 Individual Lesson Plan Format

Student _____ Classroom Teacher _____

Date _____

Familiar Book: Level:

Result of Running Record:

New Book: Level:

Targeted Skills for This Lesson:

Book Introduction:

Word Work:

Writing:

Notes:

Future Skills to Work On:

---

learner's developmental reading level. For students reading between Levels A to 3, instruction focused on the following four areas:

1. One-to-one correspondence between words and oral reading, usually exhibited by placing a finger under the word as it is read
2. Left-to-right directionality within words and across words
3. Locating known and unknown words in the text
4. Return sweep (following text to the next line)

Students reading at a developmental reading level of 4–6 benefited from lessons that focused on using early reading behaviors (directionality, one-to-one correspondence) over longer text, phasing out finger pointing in reading text, using known words to solve unknown words, rereading to check or confirm, promoting fluency, and reading for meaning (Fountas & Pinnell, 1996).

Introduction of the new book included a picture walk—the practice of discussing the cover and illustrations in the book to preview the story—to provide the student with a cognitive frame. The tutor located targeted words and taught them in advance. The student then read aloud while the teacher supported and prompted his or her reading. After reading the text, a lesson emphasizing the targeted words or skill was taught. The lesson finished with a writing activity, usually a sentence about the book. The following day's lesson would begin with this same book, now a familiar text. The teacher then collected the running record to ascertain how much new information the student applied to the rereading (Clay, 1993). This lesson format was used throughout the length of the study.

Data Sources

We measured performance growth using the DRA (1999), a performance-based comprehensive diagnostic reading assessment for kindergarten through grade 4 that measures a student's independent reading level. Designed after Clay's (1993) running records, these benchmark assessments describe a young reader's ability to consolidate graphophonics, syntax, and semantics to make meaning. We agreed to use this instrument as the dependent variable because it is the measure used by the school district to gauge reading achievement and to make decisions about retention and promotion. We also collected field notes detailing observations of reading tutoring sessions, staff development, and faculty meetings, and interviewed teachers, tutors, and the principal.

Data Analysis

We coded each of the DRA (1999) scores from Tubman and entered them into a data file. We calculated descriptive statistics, measures of central tendency, and across-group comparisons (e.g., Kerlinger, 1986). We also applied inferential statistics to this data set and calculated an analysis of a comparison of means between Tubman and Banneker cohorts using a t-test, then calculated these test statistics to compare the entire first-grade class's DRA (1999) scores for the midyear cycle (preintervention) and the end-of-year cycle (postintervention) to determine if there was a meaningful treatment effect. We performed an independent-samples chi-square test to determine if there was a meaningful difference between the number of students retained at Tubman and Banneker at the end of the school year. We also analyzed the field notes and observations using a constant comparative method.

Limitations

The limitations of this study include the fact that this intervention was implemented at one elementary school and did not include random sampling. Because the scope of this study was limited to first-grade students, we cannot generalize the results to other grade levels. In addition, the tutors who worked in this study had extensive literacy knowledge; it is not known whether tutors with less literacy knowledge would have fostered similar gains in student achievement.

Results

In what follows, we summarize several findings that emerged from the analyses on the intervention.

Would reading scores improve by providing an intervention program that supported students' literacy development? Yes, the academic booster shot was an effective way of improving student achievement. The first-grade students were not significantly different in terms of DRA (1999) scores at the outset of the study ($t = 1.52$, $df = 483$, $p < 0.13$). Following the intervention, Tubman's first-grade DRA grade-level scores in English were higher ($M = 11.55$, $SD = 7.92$) than Banneker's ($M = 10.45$, $SD = 6.31$), but the difference was not significant ($t = 1.67$, $df = 466$, $p < 0.91$). It is interesting to note that when the analysis is focused on bilingual students, the results suggest that the intervention was effective. Tubman's test scores were significantly lower than Banneker's ($M_1 = 8.28$, $SD = 6.09$ vs. $M_2 = 10.15$, $SD = 5.97$) and these differences were statistically significant ($t = 2.27$, $df = 213$, $p < 0.03$). The gains made during the intervention closed the gap between the two schools. Tubman gained 6.63 points on the assessment, while Banneker's mean gain was 5.58 ($M_1 = 14.91$, $SD = 5.61$ vs. $M_2 = 15.73$, $SD = 6.01$). Although

significantly different at the preintervention, they were no longer different postintervention ($t = 1.02$, $df = 209$, $p < 0.3$).

Would the tutoring program reduce the number of students retained in first grade? An independent-samples chi-square test statistic was calculated using dichotomous data (retained/not retained). There were seven students retained at Tubman, meaning that they would repeat the first-grade curriculum for the following school year. This is an overall 3% retention rate. In contrast, 30 students were retained at Banneker (a 12.3% retention rate) indicating that there was a significant difference in the number of students retained at the two schools (χ^2 (1, $N = 468$) $= 8.42$, $p < 0.001$). Bear in mind that the treatment school used a higher standard for retention than the comparison school or school district. The treatment school required students to achieve a DRA (1999) level 8 (English or Spanish) to be promoted to second grade, higher than the district policy of a DRA level 3 score (English or Spanish).

Would the academic progress made by tutored students be maintained in second grade? Teachers administered the DRA again in March of the following school year (second grade), eight months after the end of the intervention. Of the original March cohort, 180 students (78%) remained. The nontutored students had a mean DRA score of 22.96 in March ($SD = 6.66$), while the tutored students possessed a mean DRA score of 16.05 ($SD = 5.13$), a difference of 6.91 points. This means that the tutored students possessed DRA scores that were 30% lower than their nontutored peers. This is a striking difference from one year earlier. In March, before the intervention began, the

> It is interesting to note that when the analysis is focused on bilingual students, the results suggest that the intervention was effective.

mean DRA score for all tutored students was 3.97, while their nontutored peers had a mean score of 11.38, a relative deficit reading percentage of 65% lower than their nontutored peers. These results suggest that the gap remained closer through the eight months after the intervention was over and did not regress to pre-intervention levels.

Discussion

We attribute the success of this tutoring program to several essential elements including the provision of additional individualized instruction, ongoing assessment of progress during tutoring, and coaching support for tutors.

Additional Individualized Instruction

Students in the intervention received 30 minutes of individualized instruction over 38 lessons. This level of instruction was not possible in most classrooms as teachers had 19 other students, many of whom were performing near or at grade level. This gift of time is an important consideration in designing intervention efforts.

Ongoing Assessment During the Tutoring

The intervention sessions were centered on a recursive cycle of assessment, instruction, and reflection. Each lesson began with a familiar reading while the tutor collected a running record of the student's oral reading behavior. A new book was introduced and the child then read again. The lesson concluded with word work and writing instruction. The focus of these lessons was drawn from analysis of previous running records. In this way, the tutors used their assessments to inform instruction. The emphasis on continuous assessment and interpretation of those assessments meant that students did not participate in the same lessons, for each objective was selected based on the results of the running record collected the previous day.

Support for Tutors

The tutors identified coaching as a critical component. We conducted weekly meetings to refine practice and solve problems related to logistics or teaching. In addition, we regularly observed tutors as they worked. Accordingly, we could provide "at the elbow" coaching for the tutors. Although the tutors were enthusiastic and motivated about participating in the intervention, the intense individual nature of the work was very different from their previous teaching experiences.

As the intervention progressed, the tutors' conversations shifted from concerns about the mechanics of their work, such as room arrangements and the sequence of the lesson, to dialogue about specific students. This finding echoes the work of Fuller and Parsons (1972) who demonstrated that teacher-centered concerns dominate early phases of new and unfamiliar instructional practice. It also mirrors the results of a previous study on the arc of professional development conversations among classroom teachers at the same school (Frey & Kelly, 2002).

This study has prompted other questions that remain unanswered. In particular, what are the effects of a series of academic booster shots during the early elementary years? We suspect that a multiyear program that offers short, intensive instruction for a limited period of time can produce a positive effect over time. A related question is whether a similar project might fit into a school's Response to Intervention (RtI) program. This process is now required by the Individuals with Disabilities Education Act of 2004. RtI programs are designed to offer intensive intervention before a student is referred for special education testing. While most RtI programs are conducted by general and special education teachers, our results suggest that trained tutors supervised by knowledgeable school personnel can also provide beneficial learning opportunities.

Implications

Our results suggest that a reading intervention tutoring program that is made available to students when they first show signs of falling behind can help them acquire more efficient habits that translate into higher reading achievement. In addition, we believe that it is vital to track the progress of students who have received tutoring for the purposes of intervention. It is unlikely that a one-shot tutoring program will be enough for stu-

dents who are falling behind. Therefore, it is prudent to plan tutoring programs with an academic booster shot approach, and to design follow-up tutoring for the student over several years.

Words of Advice

In-school tutoring and intervention efforts can result in improved student achievement and reduced numbers of students retained at grade level. However, there are a number of considerations necessary when designing such programs. We have included a number of questions that program developers might want to consider when implementing an intervention such as the one described here. We have organized the questions into a number of categories, including before tutoring, during tutoring, and after tutoring (see Table 3.1).

Table 3.1 Intervention Design and Critical Questions

Elements of Intervention Design	Critical Questions
Before the intervention: Communication and logistics	• Who will coordinate? • How will stakeholders (teachers, administrators, families) be consulted? • How will tutors be identified? • What materials will be used? How will they be obtained? • What are the space requirements? • What are the scheduling requirements? • What is the budget for the intervention?
Before the intervention: Establishing practices	• What is the intent of the intervention? • What is the method of delivery? • What lesson framework fits the intent? • What is the duration and frequency of the intervention? • What formative assessments will be used? • How will data be collected?
During the intervention: Ongoing support	• How will tutors be trained? • How will they be coached while tutoring? • How will they access professional development? • How will they communicate with classroom teachers? • How will ongoing assessments be used to make instructional decisions?
After the intervention: Making decisions about next steps	• What does the collected data, both qualitative and quantitative, indicate about the intervention? • What improvements can be made for the next intervention? • How will students gain access to the next intervention?
After the intervention: Academic booster shots	• At what interval will subsequent interventions occur? • How will continuity from one intervention cycle to the next be assured?

In particular, we advise the following:

- Tutoring programs such as this should begin with the identification of a coordinator who will gather information, meet with stakeholders, and monitor program fidelity. A complex task such as this has to "belong" to someone, or else it will belong to no one.

- In addition, the need for communication between classroom teachers and tutors is critical. The two groups have a great deal to offer one another, yet during busy school days it is easy for this to be pushed aside.

- Further, it is essential that classroom teachers are the ones to administer progress assessments. This allows for independent measures of progress and builds program buy-in among teachers.

REFERENCES

Clay, M.M. (1993). *Reading recovery: A guidebook for teachers in training*. Portsmouth, NH: Heinemann.

Clay, M.M. (2001). *Change over time: In children's literacy development*. Portsmouth, NH: Heinemann.

Dauber, S.L., Alexander, K.L., & Entwisle, D.R. (1993). Characteristics of retainees and early precursors of retention in grade: Who is held back? *Merrill-Palmer Quarterly*, *39*(3), 226–243.

Fountas, I.C., & Pinnell, G.S. (1996). *Guided reading: Good first teaching for all children*. Portsmouth, NH: Heinemann.

Frey, N., & Hiebert, E.H. (2003). Teacher-based assessment of literacy learning. In J. Flood, D. Lapp, J.R. Squire, & J. Jensen (Eds.), *Handbook of research on teaching the English language arts* (2nd ed., pp. 608–618). Mahwah, NJ: Erlbaum.

Frey, N., & Kelly, P.R. (2002). The effects of staff development, modeling, and coaching of interactive writing on instructional repertoires of K–1 teachers in a professional development school. In D.L. Schallert, C.M. Fairbanks, J. Worthy, B. Maloch, & J.V. Hoffman (Eds.), *51st yearbook of the National Reading Conference* (pp. 176–185). Oak Creek, WI: National Reading Conference.

Fuller, F.F., & Parsons, J.S. (1972, April). *Current research on the concerns of teachers*. Paper presented at the annual meeting of the American Educational Research Association, Chicago, IL.

Invernizzi, M.A. (2001). The complex world of one-on-one tutoring. In S.B. Neuman & D.K. Dickinson (Eds.), *Handbook of early literacy research* (pp. 459–470). New York: Guilford.

Johnson, R.B., & Onwuegbuzie, A.J. (2004). Mixed methods research: A research paradigm whose time has come. *Educational Researcher*, *33*(7), 14–26. doi:10.3102/0013189X033007014

Juel, C. (1988). Learning to read and write: A longitudinal study of 54 children from first through fourth grades. *Journal of Educational Psychology*, *80*(4), 437–447. doi:10.1037/0022-0663.80.4.437

Kerlinger, F.N. (1986). *Foundations of behavioral research* (3rd ed.). Orlando, FL: Harcourt Brace Jovanovich.

Morris, D., Tyner, B., & Perney, J. (2000). Early Steps: Replicating the effects of a first grade reading intervention program. *Journal of Educational Psychology*, *92*(4), 681–693. doi:10.1037/0022-0663.92.4.681

San Diego Unified School District. (2001, March). *The blueprint for student success: Expanded strategies for prevention, intervention, and retention*. San Diego, CA: Author.

Santa, C., & Hoein, T. (1999). An assessment of Early Steps: A program for early intervention of reading problems. *Reading Research Quarterly*, *34*(1), 54–73. doi:10.1598/RRQ.34.1.4

Stanovich, K.E. (1986). Matthew effects in reading: Some consequences of individual differences in the acquisition of literacy. *Reading Research Quarterly*, *21*(4), 360–407. doi:10.1598/RRQ.21.4.1

Stuebing, K.K., Fletcher, J.M., LeDoux, J.M., Lyon, G.R., Shaywitz, S.E., & Shaywitz, B.A. (2002). Validity of IQ-discrepancy classifications of reading disabilities: A meta-analysis. *American Educational Research Journal*, *39*(2), 469–518. doi:10.3102/00028312039002469

Vellutino, F.R., & Scanlon, D.M. (2001). Emergent literacy skills, early instruction, and individual differences as determinants of difficulties in learning to read: The case for early intervention. In S.B. Neuman & D.K. Dickinson (Eds.), *Handbook of early literacy research* (pp. 295–321). New York: Guilford.

ABOUT THE CONTRIBUTORS

Nancy Frey *is a professor of Literacy in the School of Teacher Education at San Diego State University (SDSU) and a teacher at Health Sciences High and Middle College, both in San Diego, California, USA. Before joining the university faculty, she was a teacher in the Broward County (Florida, USA) Public Schools, where she taught students at the elementary and middle school level. She worked at the state level for the Florida Inclusion Network helping districts design systems for supporting students with disabilities in the general education classroom. E-mail: nfrey@mail.sdsu.edu*

Diane Lapp *is a distinguished professor of Education in the Department of Teacher Education at San Diego State University who has taught in elementary and middle schools and now teaches*

English at Health Sciences High and Middle College, San Diego, California, USA. Her major areas of research and instruction have been of issues related to struggling readers and their families who live in urban, economically poor settings. She is also a member of both the California and the International Reading Halls of Fame. E-mail: lapp@mail.sdsu.edu

Douglas Fisher *is a professor of Language and Literacy Education at San Diego State University and a classroom teacher at Health Sciences High and Middle College, both in San Diego, California, USA. An early intervention specialist and language development specialist, he has taught high school English, writing, and literacy development to public school students. E-mail: dfisher@mail.sdsu.edu*

CHAPTER 4

"You Gotta Read It With Awake in You": Marginalized High School Readers, Engagement, Agency, and Reading as Performance

Mellinee Lesley

As members of a homeroom reading tutoring group in an urban high school, six sophomore and junior students explored possible texts to read. Following is an excerpt from a transcript of the first reading tutoring session of the adolescent literacy group described in this study.

Mellinee:	Ms. S just printed this [poem bearing the title of the book it is published in] off of the Internet, "The Rose That Grew From Concrete."
Lisa:	We gonna read this?
Mellinee:	We can read whatever you want, Lisa. What do you want to read? But this is Tupac Shakur's book of poetry. Have y'all read that?
Mando:	Are we, are we gonna read that?
Keonte:	I wanna read that. I done read the book.
Mellinee:	We can find it. We can get it online. And we can, we can get that one. We just want to know what you-all want to read. And, what all do you feel about that book?
Tara:	These all your books?
Mellinee:	Yeah, I'll share. I'm happy to share. So what do you-all think? [Group discussing quietly, passing around books.]
Keonte:	I wanna read this.
Mellinee:	Okay, so what do y'all think?
Shawna:	I like a lot of these books.
Mellinee:	Do they all sound good? Well, we can work our way through them. We've got a lot of time.
Tara:	I wanna read this book.
Keonte:	I wanna read this one.

Shawna: I like that one and that one and the Hollis Woods.

Tara: I wanna read all of 'em.

Mellinee: Okay, well let's talk about this. Do you want to read them all together, or do you want to read different books?

Keonte: I wanna read the one Lisa's [inaudible word]. [Laughing]

Shawna: I wanna read 1, 2, 3, 4 books.

Mellinee: Okay, well, let's choose. Let's take a vote.

A great deal has been written about struggling, at-risk, reluctant, marginalized, and resistant adolescent readers' lack of engagement with texts as a significant obstacle in their reading comprehension (Irvin, Buehl, & Klemp, 2006; Lenters, 2006; Tovani, 2000). In fact, research pertaining to adolescent literacy is fundamentally concerned with finding ways to foster comprehension through student engagement with school-based texts (Alvermann, 2001; Alvermann & Heron, 2001). The beginning vignette in this chapter, however, captures a different portrayal of marginalized, academically at-risk adolescents as fully engaged, enthusiastic readers.

As in other work that has examined the connections between self-selection of texts, self-regulation, and engagement for struggling adolescent readers (e.g., Tovani, 2000), the riddle of engagement for these students resided in their interpretive authority or ability to claim knowledge about a text afforded them within the tutorial setting. Selecting the texts to be read as a group of identified struggling high school readers was only the beginning. Through a yearlong endeavor of reading together with adult mentors, these students revealed that engagement with reading is not a dichotomous process of all or nothing ("I'm a reader" or "I'm not a reader") or school-sanctioned texts versus nonschool or authentic texts (e.g., zines or teen-created magazines, websites, video games, graffiti). Rather, engagement involves a complex and contingent weaving together of definitions of literacy, agency, and reading identity within the context of multifaceted purposes for literacy. In this manner, adolescent engagement with texts is fluid and often mercurial in nature. Moje (2002) describes this phenomenon as a derivative of youth culture.

Translating such authentic practices of youth-driven literacies into classroom settings, however, is problematic. Guzzetti and Gamboa (2004) argue that simply adding new types of assignments such as zine projects for adolescents is not the seemingly axiomatic solution to translating youth literacies into classroom practice in the hope of fostering engagement with texts. Rather, a greater understanding of the complexities of adolescent engagement with print-based texts is needed. Based on their at-risk status for academic failure, the students involved in this study were all participants in the Communities in Schools (CIS) program, which is the nation's largest drop-out prevention program.

As an externally funded agency created to promote student success, CIS defines at-risk status based on a student's probability for dropping out of high school. Risk factors include the following:

- failure of two or more classes
- having not been promoted to the next grade level

- pregnancy or teen parenthood

- homelessness

- eligibility for free lunch

- eligibility for Temporary Assistance for Needy Families (TANF)

- failure of a state-required standardized test

- being on academic probation

- currently in a family crisis

- having an incarcerated parent

The high school in which this study took place is located in a low socioeconomic community composed of a predominantly minority population in a city in the southwestern United States. At the time of the study, the student body of the high school consisted of 48% African American students, 46% Latino students, and 4% white students. Seventy-nine percent of the student body was eligible to receive free or reduced-cost lunch. The school was also identified as a low-performing campus based on state-mandated standardized test scores. The reading group sessions occurred once a week.

> "Language has meaning only in and through social practices."

Amid tremendous fluctuations such as new tutoring participants drifting in for a few sessions, students leaving due to pregnancy, changes in CIS staff, and uncertain classroom settings, we managed to create a solid and consistent tutoring project. As such, this research is primarily the story of six at-risk high school students and their interactions with texts, peers, and mentors within a reading group that met in the middle of a high school day.

Question Guiding the Research

Pragmatically, the reading tutorial group functioned as a place where students collectively selected, read, and discussed texts together. As an educator, I wanted the literacy group to be a place where adults listened to adolescents and mutual planning and goal setting occurred between all members in the group. As a researcher, my objective in conducting this study was to develop a greater understanding of the ways at-risk adolescents approach text. Specifically, I wanted to explore the circumstances under which adolescents deemed to be at risk for academic failure become engaged in reading text. To this end, I developed the following primary research question to guide this study:

- How do struggling adolescent readers identified as at risk for academic failure select and respond to texts in a reading tutorial setting designed to foster literacy strategies considered appropriate for reading in high school course work?

Theoretical Background and Perspectives

Gee (2005) writes, "*language has meaning only in and through social practices*" (p. 8, italics in original). The social practice of language in this study resided largely in the interactions among students, mentors, and texts. Therefore, I used discourse analysis (Gee, 2005) as a way to examine students' use of language in response to texts in this tutorial setting. Beyond discourse analysis as a tool to investigate language use, I also drew on theories of struggling adolescent readers (e.g., O'Brien, 2006), transactional theories of reading (e.g., Rosenblatt, 2004), and theories of literacy identities as a form of agency (e.g., Moore &

Cunningham, 2006) to provide a lens for analysis in this work.

Because of the analytical focus of this research on social interactions and language, methodologically this study is grounded in sociocultural literacy theories (Dyson, 2004; Gee, 2004; Heath, 2004). Sociocultural theories of literacy are predicated upon the notion that literacy events and learning take place within social contexts and culturally defined discourse communities.

Methodology

For purposes of data collection, I used qualitative research methods predicated on a teacher research stance (Bauman & Duffy-Hester, 2002). Although this was not a traditional teacher research study in many respects, I served as a classroom teacher in the reading tutorial setting.

Participants

All of the students involved in the literacy group met one or more of the previously mentioned CIS criteria for being at risk. In addition to the CIS criteria, two of the students were receiving services for special education in all subject areas. At the completion of this study, most of the students were juniors in high school. Five of the students were African American; one student was Latino. Lisa (female) was 17, Keonte (male) was 16, Tara (female) was 17, Mando (male) was 17, Michael (male) was 16, and Shawna (female) was 17.

Data Sources

Data sources for this study included the following:

- Participant-observation analytic field notes (Spradley, 1980) of weekly group sessions
- Transcriptions of audiotapes of each group session

- Semistructured interviews conducted with four of the participants in the study at the conclusion of the project
- Periodic formal and informal interviews with a key informant in the high school setting
- A collection of student writing samples generated during the group sessions as well as writings the participants shared spontaneously arising from other venues (e.g., school assignments)
- Personal writing (or what Mahiri [2004] calls "street scripts")
- My reflective journal notes of each weekly session

Data Analysis

I analyzed data for this study through a grounded theory approach (Harry, Sturges, & Klingner, 2005). I also used discourse analysis (Gee, 2005) to analyze transcripts of the tutorial sessions. I began by developing open codes for the data sources and then refined these codes into axial codes, which consisted of combining codes with similar patterns together. Finally, I developed selective codes containing two predominant themes or theoretical codes from the axial codes pertaining to students' definitions of reading. To deepen my understanding of these themes, I engaged in discourse analysis with excerpts from the transcripts that I had identified as exemplifying these themes.

I relied on Gee's (2005) seven building tasks of language to guide my discourse analysis. These building tasks include significance, activities, identities, relationships, politics, connections, and sign systems and knowledge (pp. 11–13). Through discourse analysis I was able to better understand the students' perspectives about processes of reading within this setting.

To verify my analysis, I followed up the group sessions by conducting interviews with four of the students participating in the group. I did not conduct interviews with all six because by the conclusion of the tutoring project, one of the six students had left the high school and one student declined to participate in an individual interview. In these interviews, I asked students about their views of the group and their roles as readers both within and outside of the group. In an effort to further establish trustworthiness of the data analysis, I also engaged in periodic debriefing with a fellow reading educator who had attended some of the tutoring sessions as well as with the CIS Campus Youth Coordinator, who attended the group meetings on a regular basis.

Limitations

This study is limited by the small number of participants. It is also limited by the fact that the students involved in this project are not necessarily representative of other high school students across the United States. All of the students came from the same urban neighborhood in the southwestern United States.

Results

Through analysis of the data sources, I discovered the students in this study constructed definitions of reading and positioned themselves as readers around reading as a public performance and these definitions dominated the students' views of reading.

> The students in this study constructed definitions of reading and positioned themselves as readers around reading as a public performance.

Performance as Embedded Narrative

In the following exchange, Lisa takes control of the discussion surrounding the text *Pictures of Hollis Woods* (Giff, 2003).

Mellinee:	Was she with, was she with Josie?
Lisa:	No.
Mellinee:	How old was she, do you think?
Lisa:	How old was, uh, Hollis? Well, she be probably like 11, 12—10 through 12.
Mellinee:	When she, when she had the doll?
Lisa:	I don't know. How old are you?
Shawna:	13.
Mando:	Probably [long pause]
Lisa:	8, 9, 10.
Mellinee:	Maybe but—
Education Professor:	She was pretty young.
Mellinee:	Yeah, I mean, when do kids play with dolls and talk to dolls like that typically?
Lisa:	Well, my niece 12. She still play with dolls. One my niece 10, she still play. And, like, if I still, when I play with 'em I just do the hair.
Mellinee:	So, it could be, it could have been her age now because she looks about how old she is right now in the story. Or it could have been when she was younger.
Lisa:	Uh huh.
Mellinee:	But, was it with Josie?
Lisa:	She probably with Steve and them.
Mellinee:	What do you think Shawna?
Lisa:	No, she with Steve and them.
Mellinee:	Was it with Josie?
Shawna:	I don't know.

The activities captured in this excerpt of dialogue constituted primarily a question-and-answer session between the students and me. Throughout this exchange, Lisa asserted her interpretive authority and knowledge of the text by dominating the discussion. She did this by including an embedded narrative about her nieces and their ages and the ways they play with dolls. She also did this by continuing to answer my questions (e.g., "Was she with Josie?") when I repeated and directed them to other students.

Another education professor in attendance during this group discussion tried to guide the interpretation of the text by offering, "She was pretty young." This interjection could have distracted Lisa from her interpretation of the character's age. Even though I kept posing questions to the group trying to lead them to a different conclusion and understanding of the concept of a flashback in this novel, Lisa continued to respond without compromising her initial answer. In fact, Lisa exerted authority in the wake of my lack of satisfaction with some of her responses.

In the first instance, Lisa took on a defiant, challenging posture retorting, "I don't know. How old are you?" This question was a defensive response implying she did not want me to undermine her interpretive authority. As my colleague and I attempted to guide the group's understanding of the text with additional questions and statements, Lisa then interjected a narrative from her personal experiences to support her original assertion about the character's age in the flashback scene. Both of these moves were used to ensure Lisa's interpretive authority with the text and dominate the meaning making occurring within the group discussion.

Because Lisa dominated the responses to such an extent, by the end even when other students were asked to respond directly, they virtually refused to offer an opinion. Shawna's response of "I don't know" indicated a resignation from taking any type of further interpretive authority of her own or siding with either my interpretation or Lisa's. Earlier in the transcript, she had responded with the answer, "13."

An interesting intersection of power emerged from my not validating Lisa's, Shawna's, and Mando's responses by continuing to ask questions and from Lisa dominating the responses. Lisa did not respond to my questions and play for interpretive authority by changing her answer until she received approval from me. Instead, she asserted her opinion repeatedly and presented an embedded narrative to support her response.

Performance as Knowledge of Textual Conventions

In the following example occurring toward the end of the group sessions, Tara demonstrated an instance where the performance of reading included knowledge of school-sanctioned conventions of text. In this discussion over a poem by Tupac Shakur (1999), Tara turned to information from her English class to help her successfully construct meaning and thus perform as a reader.

Tara: It's like a fig-u-a, figurative language. You know what that mean?

Mando: No. [gives a slight, nervous laugh]

Tara: It's not really all happening in the book.

Mellinee: Okay. Excellent. So, it's not literal. When you say it's, it's figurative it's not—

Tara: Let me see my literary terms, you know, and [inaudible] something.

Mellinee: [laughs slightly] Are you learning this in English?

Tara: [reading from a paper she has fished out of her backpack] "Figurative language means something besides what is said literally and is often used in poetry."

Mando: Yep.

Through this brief exchange, Tara asserted interpretative authority by making reference to her knowledge of textual conventions. Specifically, Tara interpreted text by referencing information pertaining to literary analysis from her English class. In doing so, she took on the role and performance of a classroom teacher with some degree of ventriloquism when she asked Mando, "You know what that mean?" and explained the concept to him through both her own paraphrase as well as a dictionary definition. Tara's questioning Mando was not belittling in nature. She did not speak for him the way Lisa did at different times with various students. She did, however, follow up with posing a question by providing a definitive answer as opposed to leading a discussion in the manner that I typically did, which further highlighted her taking on the role of a classroom teacher to read the text. The social good expressed in this excerpt was interpretive authority exhibited through the correct answer. In this case the correct answer was derived from an external, school-sanctioned form of information.

Performance as Reading Aloud in a Fluent Manner

Shortly after the exchange about figurative language took place, we began to read another poem by Tupac Shakur (1999) that elicited advice about the importance of reading aloud in a fluent (including attention to prosody) manner (Kuhn & Stahl, 2004).

Mellinee: Let's look at the next poem, "Life Through My Eyes." Who wants to read?

Mando: Me!

Michael: I'll read it.

Mellinee: Do you want to read Shawna? Okay, thank you.

Lisa: You gotta read it with awake in you, like...make it sound—

Mando: Interesting.

Lisa: Yeah. Don't just.... "Life through my bloodshot eyes" [spoken in a flat tone of voice simultaneously with Tara]

Shawna went on to read the poem in a soft voice, quickly but accurately.

Reading texts aloud in the reading group was a privilege for which the students vied. In the previous exchange, both Mando and Michael volunteered to read this poem, but I invited Shawna because she had not yet had a turn to read. Once Shawna agreed to read the poem, Lisa, Mando, and Tara gave her advice on how she should read aloud. In doing so, they asserted identities as experts in reading aloud performance and in this manner asserted interpretive authority. They coached Shawna on how to interpret the reading with inflection and prosody. They also intimated, through their imitation of monotone reading, that Shawna had been guilty of reading in this manner in past tutorial sessions.

This was an example of ventriloquism, where Tara and Lisa presented two instances of ways people read text that are good and bad. With the advice for reading, Lisa and Tara related to Shawna as authorities. In effect, Lisa and Tara usurped Shawna's interpretive authority with their implicit criticism of her ability to perform text. Shawna did not outwardly protest this behavior. After the interpretive advice, however, Shawna read the text rapidly, in a soft voice with little inflection.

In this excerpt, emphasis was placed on the correct way to perform a text through reading aloud. Successful reading was equated to oral fluency and prosody. There was also an assumption presented that there is one way to read a text that is preferred over other ways.

Discussion

I opened this chapter with an excerpt from the first literacy group session that demonstrated the energy and interest at-risk adolescents exhibited toward the prospect of reading books. Through my subsequent work with this group of students, I came to see the intricacies of their engagement with texts as centered around their views of reading as a performance. Similar to Alvermann, Young, Green, and Wisenbaker's (1999) research, I discovered the students' models of reading were outgrowths of school and peer models of reading.

In individual interviews with the students, I was able to get a sense of the kinds of significant school reading experiences each student brought to the group. Through such an exploration, I discovered that all of the students had been steeped in years of classroom reading experiences that involved traditional, whole-class reading instruction predicated upon teacher lecture and read-alouds, round-robin reading, and teacher-directed question-and-answer sessions.

Reading as performance is a notion that is reinforced in many high school classroom settings where such traditional reading techniques are relied upon as a typical mode for reading instruction across the content areas. Instances of transactional theories of reading rarely figured into the students' previous reading experiences. Good readers, thus, are those students who do not stumble over pronunciation of words, read with a sense of prosody, and answer comprehension questions about the text "correctly." Given these experiences, it is not surprising that such models of reading instruction would filter into the ways the students in this study constructed definitions of reading around performance and, furthermore, that engagement with texts also hinged on the ways students constructed themselves as good readers through their reading performances.

> "We need to turn our focus to the relationships that we build with youth inside the classroom."

Implications

Franzak (2006) notes of the educational settings for marginalized adolescent readers, "we need to turn our focus to the relationships that we build with youth inside the classroom, relationships that have the power to value individuals, cultural backgrounds, and a range of textual and discursive practices" (p. 228). Franzak speaks to the influence and overlap that occurs between adolescents and adults in school settings. Offering a similar concern about the ways teachers relate to adolescents, Moje (2002) writes,

> What we have not done, and where we need to direct our attention in the future, is to examine how youths' literacy practices reflect the intersection of multiple groups (e.g., ethnic groups, youth cultural groups, social class groups, to name just a few), and to examine how the knowledges [sic], ways of knowing, and identities they build from those group experiences intersect with the advanced, deep content learning teachers, parents and administrators expect young people to do in secondary school classrooms. (p. 213)

In essence, Moje advises that much more research devoted to sociocultural aspects of secondary content area literacy with at-risk adolescents is warranted.

What I have learned through my work with these students in a tutorial scenario is this: Marginalized adolescent readers need spaces to explore literature without fear of reprimand or embarrassment. It is also important that such spaces are legitimized by literacy experts and as much as possible by peers. Students need to be able to make assertions about texts without feeling as though they have failed in their ability to perform as readers. They need to verbalize their seemingly idiosyncratic and personal narrative connections. They need to be permitted to mispronounce words and stumble over language without being made to feel humiliated and as if success as a reader is contingent upon a public performance of reading rate and accuracy in pronunciation. They need to feel like fully functional members of school-sanctioned learning.

With this connection between reading performance and engagement with texts in mind, one of the implications for this study is the importance of successful public performances in reading for struggling adolescent readers. The findings from this study suggest that agency (Ahearn, 2001) and engagement are complementary processes for adolescents who are identified as struggling readers and at risk for academic failure. Adolescents become engaged with nonschool texts because they feel a sense of agency and interpretive authority over the task of reading in nonschool settings (Moje, 2000). The challenge for educators, consequently, is not so much to adopt the literacies perpetuated by youth culture (e.g., zines) through class assignments, but rather to re-create the authority adolescents experience within discourse communities delineated by youth culture. Ultimately, interpretive authority with texts is a key ingredient to fostering reading engagement for at-risk adolescents.

Words of Advice

The following ingredients proved to be crucial in facilitating student success in this project:

- Feedback predicated upon a right/wrong, evaluative stance of student response serves to alienate adolescents from reading tasks whereas a more process-oriented stance to question-posing and student response facilitates greater student engagement.

- Encouraging students to participate in the selection process of texts is important for fostering student engagement.

- Incorporating popular media texts with which adolescents have prior knowledge helps foster textual authority. Not only are adolescents better equipped to interpret the writings of popular media texts because of their familiarity with them but also they are more interested in working at interpreting such texts.

REFERENCES

Ahearn, L.M. (2001). Language and agency. *Annual Review of Anthropology, 30*(1), 109–137. doi:10.1146/annurev.anthro.30.1.109

Alvermann, D.E. (2001). Reading adolescents' reading identities: Looking back to see ahead. *Journal of Adolescent & Adult Literacy, 44*(8), 676–690.

Alvermann, D.E., & Heron, A.H. (2001). Literacy identity work: Playing to learn with popular media. *Journal of Adolescent & Adult Literacy, 45*(2), 118–122.

Alvermann, D.E., Young, J.P., Green, C., & Wisenbaker, J.M. (1999). Adolescents' perceptions and negotiations of literacy practices in after-school read and talk clubs. *American Educational Research Journal, 36*(2), 221–264.

Bauman, J.F., & Duffy-Hester, A.M. (2002). Making sense of classroom worlds: Methodology in teacher research. In M.L. Kamil, P.B. Mosenthal, P.D. Pearson, & R. Barr (Eds.), *Methods of literacy research: The methodology chapters from the* Handbook of Reading Research (Vol. 3, pp. 1–22). Mahwah, NJ: Erlbaum.

Dyson, A.H. (2004). Writing and the sea of voices: Oral language in, around, and about writing. In R.B. Ruddell & N.J. Unrau (Eds.), *Theoretical models and processes of reading* (5th ed., pp. 146–162). Newark, DE: International Reading Association.

Franzak, J.K. (2006). *Zoom*: A review of the literature on marginalized adolescent readers, literacy theory and policy implications. *Review of Educational Research*, 76(2), 209–248. doi:10.3102/00346543076002209

Gee, J. (2004). Reading as situated language: A sociocognitive perspective. In R.B. Ruddell & N.J. Unrau (Eds.), *Theoretical models and processes of reading* (5th ed., pp. 116–132). Newark, DE: International Reading Association.

Gee, J.P. (2005). *An introduction to discourse analysis: Theory and method*. New York: Routledge.

Guzzetti, B.J., & Gamboa, M. (2004). Zines for social justice: Adolescent girls writing on their own. *Reading Research Quarterly*, 39(4), 408–436. doi:10.1598/RRQ.39.4.4

Harry, B., Sturges, K.M., & Klingner, J.K. (2005). Mapping the process: An exemplar of process and challenges in grounded theory analysis. *Educational Researcher*, 34(2), 3–13. doi:10.3102/0013189X034002003

Heath, S.B. (2004). The children of Trackton's children: Spoken and written language in social change. In R.B. Ruddell & N.J. Unrau (Eds.), *Theoretical models and processes of reading* (5th ed., pp. 187–209). Newark, DE: International Reading Association.

Irvin, J.L., Buehl, D.R., & Klemp, R.M. (2006). *Reading and the high school student: Strategies to enhance literacy* (2nd ed.). Boston: Allyn & Bacon.

Kuhn, M.R., & Stahl, S.A. (2004). Fluency: A review of developmental and remedial practices. In R.B. Ruddell & N.J. Unrau (Eds.), *Theoretical models and processes of reading* (5th ed., pp. 412–453). Newark, DE: International Reading Association.

Lenters, K. (2006). Resistance, struggle, and the adolescent reader. *Journal of Adolescent & Adult Literacy*, 50(2), 136–146. doi:10.1598/JAAL.50.2.6

Mahiri, J. (2004). *What they don't learn in school: Literacy in the lives of urban youth*. New York: Peter Lang.

Moje, E.B. (2000). 'To be part of the story': The literacy practices of gangsta adolescents. *Teachers College Record*, 102(3), 651–690. doi:10.1111/0161-4681.00071

Moje, E.B. (2002). Re-framing adolescent literacy research for new times: Studying youth as a resource. *Reading Research and Instruction*, 4(1), 211–228.

Moore, D.W., & Cunningham, J.W. (2006). Adolescent agency and literacy. In D.E. Alvermann, K.A. Hinchman, D.W. Moore, S.F. Phelps, & D.R. Waff (Eds.), *Reconceptualizing the literacies in adolescents' lives* (2nd ed., pp. 129–146). Mahwah, NJ: Erlbaum.

O'Brien, D. (2006). "Struggling" adolescents' engagement in multimediating: Countering the institutional construction of incompetence. In D.E. Alvermann, K.A. Hinchman, D.W. Moore, S.F. Phelps, & D.R. Waff (Eds.), *Reconceptualizing the literacies in adolescents' lives* (2nd ed., pp. 29–46). Mahwah, NJ: Erlbaum.

Rosenblatt, L.M. (2004). The transactional theory of reading and writing. In R.B. Ruddell & N.J. Unrau (Eds.). *Theoretical models and processes of reading* (5th ed., pp. 1363–1398). Newark, DE: International Reading Association.

Spradley, J.P. (1980). *Participant observation*. New York: Harcourt Brace Jovanovich College.

Tovani, C. (2000). *I read it, but I don't get it: Comprehension strategies for adolescent readers*. Portland, ME: Stenhouse.

LITERATURE CITED

Giff, P.R. (2003). *Pictures of Hollis Woods*. New York: Yearling.

Shakur, T. (1999). *The rose that grew from concrete*. New York: Simon & Schuster.

ABOUT THE CONTRIBUTOR

Mellinee Lesley *teaches at Texas Tech University, Lubbock, Texas, USA, as an associate professor in both the Language & Literacy Program and the Secondary Education Program. Currently, she has over 19 years of teaching experience in high school, adult basic education, developmental reading, freshman composition, and teacher preparation settings. Her recent research direction is an exploration of the literacy development of at-risk adolescents in third space settings. E-mail: mellinee.lesley@ttu.edu*

CHAPTER 5

Literacy Partners Program:
In-School Tutoring in a School–University Partnership

Kelly B. Cartwright, Donna S. Savage, Kathryn D.S. Morgan,
and Brian J. Nichols

Kendall, a first grader, looks up to see Taylor, her tutor and Literacy Partner, walk through the classroom door. Kendall stands up beaming as she walks to greet her. "Do you have a new book for me today?" she asks.

"Yes, I have a great book for you about a family working and playing together on a Saturday morning. What kinds of things do you like to do with your family?" Taylor asks as they walk down the hall.

"Play games, go shopping, play out in the yard," replies Kendall.

As they reach the table in the corner of the school's literacy room, they sit side by side. In front of Kendall is a white dry-erase board. Taylor hands Kendall a marker and tells her to write the sight words *with, where,* and *could* several times to practice automatic, fluent word writing. Grinning broadly, she looks up at Taylor to show her what she had written:

Taylor: Great writing, Kendall. Let's look at a few books you have already read. [Taylor pulls a book out of a basket of leveled readers on the table. See Mesmer, 2008, for more information on leveled readers and various book leveling systems.] We read this book last time. Let's try it again today. [After reading a few familiar books, Taylor pulls out the new book for today's lesson.]

Taylor: This book is about a family. Let's look at the pictures. What kinds of things do you see the family doing together?

As they look at the pictures, Kendall discusses what she notices. The picture of the dog digging in the dirt makes her giggle. Kendall remembers one afternoon when her family had to get their dog out of the flower bed. Excited about the new book, Kendall begins to read. She stops and looks at Taylor when she reaches an unfamiliar word:

Taylor: That's a tricky word. What could you try?

Literacy Tutoring That Works: A Look at Successful In-School, After-School, and Summer Programs, edited by Janet C. Richards and Cynthia A. Lassonde. © 2009 International Reading Association.

Kendall: Grass?

Taylor: It could be grass. Does it end like grass?

Kendall: Grrrasss. No.

Taylor: What else could you try?

Kendall: Garden?

Taylor: Are you right? Slow check it.

Kendall: Garrrdennn, garden!

Taylor: Keep going.

Kendall: [rereading] The dog is in the garden.

Taylor: Great job. As you turn the pages, remember to check the pictures when you get stuck on a word. [Kendall stops again.]

Taylor: That's a tricky word. Get your mouth ready, look at the picture and try something.

Kendall: /P/, working?

Taylor: Mom *is* working. What is she doing in the picture?

Kendall: Painting. Painting!

Taylor: Are you right? Does that word start like *painting*?

Kendall: /P/, paaaintinng, yes! Mom is painting. [Kendall is beaming.]

As Kendall finishes the book, Taylor returns to one of the pages to point out the good reading work Kendall had accomplished:

Taylor: Show me the tricky word on this page. What did you do when you got stuck? [Kendall shows her how she looked at the first letter and checked the picture to see what the word could be.]

Taylor: I like what you did to figure that word out. You are becoming such a great reader! [Kendall smiles as Taylor stands up to take her back to class.]

Kendall: Can we read a book about dogs next time? My aunt just got a new dog, and I thought I could find out how to train her to sit down.

Taylor: Sure. It's fun to read and learn new things, isn't it?

Kendall: Yes. It is!

This opening vignette illustrates a typical tutor–student exchange that might take place in the Literacy Partners program, an in-school tutoring program that accompanies a graduate-level reading course in a Master of Arts in Teaching Program that prepares students for initial teacher licensure. University professors and elementary reading teachers provide guidance to graduate-level preservice teachers as they learn to deliver instructional support to struggling readers. Our instructional model was adapted from the well-known and effective Reading Recovery intervention (Clay, 1993). Struggling readers as well as graduate students benefit from research-based, individualized instruction in our school–university partnership.

Our program evolved over several years, and each of us has played a different role in this process. Thus, our chapter describes particular individuals' participation in the program's evolution, with most sections written in our collective voice, reflective of the partnership. We selected this structure to give readers insight on the nature and development of our Literacy Partners program.

In an effort to have every child reading well and independently by the end of third grade, The America Reads Challenge Act of 1997 prompted community service organizations, churches, and universities to partner with elementary schools in our school district. These groups provided volunteers, monies, and donations to help schools get instructional support materials and provide tutoring to struggling readers. At first, tutoring programs varied widely: Some schools started with Foster Grandparents programs, in which elderly, paid tutors read to individual students on a weekly basis. Others provided after-school volunteers to help students with homework and study skills.

As other schools were developing their programs, Donna's (second author's) school worked to find a program that would best meet its students' needs. Due to the close proximity of a major university and various churches, volunteers were already being recruited to serve the K–3 population of the school. The number of volunteers in the building at one point had reached an all-time high of close to 100. Teachers were over-

whelmed as they attempted to provide a plan for each volunteer. All too often volunteers were simply sitting with students as they completed class work. Therefore, the school recognized an unstructured program would no longer suffice. Only a structured program would make the most efficient use of the volunteers' and the students' time. At the beginning of the 1997–1998 school year, the school prepared a new, structured tutoring program.

Because Donna was a trained Reading Recovery teacher, she helped design the program around the procedures of a typical Reading Recovery lesson (Clay, 1993). The components of the lesson were sound, but the initial training of the volunteers was limited to one orientation a year. As tutors became more proficient, the lessons were strengthened. However, the effectiveness of the lessons depended more on the consistency of the volunteers' participation. Because of the transience of the volunteers, the program lacked the continuity that it needed to obtain results.

By chance in 2003 Donna met Kelly Cartwright (first author), a university professor, in the school office. Donna learned Kelly was in the process of designing an elementary reading course for the local university's new Master of Arts in Teaching (MAT) program. Our discussion led to Literacy Partners, a school/university partnership that continues to exist. This partnership provides the elementary students with tutors who are preservice teachers enrolled in a reading methods course. The preservice teachers are able to connect theory with practical experiences as they work with struggling readers. Tutors meet with two students each week: a first grader developing decoding, word recognition, and fluency skills and a third or fourth grader developing comprehension skills. We purposefully select pairings such as these to ensure that the tutors will experience a varied range of experiences, instructional needs, and challenges.

The materials to support the initial tutoring program were purchased with funds provided by the Department of Psychology, the Teacher Preparation Program, and the Office of the Dean of the College of Liberal Arts and Sciences at the university. These materials include leveled books sorted and stored in plastic baskets, read-aloud books, magnetic letters, cookie sheets, white dry-erase boards, and dry-erase markers. We store the materials in the corner of an elementary school literacy room on a bookshelf provided by the elementary school, adjacent to a table and chairs where the tutors work with their students. Tutors keep notes on tutoring sessions with forms provided for that purpose, and these notes are kept in student folders stored in a file cabinet in the literacy room (see Figure 5.1 for an example of the form). The elementary school's reading teachers also work with students in the literacy room and are thus easily accessible to the tutors to answer questions or provide feedback on the tutoring sessions.

Figure 5.1 Record Sheet Example

Student __Kendall Greene__   Grade __1__   Level __E__

Tutor __Taylor Lewis__

Date: 12/08

Fluent Writing: Kendall wrote "with," "when," and "could." "Could" wasn't automatic. Kendall needs additional practice with this word.

Reading Aloud: I read *Caps for Sale* by Esphyr Slobodkina [1987] to model fluent reading.

Rereading Familiar Book(s): Kendall reread *Brown Bear, Brown Bear, What Do You See?* by Bill Martin [2007]. Kendall made two self-corrections and showed reasonable fluency.

Making Words: Started with "car" and went to "jar" and "far," to provide background knowledge to support Kendall's later reading of "garden." Needs additional practice with onset and rime for next lesson.

Writing Activity: Kendall made a statement about losing a hat at the mall, which we wrote together, as follows: *I lost my hat at the mall.*

We used letter boxes for "lost" and "mall." Kendall knew "at" and wrote "hat" by analogy. "I," "my," "at," and "the" were all known words.

Introducing and Reading New Book: Because the new book focuses on working with your family, I talked with Kendall about things families do together to activate prior knowledge. We completed a picture walk to preview some of the story concepts. Kendall had trouble with "grass," "garden," and "painting." We need to work on using pictures, meaning, and initial letters together when reading a new text.

Other Activity (Optional): We did not do any other activities in this lesson.

Notes for Next Lesson: Find books about dogs for next read aloud and/or new book.

Planning for Literacy Partners begins when Kathryn Morgan (third author), an elementary school reading teacher, uses beginning-of-year results from the Phonological Awareness Literacy Screening (PALS; 2008) to identify students who are below grade-level benchmarks for reading. Consulting school calendars and schedules, Kathryn determines the days and times when each student is available for tutoring. She records the resulting student names and time frames on large charts that we hang on the walls of the school's cafeteria during the initial tutor orientation and training session at the elementary school. The tutors sign up for 30-minute slots on the charts within the noted, available time frames for two students: one student who is developing decoding skills and another who is developing comprehension skills. We recommend that tutors choose two times that are in close proximity, which will require them to make only one visit to the school per week.

The tutors receive a handbook at the orientation that contains university and school contact information, school calendars and schedules, an introduction, directions for tutoring, sight word lists, and information on instructional strategies (see Table 5.1). We provide strategy prompts that reduce the possibility of confusion for elementary students by ensuring a common language between the tutors and the classroom teachers. Tutor training continues throughout the semester-long tutoring period and occurs in the university classroom as well as at the elementary school. The tutors are required to observe a Reading Recovery lesson and participate in reflection sessions at the elementary school. Additionally, they are given regular opportunities to discuss the students with school reading teachers and the university professor. We have found that our combined expertise affords the university tutors the chance to gain insight on the process of reading development by readily applying theory and research to practice.

As stated previously, we adapted the tutoring lessons from Clay's (1993) successful Reading Recovery intervention in that tutors establish relationships with elementary students in a one-on-one, 30-minute tutoring model. As a result, elementary students receive consistent support on a weekly basis, and preservice teachers are able to follow students' progress across a semester of tutoring. This experience provides tutors an invaluable vantage point for observing each student's unique problem-solving and reading development firsthand. Reading acquisition occurs best when students are reading appropriately leveled or "just right" texts (Allington, 2005; Mesmer, 2008). Matching readers to texts is particularly important for struggling readers like those targeted for our tutoring program because such readers typically receive most classroom instruction in texts that are too difficult (Allington, 2001). Therefore, each student's tutoring lesson features carefully selected text and is individually designed within the student's zone of proximal development (Vygotsky, 1978). Tutors record observations of each student's problem solving on lesson records, which are used for reflection and planning purposes. Our ultimate goal for the tutoring program is to arm students with problem-solving strategies so they can work independently and on grade level.

Each lesson begins with fluent writing. Students practice writing and reading high-frequency words to achieve automaticity. The tutors record the words students know or almost know and practice those on a weekly basis. To support this activity, we provide lists of high-frequency words for each grade level (e.g., Dolch sight words, Dolch, 1936; or Fry's instant words, Fry & Kress, 2006) in the tutoring handbook. Reading aloud to the students occurs next, and varies from the Reading Recovery lesson format.

Table 5.1 Instructional Strategies for First-Grade Literacy Lessons

Component	Description
Fluent Writing	This allows the student to practice writing high-frequency words in order to quickly and easily recognize and write them in stories. Ask the student to quickly write a word on the chalk or dry-erase board. If the student doesn't know the word, kindly say, "This is how I write the word _____," and then write it, read it, and move on. Repeat this procedure for 1 or 2 more words. Keep a record of words that the child can write fluently, as well as a list of words that will require further practice. Use an Instant Word List (Fry & Kress, 2006) when planning for this task.
Reading Aloud	This allows you to model what good reading sounds like for the student, and expose the student to book language. Talking about the book with the student provides for relationship building through genuine conversation, as well as a time to recognize what good readers do as they read: match 1:1, reread to predict, make connections, create mental images, and ask questions.
Rereading Familiar Books	This promotes fluent reading: the student should "sound like talking" as she or he reads a familiar text aloud to you. After the first tutoring session, the student should reread all or part of 2–3 books that have been previously read aloud to you. Always follow the reading of a book with a question or statement related to the book's meaning.
Letter or Making Words Work	This provides the student with practice in letter recognition, word recognition, or manipulating a word part so that he or she can read and write new words featuring the same part, or "chunk." Either select a few dissimilar letters to practice, a high-frequency word that has been troublesome for the student, or select a word from the Writing Vocabulary Chart in order to move from the known to the unknown using a "chunk." Use magnetic letters or letter cards for this task.
Writing	This supports the connection between reading and writing: a student must realize that she or he can read what she or he writes, and write what is read. Composing a sentence or two for writing should arise from the genuine conversation about a read-aloud or familiar book: the favorite part, a real life connection, a question about a character or a statement about the ending, for example. This also provides the student with practice in hearing and recording sounds in words that he or she wants to write: the student should stretch the word (i.e., *caaat* for *cat*) and write the letters for the sounds that are heard.
Introducing and Reading a New Book	This provides an opportunity for you to carefully select and introduce a new book, as well as a time for the student to practice current problem-solving strategies. When planning for this task, try to select a book based on its learning opportunities for the student. Preview the book so you can tell the student what it's about when you introduce it. Look through the book with the student and briefly discuss the pictures after your introduction. Then ask the student to read the book aloud to you. If the student gets stuck on a "tricky word," ask him or her to think about and try a word that would make sense. In later lessons, if the student still can't get the word, you might use the chalk or dry-erase board or magnetic letters to show a student how to use a known word or "chunk" to figure out a longer, unknown word. The book used in this task should be recorded so it can be read again during the Rereading Familiar Books component of another lesson.

(continued)

Table 5.1 (continued)

Component	Description
Doing an Alternate Activity	In the beginning of your tutoring program, or to disengage the student from the lesson in order to reengage her or him, you may choose to do an alternate activity from the basket in the Literacy Room. It will be important for you to have a focus for the task, which may be identified by the very nature of the game.
Reflecting and Planning Notes	After returning your student to his or her classroom, you should take the time to reflect upon the lesson and record notes about what you observed or felt to be important. The notes you make should guide your planning and justify what you choose to do during the next lesson with your student.

We added this component because some struggling readers have far fewer literacy experiences at home than their more able peers (Livingston & Wirt, 2003). Reading aloud provides struggling readers with the opportunity to hear what good reading sounds like; become familiar with book language, new vocabulary, and various language structures; and just bond with their tutors. Tutors follow the Reading Recovery format for the remainder of the lesson. Students reread a familiar book for fluency, use magnetic letters for letter and word work, write a story (i.e., a sentence in response to a reading), and read a new book that the tutor carefully selects for its problem-solving opportunities.

Questions Guiding the Research

Our program developed around one main question: Do elementary school students benefit from an in-school tutoring program, delivered by preservice teachers and supervised by university and school personnel, in a school–university partnership? In particular, we wanted to determine whether Literacy Partners helped the tutored students perform on grade level like their nontutored peers.

Theoretical Background and Perspectives

Because we designed our Literacy Partners program as a field experience to accompany a graduate-level reading course for elementary preservice teachers in an interdisciplinary Master of Arts in Teaching (MAT) program, we aligned the field experience components with best practices in the research literature. The National Commission on Excellence in Elementary Teacher Preparation for Reading Instruction determined that excellent preservice teacher preparation programs engage preservice teachers in supervised field experiences, specifically designed to accompany reading course work (International Reading Association, 2003). Sailors and colleagues. (2004) found that the reading field experiences at the sites of excellence identified by the National Commission included several essential components, such as a purposeful structure, opportunities for reflective teaching and informed decision making, scaffolded experiences for preservice teachers, work with elementary students in varied contexts, and opportunities for one-on-one tutoring. As we structured our program, we attended to these features to ensure quality in the preservice teachers' experiences.

We also wanted to ensure that elementary struggling readers received a quality tutoring experience from our trained tutors. The Reading Recovery intervention (Clay, 1993) after which we modeled our program enjoys much research support as an effective intervention. Two recent meta-analyses point to the effectiveness of the intervention across multiple studies (D'Agostino & Murphy, 2004; Elbaum, Vaughn, Hughes, & Moody, 2000). Moreover, Reading Recovery is one of only 25 early reading interventions deemed effective by the Institute for Education Sciences, based on their review of the research, and included in the What Works Clearinghouse (Institute of Education Sciences, 2008). Of the 25 approved interventions, the What Works Clearinghouse evaluation shows that Reading Recovery is the only intervention that produces gains on all categories of evaluation: alphabetics (includes phonemic awareness and phonics), fluency (fast, accurate decoding), comprehension, and overall reading achievement. Additionally, other research has shown that adaptations of the Reading Recovery format are effective, such as varying intervention group size from a one-on-one to a one-on-two model (Iversen, Tunmer, & Chapman, 2005). Taken together, these findings fostered our confidence in the potential effectiveness of an adaptation of the Reading Recovery intervention for improving reading achievement for struggling elementary school readers.

Methodology

Participants

The Literacy Partners Program began in mid-October to accommodate the elementary school's beginning-of-year assessment program and the preservice teachers' fall break, which occurred in early October. Tutoring ended in mid-December when the preservice teachers' semester ended.

The elementary school where the tutoring took place is a Title I, urban, public elementary school in a school district that primarily serves minority students. Although several other interventions occurred at the school (e.g., retention, church volunteer tutoring, small-group intervention, and Reading Recovery), we selected students for this research who either received only Literacy Partners tutoring or who received no intervention at all (because they met grade-level benchmarks for reading at the beginning of the school year). We selected a total of 20 first-grade students for tutoring because they were below grade level at the time of the intervention. The control group included the 24 first-grade students in the same classes who received no intervention, which allowed us to compare the effect of our tutoring intervention to standard instruction at the students' school.

Data Sources

The school district uses the Developmental Reading Assessment (DRA, 2001) to gauge reading growth. Thus, students' DRA fluency and comprehension scores from the first and second marking periods (beginning of November and mid-January, respectively) were used to determine growth in reading proficiency across the tutoring period. Furthermore, second marking period composite DRA scores were used to gauge reading level, which was converted to Phonological Awareness Literacy Screening (PALS; 2008) equivalents, using a conversion chart on the PALS website (pals.virginia.edu), for comparison to students' beginning-of-year PALS reading levels.

Data Analysis

We conducted a quasi-experimental comparison using a pretest/posttest, control group design. We used three 2×2 repeated-measures analyses of variance (ANOVAs) to compare students' growth in reading skill across the intervention period for DRA Fluency Scores, DRA Comprehension Scores, and PALS Reading Levels. We converted PALS qualitative reading levels to ordinal numbers for this analysis (see Table 5.2).

Limitations

Although our results are encouraging, our research included only first-grade children. Thus, extensions of this program to other grade levels must be carefully monitored to ensure that students benefit from the tutoring lessons.

Results

Independent samples t-tests indicated no significant difference between tutoring and control groups on DRA Fluency scores at pretest. However, students selected for the Literacy Partners Program scored significantly lower than control students on DRA Comprehension Scores and on PALS Reading Levels (see Table

Table 5.2 PALS Reading Levels and the Numerical Equivalents for the Repeated-Measures ANOVA Examining Growth in Reading Level Across the Tutoring Period

PALS Level	Numerical Equivalent
Readiness	1
Pre-Primer 1, PALS A	2
Pre-Primer 2, PALS B	3
Pre-Primer 3, PALS C	4
Primer, 1.1	5
First, 1.2	6
Second, 2.1	7
Second, 2.2	8
Third	9
Fourth	10

Note. PALS levels derived from PALS Book Level Equivalencies chart, downloaded from pals.virginia.edu/instructional-resources/pals-instructionalresources-book-levels.asp on April 24, 2008.

5.3). A 2×2 repeated-measures ANOVA examining the growth of fluency across the tutoring period indicated no significant Group by Fluency interaction. However, planned post hoc comparisons indicated a marginally significant improvement in fluency scores for the tutored group, $p = 0.09$. Examination of the mean fluency scores for both groups across marking periods shows the tutored students improved an average of one point on the DRA Fluency scale, while the control group showed an average gain of only 0.17 point.

The 2×2 repeated-measures ANOVA examining comprehension growth over the tutoring period revealed a significant main effect of Comprehension, indicating that overall, students scored significantly lower on the DRA Comprehension subscale at pretest, $F(1, 42) = 21.97$, $p < 0.01$. Additionally, a main effect of Group indicated that the tutoring group scored significantly lower than the control group overall, $F(1, 42) = 4.17$, $p < 0.05$. However, a significant Group $\times$ Comprehension interaction, $F(1, 42) = 5.56$, $p < 0.05$, showed that although the tutored group scored significantly lower than the control group at pretest, they showed greater growth, achieving comprehension scores that were not significantly different from their control counterparts at posttest.

The 2×2 repeated-measures ANOVA for PALS Reading Level yielded a similar pattern of results. Specifically, the analysis revealed a significant main effect for Reading Level, indicating that overall, all students showed significant growth in reading level over the intervention period, $F(1, 42) = 313.59$, $p < 0.01$. Additionally, there was a significant main effect of Group, indicating the tutored students had significantly lower reading levels overall than the control students, $F(1, 42) = 22.87$, $p < 0.01$. A significant Group $\times$ Reading Level interaction, $F(1, 42) = 6.24$, $p < 0.05$, showed that both groups made

Table 5.3 Means and Standard Deviations for DRA Fluency, DRA Comprehension, and PALS Reading Levels for Students in the Tutored and Control Groups

Measure	Pretest		Posttest	
	Tutored	Control	Tutored	Control
DRA Fluency	9.45	9.63	10.45	9.79
	(2.28)	(1.97)	(2.24)	(2.21)
DRA Comprehension	10.85	15.92	17.40	18.08
	(8.54)	(4.37)	(5.17)	(3.45)
PALS Reading Level	1.65	4.08	4.75	6.42
	(0.59)	(2.98)	(0.97)	(1.59)

significant gains in reading level from pretest to posttest, with the tutored students improving an average of 3.1 reading levels, and the control students improving an average of 2.33 reading levels.

Further examination of students' reading levels at pretest and posttest indicates that prior to intervention, only one student in the tutored group was on grade level, with a PALS Reading Level of Pre-Primer 2, or PALS B. However, after tutoring, all of the tutored students were reading at a first-grade level (see Table 5.4).

We found that in only one semester Literacy Partners resulted in significant gains for the first-grade struggling readers. Our primary goal for the tutoring program was to equip struggling readers with problem-solving strategies that will enable them to read independently and operate within the average band for their grade level. The tutored students in this sample did just that. The tutored students achieved DRA Comprehension scores that were not significantly different from their nontutored peers at posttest. Our conclusion was confirmed by an examination of PALS Reading Levels at posttest, which showed that all students were reading at a first-grade level by the end of the second marking period, after tutoring had occurred. In sum,

Literacy Partners achieved the desired academic effects for our struggling readers.

Discussion

Observations of Kathryn Morgan, School Reading Teacher

In addition to clear benefits for reading achievement, I observed additional benefits for students. Literacy Partners helped the tutored, struggling readers perceive themselves as readers and writers, which was quite an improvement over the initial sense of failure experienced by so many of these students. The tutoring program helped these students know and expect success, using self-fulfilling prophecy for positive outcomes, which contributed to a narrowing of the literacy achievement gap. Tutored students exhibited an improved degree of confidence in the area of literacy in particular, which seemed to transfer to overall academics. Furthermore, the tutored students benefited because tutors learned to use the same language and strategy prompts used by classroom teachers, resulting in common language practices between the tutoring situation and the classroom.

The tutoring relationship created a supportive environment that encouraged students to become risk takers as literacy learners because

Table 5.4 Numbers of Children at PALS Reading Levels at Pretest and Posttest

Grade Level	PALS Level	Pretest		Posttest	
		Tutored	Control	Tutored	Control
Kindergarten/ First Grade	Readiness	8	1	0	0
	Pre-Primer 1, PALS A	11	5	0	0
First Grade	Pre-Primer 2, PALS B	1	5	2	0
	Pre-Primer 3, PALS C	0	5	5	3
	Primer, PALS 1.1	0	4	10	4
First Grade/ Second Grade	First, PALS 1.2	0	1	2	7
Second Grade	Second, PALS 2.1	0	0	1	3
Second Grade/ Third Grade	Second, PALS 2.2	0	1	0	4
Third Grade/ Fourth Grade	Third	0	2	0	3

Note. PALS levels and grade-level equivalencies derived from PALS Book Level Equivalencies chart, downloaded from pals.virginia.edu/ instructional-resources/pals-instructionalresources-book-levels.asp on April 24, 2008.

they were more willing and able to try strategies on their own rather than passively waiting for instruction or the answer from a teacher or tutor. Finally, I observed that Literacy Partners encouraged tutored students to become active problem solvers by helping them think about what they could do to help themselves when reading (e.g., I can get my mouth ready, look at the picture, check the word, reread), enabling the tutored struggling readers to replace ineffective strategies with effective ones and promoting more independent, strategic literacy processing. These observations were supported by our data, which indicated positive effects on tutored students' reading achievement.

Observations of Brian Nichols, School Principal

Over the course of the Literacy Partners Program, I (fourth author) observed that tutored students benefited because they received intensive, one-on-one instruction from trained, prospective teachers with appropriately leveled text, which is critical to struggling readers' success (Allington, 2001). The tutored students received a second dose of specific reading intervention that reinforced classroom instruction, while being differentiated to specific learning styles and needs within students' zones of proximal development (Vygotsky, 1978). Tutors assisted students in discovering and capitalizing on their strengths, which encouraged them to develop in areas that needed improvement. Furthermore, the tutoring program provided these students the added benefits of increased praise, valuable encouragement, and appropriate feedback in the context of a nurturing relationship with adult role models who truly viewed them as readers and writers. Over the course of the tutoring program, I observed that these features contributed to improved student attitudes toward reading, writing, and learning, in addition to improved reading levels.

In addition to the benefits to the students, the preservice teachers benefited because they had opportunities to put theory into practice in a school setting. The aspiring teachers planned, delivered, and evaluated lessons, while learning to build a positive rapport with students and staff, resulting in increased confidence in the delivery of instruction and valuable career-related experience in an authentic environment. Preservice teachers experienced a sense of accomplishment for having contributed to the success of tutored students and the school. They also benefited from the professional relationships they developed with teachers, interventionists, and administrators.

Finally, elementary school teachers also derived benefits from our school–university partnership tutoring program. Anecdotally, teachers noted that tutored students' interest in doing quality work improved, and student self-esteem and confidence increased. Furthermore, as our data showed, student reading achievement improved during the course of the tutoring program.

Implications

The results of our study are promising and have implications for those who wish to develop similar tutoring programs. First, consistent with prior work, we found that well-structured, one-on-one tutoring, delivered by trained tutors, is an effective intervention for struggling readers in first-grade classrooms. The lesson structure and tutor training we developed can be easily adapted by university personnel to support preservice teacher training or by elementary school administrators to develop an intervention program to support struggling readers in their school buildings. Classroom teachers may wish to incorporate our structured lesson format into their own intervention lessons or use our format to train classroom volunteers to support strug-

gling readers within their classrooms. Furthermore, because text choice was critical to the design and effectiveness of our tutoring lessons, university and school personnel should carefully choose reading materials that will provide students with appropriately leveled reading experiences. See Mesmer (2008) for information on matching readers to texts.

Words of Advice

- Developing a handbook for tutors is critical not only to communicate the expectations of the overall program but also to provide continuity, resources, and a common language. Be sure to include building schedules, academic calendars, and school maps for tutor reference.

- Consider respective schedules, including break and testing times for school and university, when planning the tutoring program.

- One person at the elementary school should be the liaison between the tutors, teachers, and university personnel to ensure that expectations are met, messages are consistent, and tutors receive consistent assistance in finding information.

- Tutors should document lesson notes to be used for preservice teacher instruction as well as for intervention and accountability purposes for the elementary school. University professors or school reading teachers should regularly read and respond to lesson notes to resolve misunderstandings.

- A sign-in and sign-out log will help to document the intervention, reinforce tutor accountability, and verify preservice teacher hours.

REFERENCES

Allington, R.L. (2001). *What really matters for struggling readers: Designing research-based programs.* New York: Addison Wesley Longman.

Allington, R.L. (2005, June/July). The other five "pillars" of effective reading instruction. *Reading Today, 22*(6), 3.

Clay, M.M. (1993). *Reading recovery: A guidebook for teachers in training.* Portsmouth, NH: Heinemann.

D'Agostino, J.V., & Murphy, J.A. (2004). A meta-analysis of Reading Recovery in United States schools. *Educational Evaluation and Policy Analysis, 26*(1), 23–38. doi:10.3102/01623737026001023

Dolch, E.W. (1936). A basic sight vocabulary. *The Elementary School Journal, 36*(6), 456–460. doi:10.1086/457353

Elbaum, B., Vaughn, S., Hughes, M.T., & Moody, S.W. (2000). How effective are one-to-one tutoring programs in reading for elementary students at risk for reading failure? A meta-analysis of the intervention research. *Journal of Educational Psychology, 92*(4), 605–619. doi:10.1037/0022-0663.92.4.605

Fry, E.B., & Kress, J.E. (2006). *The reading teacher's book of lists.* San Francisco: John Wiley & Sons.

Institute of Education Sciences. (2008). What works clearinghouse. Retrieved May 1, 2008, from ies.ed.gov/ncee/wwc/reports/beginning_reading/topic/tabfig.asp#tbl1

International Reading Association. (2003). *Prepared to make a difference: An executive summary of the National Commission on Excellence in Elementary Teacher Preparation for Reading Instruction.* Newark, DE: International Reading Association.

Iversen, S., Tunmer, W.E., & Chapman, J.W. (2005). The effects of varying group size on the Reading Recovery approach to preventive intervention. *Journal of Learning Disabilities, 38*(5), 456–472. doi:10.1177/00222194050380050801

Livingston, A., & Wirt, J. (2003). *The condition of education 2003 in brief* (NCES 2003–068). Washington, DC: U.S. Department of Education, National Center for Education Statistics.

Mesmer, H.A.E. (2008). *Tools for matching readers to texts: Research-based practices.* New York: Guilford.

Sailors, M., Keehn, S., Martinez, M., Harmon, J., Hedrick, W., Fine, J., et al. (2004). Features of early field experiences at sites of excellence in reading teacher education programs. In J. Worthy, B. Maloch, J.V. Hoffman, D.L. Schallert, & C.M. Fairbanks (Eds.), *53rd yearbook of the National Reading Conference* (pp. 342–355). Chicago: National Reading Conference.

Vygotsky, L.S. (1978). *Mind in society: The development of higher psychological processes.* (M. Cole, V. John-Steiner, S. Scribner, & E. Souberman, Eds. & Trans.). Cambridge, MA: Harvard University Press.

LITERATURE CITED

Martin, B. (2007). *Brown bear, brown bear, what do you see?* New York: Holt.

Slobodkina, E. (1987). *Caps for sale.* New York: Harper Trophy.

ABOUT THE CONTRIBUTORS

Kelly B. Cartwright *teaches at Christopher Newport University (CNU), Newport News, Virginia, USA, where she has taught undergraduate courses in Child Development, Cognitive Development, and Research Methods. She serves on the governing council for the interdisciplinary Teacher Preparation Program at CNU for which she designed and teaches a graduate course in reading for elementary preservice teachers. CNU's graduate reading students complete a required in-school tutoring experience, which she and elementary school-based colleagues designed. Her research focuses on the roles of cognitive development and cognitive flexibility in literacy processes, family and gender influences on literacy development, and preservice reading teacher education. E-mail: kewright@cnu.edu*

Donna S. Savage *is currently a Reading First Reading Specialist with the Virginia (USA) Department of Education. She has spent over 20 years in public education. During this time, she was a classroom teacher, Reading Recovery teacher, reading specialist, Title I reading teacher, and literacy coach in the Newport News Public School System, Newport News, Virginia, USA. Her interest in preservice teacher education led to the development of a school–university partnership which focused on a one-to-one tutoring program. She is also an adjunct instructor at Old Dominion University and Christopher Newport University where she teaches graduate courses in reading development. E-mail: DSS2@aol.com*

Kathryn D.S. Morgan *has worked with at-risk primary age students in public education for 20 years. She was a classroom teacher for Newport News Public Schools, Newport News, Virginia, USA, prior to becoming a Title I reading and Reading Recovery teacher, the position she currently holds. She also serves as the school-based* *coordinator for the tutoring program described in this chapter. She was recently honored by the Newport News Reading Council as Reading Teacher of the Year. E-mail: Kathryn.morgan@ nn.k12.va.us*

Brian J. Nichols *is currently the principal of T. Ryland Sanford Elementary School in Newport News, Virginia, USA, where he has served for three years. He has over 10 years of experience as a classroom teacher, an instructional specialist, and an administrator. His current school has been recognized as a No Child Left Behind Blue Ribbon School and is the site for the Christopher Newport University in-school tutoring program, which provides field experiences for graduate level reading students and valuable services for struggling elementary readers. E-mail: brian.nichols@nn.k12.va.us*

Transforming Reading Assessment Classes Into Professional Development School Reading Clinics: What We Have Learned

Eva Garin and W. Dorsey Hammond

In the beginning of the semester, I did not understand the need or the reason for the PDS [professional development school] reading clinic. Once I met my student, I really did not understand how I could help her because she did pretty well on the informal reading assessments for a first grader—although I did recognize some things that could use practice. And at the end of the experience I felt OK about it, but still unsure that I really helped the student in any way. Once I met with the classroom teacher I understood what my student and I gained in the PDS reading clinic. The classroom teacher was excited and felt I helped the student in various ways. In class the student gained confidence and began reading with a plethora of expression. She also went up a level in her reading group from below grade level to on grade level. I knew I had made a difference with that student. The PDS reading clinic did help me grow as a person and as an educator, as well as help a student grow as a reader. (Preservice teacher, December 3, 2007)

The opening vignette illustrates how a reading assessment class was transformed into a reading clinic, as detailed in this chapter. The name of the school in which the reading clinic took place is a pseudonym, as are all participant names. The site is designated as a professional development school (PDS), which is a collaboratively planned and implemented partnership for the academic and clinical preparation of interns and the continuous professional development of faculty of both the school system and the partnering institution of higher education. The focus of the PDS partnership is improved student performance through research-based teaching and learning (Maryland State Department of Education, 2003).

When we—two university professors from Bowie State University and Salisbury University—began teaching reading assessment classes, we believed there should be opportunities for our preservice teachers to authentically assess students' reading strengths and instructional needs. In the past, preservice teachers learned about reading assessment in the confines of their university classrooms and completed case studies with students they identified on their own. It was our desire to create a situation in which the reading assessment class was able to link theory and practice in a supervised tutoring setting. And so, the notion of a PDS reading clinic was born.

We found the procedures of Morris, Shaw, and Perney (1990), who conducted replication research on successful elementary tutoring programs, to be helpful in establishing our PDS reading clinic at Grove Elementary School. We were able to select an appropriate site, coordinate our reading assessment class with Grove Elementary staff, and provide structure and support for our preservice teachers in the areas of assessment and instruction. When establishing our reading clinic we considered the following key factors.

Identifying a PDS site. The selected site needed to be in close proximity to the university so preservice teachers would be able to attend afternoon classes. Offering the reading assessment class in the morning gave us access to elementary students who could benefit from tutoring.

Designating a coordinator. As the professor teaching the reading assessment class, Eva (first author) was one of the PDS reading clinic coordinators. She shared coordination with the reading specialist and a classroom teacher who had a full-time preservice teacher in her classroom. This teacher was able to participate in our class sessions as a guest speaker and to offer input on the structure of the clinic.

Determining who will do the tutoring. The tutors were the preservice teachers who were taking the reading assessment course. The class met every Wednesday from 9:00 A.M. until 11:30 A.M. The members of the reading assessment class were in the PDS site on Tuesdays and

Thursdays throughout the semester and participated in methods classes in reading, science, math, and social studies on Mondays and Wednesdays. This was the format for their semester prior to student teaching.

Identifying children to receive tutoring. Eva met with the principal and reading specialist to determine the reading needs of the students. During the semester of this study we decided to work exclusively with first- and second-grade students because the third and fourth graders participated in state testing when our tutoring sessions met.

Selecting assessment materials. To select the assessment materials, we used two sources: the textbook for the reading assessment class (Cooper & Kiger, 2008) and input from the PDS reading specialist and classroom teachers. We used the following assessment materials:

- Reading interest survey—Preservice teachers prepared a reading interest inventory to administer to their students at the first session of the PDS reading clinic. Tutors used students' responses on the interest survey to guide selection of materials for each tutoring session.

- Informal reading inventory (IRI; Prince George's County Public Schools, 2001; Valencia, 1996)—Preservice teachers learned to use word lists to determine what level at which to begin students' assessment on the reading passages. The tutors administered both silent and oral comprehension checks. Preservice teachers learned about miscue analysis and students' learning styles.

- Emergent literacy assessments (Cooper and Kiger, 2008; Prince George's County Public Schools, 2001; Pikulski, 1996)— We selected these assessments on an as-needed basis depending on the level of the student referred to the PDS reading clinic. During the semester of this study, we concentrated on word writing, sentence dictating, and rhyming.

- Fluency checklist—We used the fluency checklist and associated rubric adapted from Fountas and Pinnell (2001). Preservice teachers learned about rubrics and fluency by administering this assessment. For accurate analysis, they tape recorded their students as they were reading familiar text aloud.

- Writing—We used a variety of informal writing assessments throughout the PDS reading clinic. One assessment was the writing spree as noted in the school district curriculum (Prince George's County Public Schools, 2001). The writing spree is used to assess a student's ability to independently recall and correctly write known words in a 10-minute period. In addition, informal writing opportunities linked to reading were used as additional writing assessments.

- Classroom observation—Toward the conclusion of the PDS reading clinic, preservice teachers observed their students in the classroom during instructional and noninstructional times.

Selecting what students read. Preservice teachers took three read-aloud books to each of the tutoring sessions. For the first session, they decided on these books by reading the teacher referrals. In subsequent sessions, they used the results from the student reading interest inventory and what they learned from the reading assessments to select readings. Preservice teachers presented each of the books using a book talk model; then the student chose the book for the read-aloud and ex-

plained his or her choice. Classroom teachers provided additional reading materials. During class Eva talked about the role that choice and self-selection play in reading motivation.

Student writing. For each session, preservice teachers encouraged their students to write about what they read during the PDS reading clinic. Students and preservice teachers discussed the books read, and then students wrote a response to an open-ended question or they engaged in free writing. The length and complexity of the piece was dependent on the grade level of the child.

Modeling. This occurred on two levels: Whatever we asked preservice teachers to do, we modeled for them first. If they were to conduct an interactive read-aloud, then we read aloud to them at each session and modeled the components of an interactive read-aloud (Fisher, Flood, Lapp, & Frey, 2004). Preservice teachers also modeled research-based reading strategies during the tutoring sessions.

Training. Training became one of the most important aspects of the PDS reading clinic. Each preservice teacher received a notebook of assessments. The first component of our training was to review the assessments and the directions for administering them. Using role playing, preservice teachers practiced delivering the assessments with one another. Running records were the most challenging of the assessments for preservice teachers. Therefore, they also observed either the reading specialist or a classroom teacher administer and score a running record. For the next part of the training, preservice teachers conducted and analyzed a running record at their PDS site under the supervision of a classroom teacher or reading specialist. Afterward, preservice teachers reported they felt prepared to independently complete all of the components of the IRI (Prince George's County Public Schools, 2001; Valencia, 1996).

Pacing the tutoring sessions. During the first two sessions of the PDS reading clinic, pacing was uniform. Preservice teachers administered the same beginning assessments and read-alouds. Later, pacing became different for each tutoring pair. We determined that each tutoring session would run between 30 and 40 minutes. With each candidate doing different lessons, our roles changed from instructors to observers of the tutoring pairs. Sometimes we had to step in and change the pacing of lessons. This happened most often when we noticed that a student was unable to concentrate further on assessments, and we encouraged the preservice teacher to return to that assessment the following week. Preservice teachers needed to discover the right balance between assessment and instruction and not attempt to complete all of the assessments in a short period of time.

Coordinating with classroom instruction. Teachers completed a referral for a student to the PDS reading clinic where they indicated the student's strengths and areas of need. We asked that the classroom teacher send familiar reading or any class work in reading for which the child needed individual attention. At the end of each semester, preservice teachers met with the referring teachers to discuss what they learned about the students and to share what recommendations they had for future instruction.

Each session of the PDS reading clinic followed the same general format. For the first two sessions, we distributed model agendas for the clinic. In subsequent sessions, preservice teachers developed their own agendas and individual plans following the format of a template that Eva distributed. We reviewed their plans at the beginning of each class and again at the end of class. Table 6.1 illustrates a typical schedule in our PDS reading clinic.

Preservice teachers are provided with several opportunities to share their PDS reading clinic case studies with university faculty, PDS faculty, and other preservice teachers. Each semester preservice teachers present their case studies in an informal poster session. These case studies are also presented in class as a portion of the final examination for the reading assessment class. In May, preservice teachers share their case studies at the Bowie State University PDS Conference.

Table 6.1 Schedule for a Typical Clinic Session

Time	Activity
9:00–9:25	Setting up for the PDS reading clinic and review of the plans. As preservice teachers arrive in class, we begin individually checking plans and discussing questions. Many preservice teachers begin arriving as early as 8:30 for these meetings.
9:30–10:00	Working with students. Preservice teachers follow agenda, which includes schedule of assessments, interactive read-aloud modeling, choice/self-selection, discussion of the reading, writing linked to reading, and familiar reading for fluency.
10:10–10:30	Preservice teachers' journal writing. Each week preservice teachers respond to the following questions: What did you learn about your child today that you didn't already know? What else would you like to learn about your child? What did you do today during reading clinic? What are your plans for next week?
10:30–11:30	Discussions/planning for next PDS reading. Class ends with individual and group discussions about the tutoring session, reading strategies, and assessment instruction.

Questions Guiding the Research

The following questions led our research:

- What is the impact of the PDS reading clinic on the students' learning?

- What is the impact of the PDS reading clinic on the preservice teachers' professional development?

Theoretical Background and Perspectives

To structure a PDS reading clinic at Bowie State University, we relied on the professional development schools' literature (Maryland State Department of Education, 2003; Teitel, 2001) to provide a rationale for situating the clinic in a PDS site. In the state of Maryland our work with professional development schools is guided by the document *Professional Development Schools: An Implementation Manual* (Maryland State Department of Education, 2003). Offering classes at a PDS site is encouraged as an opportunity for PDS faculty and university faculty to work together to develop curricula for preservice teachers. As the manual states, "When this occurs, theory and practice naturally merge to produce an integrated teacher preparation program. Higher education faculty team teach with PDS faculty to focus on student achievement" (Maryland State Department of Education, 2003, p. 19).

> We wanted to raise a generation of new teachers who would believe that reading is about making meaning from print.

Hunt (1997) provides much of the philosophical constructs around the PDS reading clinic. We knew that we wanted teacher candidates to be proficient in using a variety of reading assessments with students and we wanted to steer them away from the deficit model in which there is a preoccupation with counting mistakes. We wanted to raise a generation of new teachers who would believe that reading is about making meaning from print. We also wanted our teacher candidates to believe that when students are given opportunities to select their own reading materials by focusing on interest, they can transcend instructional level. We also aimed to model the power of self-motivation and instill in our teacher candidates the idea that choice in reading makes a difference. We also wanted our teacher candidates to believe that comprehension in oral and silent reading may differ and that when "oral reading is inadequate, it should be used less" (Hunt, 1997, p. 281).

Pikulski (1994) reviews five successful reading programs for at-risk, first-grade students—Success for All, The Winston-Salem Project, Early Intervention in Reading, The Boulder Project, and Reading Recovery—and identifies 11 critical features of successful reading programs for at-risk first graders. Pikulski's 11 critical areas are as follows:

1. Relationship to regular classroom instruction

2. Organization of the intervention

3. Increased amount of instructional time for reading

4. Length of the reading intervention

5. Use of a great variety of text and materials

6. Use of text-level strategies, emphasis on reading as a meaning-constructing process

7. Use of repeated readings with books and other texts, including word-level strategies

8. Use of writing strategies

9. Use of regular, ongoing assessment

10. Connections with the home

11. Inclusion of teacher training

We used these 11 critical features to support the structure of our PDS reading clinic. One of our goals was to link the tutoring sessions to the students' classroom instruction. We made sure that the students we tutored did not miss reading instruction in their classrooms (Allington, 2006). Pikulski (1996) finds that one-to-one tutoring is very powerful; we organized our tutoring program in that fashion. We also stressed the use of authentic literature that was interesting and motivating. We emphasized that reading is a process of making meaning, and we prohibited the use of worksheets and isolated skills practice. Each tutoring session also included writing that related to reading. Additionally, our PDS reading clinic supported Pikulski's critical features of regular ongoing assessment, teacher training, and repeated readings.

Allington (2006) offers further support for our PDS reading clinic, focusing on components of designing research-based programs for struggling readers. Allington maintains that students need to read a lot. Students participating in the reading clinic read 30 to 40 additional minutes per week over their nontutored peers. By using an IRI early in the reading clinic, preservice teachers were able to identify books that the students could read. Tutors focused a portion of their time on fluency interventions suggested by Allington, including paired reading with tutors, audiotaping, checking and charting fluency, echo reading, and tutor modeling.

Methodology

Participants

Nine preservice teachers participated in the PDS reading clinic. They tutored nine students rang-ing in grades from K to 3. The children were at least two years below grade level in reading.

Data Sources

To address the first research question on the impact of the tutoring on elementary school students, we collected an attitude survey, writing samples, student interview protocols, records of meetings between preservice teachers and classroom teachers, and preservice teachers' journal entries. Additionally, we collected anecdotal information from students and information from the referring teachers.

We administered a pre- and postintervention attitude survey, adapted from Fountas and Pinnell (2001). We asked students to rate themselves on a variety of statements including "How do you feel when you read a book in school during free time?" and "How do you feel when you read out loud?" Results from these surveys did not yield significant changes in students' reading attitude. This was a surprising finding given the informal and observational data available to tutors and classroom teachers. It is likely that the instrument was not sensitive enough to reflect the valid perceptions of the students during such a short period of time.

To answer the second research question regarding the impact of the tutorial program on the preservice teachers, we collected pre- and postintervention survey data on attitudes and self-reflections from teacher candidate journal entries.

Data Analysis

We analyzed the effectiveness of the PDS reading clinic through action research. Kemmins and McTaggart (1992) define action research as a deliberate, solution-oriented investigation that is group or personally owned and conducted. It is characterized by spiraling cycles of problem identification, systematic data collection, reflection analysis, data-driven action taken, and problem redefinition.

We chose action research as our methodology because it encourages researchers to redefine their research questions by using data to inform these changes. We also chose action research because this methodology is flexible in what counts as data (Calhoun, 2002).

We used qualitative research procedures such as clustering of data sources to identify common themes. According to Bogdan and Biklen (2007) the questions used to guide a qualitative study need to be open-ended and concerned with process and meaning rather than cause and effect. We analyzed the data sources independently. We then collaborated on the interpretation of our data by reanalyzing our data together to see how our findings were consistent or different. Eva shared our findings with preservice teachers and PDS teachers to check for consistency and to test our assertions and responses. We used these discussions to redesign our action research questions and to design new data sources to more fully answer our research questions. An example of adding a new data source occurred during one of our initial data analysis meetings when we decided to have tutors interview one another's students to learn more about the impact of the PDS reading clinic on the students being tutored.

Limitations

There are several limitations to this study. There were only nine tutors during the semester in which the study was conducted. Therefore, we plan to continue collecting data over the next two semesters to add to our sample. Another limitation was our communication with referring teachers. Although we communicated at the end of the semester, during the semester contact between the referring teacher and tutors was informal and lacked consistency. In the fu-

ture we will use electronic journals so that referring teachers know more specifically what we are doing in the reading clinic and will have a convenient way of communicating with the tutor and the professor. Finally, Grove Elementary School is an established PDS site; we are, therefore, uncertain how this format for teaching reading assessment courses would work at a site without a history of a mature partnership between the school and a university.

Results and Discussion

Effects of the Tutorial Experience on the Students

We collected data regarding reading attitudes from the students' writing samples about the PDS reading clinic. These writing samples included captions written by students for their individual photographs with their tutors. We learned that the students had positive attitudes about coming to the PDS reading clinic. Some of the students included either a reading skill or comment about reading in their caption, such as the following:

- "I like to read; it was fun."
- "I like to rhyme."
- "We are having a fun and happy time reading a book."
- "I feel excited, awesome, good."

We used interviews with the students to add to our data about students' attitudes toward reading (see Figure 6.1). During one session of the PDS reading clinic, preservice teachers interviewed one another's students to further explore the impact of the reading clinic on the students being tutored. What we learned from these interviews is that students looked forward to attending the PDS reading clinic, they liked to read with their tutors, they enjoyed partici-

---

Figure 6.1 Student Interview

---

1. I like reading to my Bowie State University tutor.

     YES   NO   SOMETIMES   NEVER

2. I like it when my Bowie State tutor reads to me.

     YES   NO   SOMETIMES   NEVER

3. I look forward to working with my Bowie State University tutor.

     YES   NO   SOMETIMES   NEVER

4. I feel like I am a good reader when I read to my Bowie State University tutor.

     YES   NO   SOMETIMES   NEVER

5. Tell me three words that describe how you feel when your Bowie State University tutor meets with you on Wednesdays.

---

pating in interactive read-alouds, and they felt like good readers when they read with their tutors. The students' feelings of being good readers illustrate the confidence level that students had during their individual tutoring sessions.

Preservice teachers were able to share anecdotal information in their weekly journal entries that supported the conclusion that students attending the PDS reading clinic were progressing in reading, as the following journal excerpt exemplifies:

> I saw that Mandy really heard my suggestion about the rhyming words. Whenever she got to one of the words that didn't make sense, she scanned the pages to find the rhyming word that did make sense. At times I feel she doesn't understand that there are ways to break down what she is reading but today she showed me that she can read the story and use the strategies we have worked on and find meaning in what she reads.

We scheduled meetings with Bowie State University preservice teachers and classroom teachers at the end of each semester. We analyzed audio recordings of these meetings, which further supported that there was a positive change in the students tutored in the PDS reading clinic. Each of the classroom teachers described in detail how enthusiastic their students were to attend tutoring sessions and their disappointment on the last day of the reading clinic. Students proudly shared the books that the preservice teachers gave them as keepsakes of their experiences in the PDS reading clinic.

In the final conference, as preservice teachers shared their case studies with classroom teachers, we learned that the classroom teachers valued what the preservice teachers shared and were impressed at how well they came to know the students as readers in six 30-minute tutoring sessions. We observed classroom teachers taking notes as preservice teachers shared the results of the assessments, their observations, and the reading instruction they provided. We also observed the nonverbal behaviors of the classroom teachers. Throughout the conferences they nodded their heads in agreement with what the preservice teachers reported.

In some cases the preservice teachers were able to suggest strategies to the classroom teachers. For instance, an early childhood/special education preservice teacher spoke of the multi-sensory approaches he used for letter formation and said, "As a special educator I see grade levels differently." The teacher seemed appreciative of the opportunity to revisit other approaches. For another student struggling with reading and consequently other subject areas, a preservice teacher identified that without oral reinforcement the student was lost. The preservice teacher used a piece of plastic plumbing pipe for the student to read into so that he could hear the content. This became a learning station in the teacher's upper-grade classroom.

Louise, a teacher who often refers students to the Bowie reading clinic, reported data that helped us learn what happened to the students who participate in the PDS reading clinic. Of the approximately 25 students she has referred for tutoring over a two-year period, she reported an increase in interest and passion for independent reading and an expansion of the types of books students chose to read. She also reported that she learned from family conferences that these students also read more at home. All of the students she referred to the PDS reading clinic have shown more gains in reading levels than her other students. Her comments about the preservice teachers are also worth noting:

> I learned more about those particular students as readers from discussions with the Bowie State tutors—what they enjoyed reading and their perceptions of my students' reading. The tutors were surprisingly sophisticated in their ability to assess reading needs. I would have reading groups four times a week and my students would never ask when reading groups

[were] but they always wanted to know when their Bowie tutor was coming.

These findings supported the conclusion that students profit from being tutored by preservice teachers taking a reading assessment course. Although we administered no standardized measures, there is evidence from students, tutors, and classroom teachers that participation in the PDS reading clinics positively affected students' reading achievement and attitudes. This achievement took various forms including increases in word knowledge and language growth, comprehension, fluency, and metacognition. Moreover, PDS faculty reported that students who received the tutoring appeared to outpace those students who did not participate in the PDS reading clinic. All stakeholders are consistent in their observations that students showed measurable growth in their literacy skills.

In addition, there is consistent evidence across the stakeholders that the students profited in their attitude toward reading and their opportunity to relate on an individual basis with a young adult. We believe that this positively affected their self-concepts and their dispositions toward reading and learning. We found this apparent growth in both achievement and disposition particularly satisfying—even more so given the relatively short duration of time the student and preservice teacher spent together.

Effects of the Tutorial Experience on Preservice Teachers

The second research question addressed the effect of the tutorial experience on preservice teachers. To answer this question we collected pre/post surveys of preservice teachers, conferences with referring teachers, and journal entries.

We administered pre- and postintervention surveys (see Figure 6.2) based on the self-efficacy component of Albert Bandura's social cognitive

Figure 6.2 Preservice Teacher Self-Efficacy Survey

Rate each of the following questions using the following scale:

   5 = Very confident
   4 = Confident
   3 = Somewhat confident
   2 = Not confident
   1 = Not at all confident

_____ How much confidence do you have that you can assess a child's strengths and weaknesses in reading?

_____ How confident are you that you can select an appropriate read-aloud book for your PDS reading clinic child?

_____ How much confidence do you have in your ability to write a reading interest survey and use the results in the PDS reading clinic?

_____ How confident are you that you can administer an Informal Reading Inventory?

_____ How confident are you that you can analyze the results of an Informal Reading Inventory to inform your instruction and interventions in the PDS reading clinic?

_____ How confident are you that providing choices in reading material will make a difference with your PDS reading clinic child?

_____ How confident are you that you can influence a child's reading fluency?

_____ How confident are you that you can inform the child's classroom teacher regarding what kind(s) of reading support is needed in the classroom?

_____ How confident are you that the classroom teacher will value what you have to say about the child you work with?

_____ How confident are you that providing choice of reading materials will influence your PDS reading clinic's student reading motivation and interest?

_____ How confident are you that participating in the PDS reading clinic as part of your reading assessment class will be a valuable learning experience for you?

Please answer the following questions, as well:

What do you hope to learn during the PDS reading clinic that will help you be an effective classroom teacher?

What concerns do you have about your performance in the PDS reading clinic?

What kinds of support from your professor would give you more confidence in your participation in the PDS reading clinic?

What have you heard from other BSU students about the PDS reading clinic?

theory (cited in Pajares, 1996). The survey contained 11 statements regarding the PDS reading clinic and gave preservice teachers the choice of rating themselves as very confident, confident, somewhat confident, not confident, or not at all confident. For each of the survey questions, preservice teachers' responses indicated a positive change in their self-efficacy. Overall, the postintervention survey results about self-efficacy indicated preservice teachers' growth in levels of self-efficacy in the areas of assessment, selection of reading materials, development of reading interest surveys, delivery and analysis of IRIs, belief in the value of choice, and ability to increase students' reading fluency.

We administered the pre- and postintervention surveys during the spring 2008 term to nine preservice teachers. The first question asked preservice teachers to rate their confidence level in assessing a child's reading abilities. The preintervention survey results indicated three preservice teachers felt confident or very confident in this area of assessment. Postintervention survey results indicated that all nine preservice teachers felt either very confident or confident to assess a child's reading abilities.

> "This is truly a unique experience that you will learn from and remember and take with you into each and every classroom you enter."

The focus of the next survey question was selecting appropriate reading materials. In the preintervention survey, seven of the preservice teachers felt confident in this area. In the postintervention survey, nine rated themselves as very confident or believed they could inform the referring classroom teachers regarding the reading levels and needs of the students participating in the PDS reading clinic. In response to the question "How confident are you that you can inform a child's classroom teacher regarding what kind(s) of reading support is needed in the classroom?" we noted a positive change in self-efficacy. In the preintervention survey, five preservice teachers felt either very confident or confident, and in the postintervention survey eight preservice teachers felt very confident or confident. The same eight respondents felt confident or very confident that the classroom teachers would value what they had to say.

In the postintervention survey, we asked preservice teachers to project their level of confidence into their future classrooms. In response to the question "How confident are you that you can influence a child's reading fluency in your own classroom?" eight preservice teachers rated themselves as very confident and one as confident. On the preintervention survey, each of the nine preservice teachers projected that participating in the PDS reading clinic would be a valuable learning experience. The postintervention survey results indicated that seven of the preservice teachers felt very confident and two felt confident that the reading clinic was a valuable learning experience.

The responses to the open-ended question "What will you tell other preservice teachers about the PDS reading clinic?" were overwhelmingly positive, as indicated by the following remarks:

> I would tell other BSU students that this reading clinic is a wonderful teaching experience. Instead of learning about how to assess a student's reading ability from a textbook, the reading clinic allows you to gain practice and experience. The reading clinic seems intimidating at first, but once you start working with your student one-to-one you gain confidence and practice needed to make important instructional decisions.

> This is truly a unique experience that you will learn from and remember and take with you into each and every classroom you enter.

I had a very beneficial and enlightening experience and I did make a difference!

We found these data to be confirming across data sources: The tutoring experiences helped develop confidence in the preservice teachers' perception of themselves as teachers of literacy. They experienced learning up close and personal with one individual student. The preservice teachers knew that they had a role in the literacy growth of their students, and themes of self-confidence and empowerment were highly evident in the data. Preservice teachers valued their tutoring experience and believed it was an integral part of their preparation as teachers of literacy. And, they readily stated they would recommend this teacher-preparation component to their peers.

Implications

Teaching reading assessment classes through a reading clinic design as described in this chapter is mutually beneficial to the elementary school and to the university. The elementary students receive targeted, individual tutoring that they otherwise might not have. The elementary students appear to profit not only from the tutoring but also from having the opportunity to establish a positive relationship with another adult in the school setting.

The preservice teachers benefit because they work closely with one student as part of their reading assessment course work, which helps them to see the relevancy of their assessments and to make adjustments to their instruction in a timely fashion. Additionally, it appears that opportunities are enhanced for "on-the-run" types of assessments. Preservice teachers like the idea that they are tutoring in a school setting, which makes their development as a teacher more realistic.

Words of Advice

As you plan to set up a reading clinic in a PDS site, consider the following suggestions:

- Implement the tutoring component of the reading assessment class no earlier than the third class meeting. Preservice teachers are more confident after practicing assessments through role playing.

- Plan with the school site at least two to three months before implementing the reading clinic. School and university schedules and expectations often differ.

- Set realistic goals for the preservice teachers and referring teachers by constructing a structured referral process for the reading clinic.

REFERENCES

Allington, R.L. (2006). *What really matters for struggling readers: Designing research-based programs* (2nd ed.). Boston: Pearson Education.

Bogdan, R.C., & Biklen, S.K. (2007). *Qualitative research for education: An introduction to theories and methods* (5th ed.). Boston: Pearson Education.

Calhoun, E.J. (2002). Action research for school improvement. *Educational Leadership, 59*(6), 18–24.

Cooper, J.D., & Kiger, N.D. (2008). *Literacy assessment: Helping teachers plan instruction* (3rd ed.). Boston: Houghton Mifflin.

Fisher, D., Flood, J., Lapp, D., & Frey, N. (2004). Interactive read-alouds: Is there a common set of implementation practices? *The Reading Teacher, 58*(1), 278–282. doi:10.1598/RT.58.1.1

Fountas, I., & Pinnell, G.S. (2001). *Guiding readers and writers grades 3–6: Teaching comprehension, genre, and content literacy.* Portsmouth, NH: Heinemann.

Hunt, L.C., Jr. (1997). The effect of self-selection, interest, and motivation upon independent, instructional, and frustration levels. *The Reading Teacher, 50*(4), 278–282.

Kemmins, S., & McTaggart, R. (1992). *The action research reader.* Geelong, VIC, Australia: Deakin University Press.

Maryland State Department of Education. (2003). *Professional development schools: An implementation manual.* Baltimore: Author.

Morris, D., Shaw, B., & Perney, J. (1990). Helping low readers in grades 2 and 3: An after-school volunteer tutoring program. *The Elementary School Journal, 91*(2), 132–150. doi:10.1086/461642

Pajares, F. (1996). Self-efficacy beliefs in academic settings. *Review of Educational Research, 66*(4), 543–578.

Pikulski, J. (1994). Preventing reading failure: A review of five effective programs. *The Reading Teacher, 48*(1), 30–39.

Pikulski, J. (1996). *Emergent literacy survey/K–2: With phonemic-awareness screening* (pp. 2–30). Boston: Houghton Mifflin.

Prince George's County Public Schools. (2001). *Balanced literacy instruction: Training packet 2–3 classrooms*. Upper Marlboro, MD: Author.

Teitel, L. (2001). *How professional development schools make a difference: A review of the research*. Washington, DC: The National Council for Accreditation of Teacher Education.

Valencia, S. (1996). *Informal reading inventory (Test Manual)*. Boston: Houghton Mifflin.

ABOUT THE CONTRIBUTORS

Eva Garin *is an assistant professor of Education at Bowie State University, Bowie, Maryland, USA, where she teaches graduate and undergraduate courses in reading and coordinates the Professional Development Schools. Her current research interests include literacy, professional development, and teacher education. She holds an M.Ed. from the Pennsylvania State University and an Ed.D. from the University of Maryland. Other professional experiences include Coordinator of Professional Development Schools for the University of Maryland and Howard County Public Schools. While with Prince George's County Schools she served in a variety of roles including reading specialist and coordinator of teacher research. In 2001 she was named as Outstanding Educator for that school district. E-mail: egarin@bowiestate.edu*

W. Dorsey Hammond *is a professor of Education at Salisbury University, Salisbury, Maryland, USA. Prior to that, he was Professor of Education at Oakland University, Rochester, Michigan, where he taught reading courses and directed or codirected university reading clinics for more than 30 years. While at Oakland University, he received the Excellence in Teaching Award in 1990 and was awarded a distinguished professorship by the Michigan Governing Boards of Universities in 1991. He began his career as a fourth-grade teacher, and he holds an M.Ed. and a Ph.D. from the University of Delaware. E-mail: wdhammond@salisbury.edu*

SECTION II

After-School Literacy Tutoring Programs

The chapters in Section II represent various motivational and volitional factors to influence reading behaviors during after-school (including weekend) literacy tutoring programs. In these chapters, tutoring programs integrate literacy activities and motivating environments. Even students who were less successful at reading and writing became engaged and succeeded in these highly motivating experiences.

To start off, in Chapter 7, Denise L. McLurkin shares her study of a community-based tutorial program called the Family Learning Institute. The study looks at family and staff perceptions of family involvement in their children's literacy development.

Neva Ann Medcalf, Karen Bessette, and David Gibbs look at the effectiveness of a school–higher education partnership to improve reading abilities and motivation to read. Chapter 8 describes the changes families and teachers observed in the students who participated, the passage rate of participants on the state-mandated reading tests, and how linking theory and practice affected graduate students' teaching practices and self-confidence regarding teaching abilities.

Chapter 9 asks, How can the arts combined with literacy engage students in critically and personally relevant learning? Nancy Rankie Shelton and Morna McDermott relate how participating students rendered comprehension and personal meaning of texts through artistic applications (e.g., poetry, drama, painting). The authors also look at how preservice teachers working with these students broadened their perspectives and explored their personal biases and tendencies to stereotype students.

Sharon M. Peck explores in Chapter 10 how offering reading clinics in authentic settings can provide opportunities for graduate students to become acquainted with urban communities and encourage their critical reflection. The chapter presents qualitative research on critical aspects of literacy clinics, instructional methods, and urban teaching.

Kathleen B. Quinn, in Chapter 11, describes a successful after-school program that was part of a long-term university–school partnership that took place from 2004 until 2007. This partnership emphasized professional development for teachers as they prepared to become reading specialists.

In the concluding chapter of this section, Chapter 12, Nina L. Nilsson presents a multiple case study examining the transformation of three graduate student mentors who worked with tutors in an after-school tutoring program for struggling readers. Consistent with the program's community-of-practice framework, mentors guided small groups of tutors in problem solving, administering assessments, and making children's book selections.

We invite you to think about all of the possibilities of these after-school programs and how they might be adapted for use in your setting.

CHAPTER 7

Two Families in an After-School Community-Based Reading Tutorial Program for Upper Elementary and Middle School Learners

Denise L. McLurkin

They [the people at the Family Learning Institute] was telling me, "Do you like to read with your kids?"...It was all about reading. I said, every time I go up there, it's something about reading. Let me begin to read to them. Then I just got it and we started reading. And now, around 8 or 9 sometimes, we'll go to bed and we have our books and we'll read to about 9 or 9:30, sometimes 10 cause the book get too interesting. We just been doin' that ever since. (verbalized by Brittany's mother, Margo)

The study discussed in this chapter took place at the Family Learning Institute (FLI), a nonprofit organization located in Ann Arbor, Michigan, USA. The FLI was created in the fall of 1999 by a retired elementary school teacher and a community services professional, with the goal of improving the literacy skills of children and adolescents in grades 3 through 8. Currently, the FLI serves over 100 low-income children who are at least two years behind their grade level in their literacy development. The tutoring services provided by the FLI are based on a family's annual income. Services are free for families who qualify.

Tutoring sessions take place on Mondays, Tuesdays, Wednesdays, and Thursdays during two separate sessions on each day (4:00 P.M. to 6:00 P.M. and 6:00 P.M. to 8:00 P.M.). The tutoring sessions include a 50-minute one-on-one session with a volunteer reading tutor during which tutors emphasize phonics, comprehension, and vocabulary development (see www.familylearn inginstitute.org). The students are also involved in a 20-minute discussion group where four students and a discussion leader, who is usually a college student, discuss a book chapter or a magazine article. Additionally, tutees spend approximately 35 to 40 minutes writing on computers.

Because families are vital to students' academic success, family involvement is strongly encouraged at the FLI. Approximately one year after opening, Doris Sperling, the director of the FLI at the time, became concerned because of what she perceived as a "lack of family involvement." In her interview, Doris went on to state, "most bring them here, but I don't think that they are making them read at home." To rectify lack of family involvement, Doris hired a Family Empowerment Specialist who contacted families on a regular basis, offered families suggestions and support to help their children with reading development, and created and presented workshops geared specifically for families of students at the FLI. When the individual she hired did not work out as planned, Doris took on the role of Family Empowerment Specialist during the time my study was conducted.

Questions Guiding the Research

The purpose of my study was to examine family involvement at the FLI, an after-school community-based reading tutorial program. The guiding questions for my research included the following:

- What did families of students in the program think their roles and responsibilities were in their children's literacy development?
- How did families of students in the program assist their children's overall literacy skills?
- What did the program's staff think the families' role and responsibilities were in the student's literacy development?
- In what ways did the program's staff assist and support families in the program?

Theoretical Background and Perspectives

There is a substantial body of evidence that shows family involvement is significant to chil-

dren's overall educational experience. For instance, Eccles and Harold (1993) find family involvement to be important to a child's educational success even through high school. Baker, Serpell, and Sonnenschein (1995) explain that family beliefs and attitudes about reading and writing influence children's literacy development. Conversely, a study by Hoover-Dempsey, Bassler, and Burow (1995) suggests families may become upset or even embarrassed when they are asked to assist their children with homework when they do not know how to help. Although there are a number of studies on the influence of family involvement on children's overall educational experience, at this time the number of studies examining family involvement in after-school reading tutorial programs is sparse.

A review of the literature on after-school reading tutorial programs shows that the majority of studies focus on the following characteristics:

- The training tutors receive (Baker & Wigfield, 1999; Cohen, Kulik, & Kulik, 1982; Elbaum, Vaughn, Hughes, & Moody, 2000; Juel, 1996; Shanahan, 1998; Vadasy, Jenkins, Antil, Wayne, & O'Connor, 1997; Wasik, 1998; Wasik & Slavin, 1993)
- Program effectiveness (Fitzgerald, 2001; Invernizzi, Juel, & Rosemary, 1996; Morris, Shaw, & Perney, 1990; Scales, Morris, & George, 1998)
- Families' perceptions of the effectiveness of after-school programs in which their children participate (Morris et al., 1990; Scales et al., 1998)

According to Jayroe and Brenner (2005), in a study of family involvement in an after-school program housed in a school, family involvement not only benefits children's literacy development but also stimulates families' motivation to read with their children. Scant research has examined families of upper elementary and middle school students who participate in literacy tutoring programs, which was the objective and purpose of this research.

The theoretical framework undergirding my study is self-efficacy theory (Bandura, 1997). Self-efficacy is a person's belief about his or her ability to effectively perform a task to fruition (Bandura, 1997). Generally speaking, success raises self-efficacy levels and failure lowers it (Wigfield & Guthrie, 1997). It is self-efficacy that drives or motivates a person to set a certain goal, determines how much energy they are willing to expend to reach that goal, and establishes how long he or she will persevere if the task gets difficult (Wigfield & Guthrie, 1997). Additionally, a person's skills and knowledge, expectations about the outcome of a task, and perceptions of the value of the task he or she is trying to learn all factor into a person's level of self-efficacy (Wigfield & Guthrie, 1997). Thus, a person can have a high level of self-efficacy, but that alone may not produce gains in performance if the requisite skills and knowledge are lacking (Wigfield & Guthrie, 1997).

Methodology

This chapter emerges from a comprehensive study in which I focused on the improvement or lack of improvement of adolescent students' reading skills in an after-school community-based reading tutorial program (McLurkin, 2004). For this chapter, I present two of a larger compilation of case studies.

Participants

For the first case, I present Brittany, an African American female who was in the sixth grade, and her mother, Margo. For the second case, I present Randy, an African American male who was in the fifth grade, and his mother, Michelle.

Data Sources

The data sources I used for the case studies were semistructured one-on-one interviews and short-answer questionnaires with the families of the students as well as with Doris Sperling, each student's classroom teacher, and each tutor. Although the students were interviewed, I did not ask them to fill out a questionnaire. I was aware they were at the FLI because they had difficulty with reading; therefore, data received from the questionnaires might not be valid or reliable.

Data Analysis

I used constant comparative methods (CCM) of analysis (Glaser & Strauss, 1999; Strauss & Corbin, 1990) to analyze the open-ended sections of the questionnaire, interviews, and documents. CCM is an analytic approach that uses systematic sets of procedures to produce an inductively derived grounded theory about a phenomenon (Glaser & Strauss, 1999; Strauss & Corbin, 1990). There are three types of coding with CCM: open coding, axial coding, and selective coding. Although each of these three coding types has distinct characteristics and can be performed individually, they are typically used in a constant comparative manner, meaning that the researcher constantly compares and reflects on his or her data (both old and newly introduced data) with each of these coding types at different times throughout the analysis phase of his or her study (Strauss & Corbin, 1990).

> A person can have a high level of self-efficacy, but that alone may not produce gains in performance if the requisite skills and knowledge are lacking.

Limitations

There are several limitations to the study that must be addressed. I employed a short-answer questionnaire that may have been difficult for some families to read and respond to. For example, some of Margo's answers were sparse and did not address the questions on the survey. Another limitation was that I had to rely on families' comments as truth. I did not observe families as they engaged in home literacy activities.

Results

Two case findings are presented here. As previously noted, these cases emerged from a comprehensive study of students' reading skills. I chose to share these particular cases because, after a lengthy discussion with Doris Sperling about family involvement at the FLI, we felt these two cases exemplified the possibilities of what could happen when the staff members of after-school reading tutorial programs work closely with families of students in these programs.

Case 1—Brittany and Margo

Brittany is an African American girl who lived with her identical twin sister and mother in a two-bedroom apartment in an area that her mother, Margo, described as "not really where I want to be, but it's the best I can do right now." There are older siblings who did not live with their mother and the twin sisters; however, they did have contact with them. Margo described herself as a recently widowed homemaker and stated she was currently unable to work or drive because she suffered from seizures. She received disability benefits as her sole income. According to Margo, "Boy, it's tight, but we getting better."

At the time of our interview, Brittany was an 11-year-old sixth grader at a local middle school. Brittany claimed she enjoyed being in middle school because "You get to switch classes around and I don't have to be with the same teacher. And we get to have more stuff at lunch."

Brittany's favorite subjects in school were gym and science. She stated that she enjoyed doing ex-periments in her science class. Brittany expressed a desire to go to the University of Michigan and wanted to be a pediatrician, actress, or teacher when she got older, explaining, "I don't know which one right now. I'll decide later."

In her interview, Margo stated that she recalled having trouble with reading ("sounding out words and some of the understanding of words") and believed that she still had trouble with reading. Margo reported that as a child herself she was placed in a full-day special education program in elementary school and remained there until she graduated from high school. Margo became concerned because although Brittany received resource help for speech and language impairment, Brittany's reading development and math scores were so poor that the school was considering testing her for full-day special education placement. Because of her experiences, Margo did not want her children to suffer the way she did in school. She said, "I was willing to try just about anything from keepin' my babies out of special ed."

It was then that Margo found out about the FLI through Brittany's school. Margo explained, "The school was telling me because both of them [Brittany and her twin sister] was having a problem with their reading, 'cause like I said, they was at a second-grade level in the fourth grade, and they turned me on to...and I called them one day, and we just been with them ever since." The administrators and her classroom teacher at her elementary school agreed to postpone special education testing for Brittany when Margo enrolled her at the FLI. At the time of the study, Brittany had attended the FLI for approximately a year and a half.

WHY BRITTANY NEEDED HELP WITH HER READING DEVELOPMENT. Margo believed Brittany's father's unexpected death and Brittany's attention-deficit hyperactivity disorder diagnosis and speech and language impairment all brought havoc to Brittany's reading development. As far as Brittany's ability to pay attention, according to Margo, "If a fly is on the wall down the hall, she know about it." Margo said that Brittany's elementary school teachers were reporting to her that Brittany's inability to concentrate was negatively affecting her schoolwork and ability to learn. "She always has had trouble focusing [but] not being hyper," Margo remarked.

Margo finally got help through Brittany's pediatrician who "was the one who really advised me to, like, think about the medication and see would that help them [Brittany and her twin sister] focus on their work." At the time of her interview, Brittany and her sister were taking Adderall once in the morning. According to Margo, "and I noticed...it did the job. It had them calm down and focus and understand what's going on instead of being hyper the way they were."

The Family Learning Institute and Changes at Home. When asked what she had been told by the staff at the FLI about how she might help her children improve their literacy skills, Margo stated, "to get them there on time. I drops them off at four and picks them up at six."

Close communication with Doris Sperling on a regular basis and the influence of another FLI staff member encouraged Margo to share her story with her girls. Margo quickly began to make the effort to bring up examples her girls could understand to encourage them to continue to improve their reading skills. The following is an example of how she encouraged her girls:

> By seeing that what I had to go through in life, with my disabilities, I don't want them to have to go through life with that. I tell them, either you get this now or later you'll pay for it in life. If you're an adult and you don't know how to read, it's kind of bad. When you can't get things you want because you can't read what's there. And it's hard. And you know, you don't want to be

asking people, "What is this word? Is this bread? Is this the right kind of bread? Is this wheat?" You know what I'm saying? And if you read and get better with it, it'll pay off in the long run.

Margo stated that she also learned that she needed to not only encourage her children to read, but to also make sure that they read every night. The vignette that opens the chapter shows how Margo started to read with her children every night. One of the things Margo found out when she started encouraging her girls to read and she began reading herself was that she was still having trouble with her own reading skills. However, Margo was pleased to inform me that she had seen some improvement in her own reading skills as a result of taking the time to read with her girls. According to Margo, "by me reading with my kids and pushing the issue, I done progressed a lot myself." Another area in which she felt she had made progress was finding help when she did not have the answer. According to Margo, Doris suggested that if during their nightly reading time Brittany doesn't understand something, "We writes it down and then she can take it to school or the FLI." Brittany and her family continue to read books every night before bed.

When asked to sum up what she had learned by working with the staff, and Doris in particular, at the FLI, Margo stated, "We need to work hard and keeping that communication goin'. I also need to be supportive and listen to my kids. That's the important things." When asked why she is doing everything she is doing, she stated, "without reading, you won't accomplish nothing."

> "Without reading, you won't accomplish nothing."

Margo stated she believed Brittany's reading improved a lot. According to Margo,

> She's doing a lot better. When they started going to the FLI, she was reading at like a second-grade level. And she was like in the third grade

going to the fourth grade. And now her reading processes is at the right level. Thank you. That's a blessing.

Case 2—Randy and Michelle

Randy lived in a house with his mother, Michelle, a one-year-old brother, and his maternal grandmother. At the time of the interview, Randy was in the fifth grade in a local elementary school. He stated he enjoyed playing video games, football, and basketball. In school, he liked gym and music. His favorite subjects were math and science because, "you get to play games in math and do experiments in science." Randy was unsure about what he wanted to do when he grows up. He told me he believed he would graduate from college, but "after that, I'm not really sure. I used to want to be a police officer. But now I don't know."

> "'Cause I feel like if you don't know how to read it like stops you from being able to have a career, a job, being able to get through your daily life."

According to Randy, he does not read for fun, but "to improve my reading." When asked why that was important, Randy stated, "you have to know how to read in order to do good in school and stuff. I want to be smart, so I have to learn how to read." When asked how he was improving his reading, Randy said he needed to read more and concentrate on reading. Randy told me, "I really spend time reading and the book that I'm reading right now is [one of the] Harry Potter [series] and it's good and it's kinda exciting. A lot of stuff happening in there."

Randy's mother, Michelle, a self-described avid reader, had some college credits and worked in a county Human Services agency. When talking about her schooling experiences, Michelle recalled, "School was pretty easy for me. I mean, I was like average. I didn't have any problems in school as far as my learning." She went on to state,

> I remember—I don't know how old I was—I just remember I liked reading and I can just always remember being in the car and I would just read anything I saw—just everything in the car. "Oh, that's that." I was always reading.

When asked what she wanted most for her son, Michelle said, "for him to improve his reading skills." She said,

> 'Cause I feel like if you don't know how to read it like stops you from being able to have a career, a job, being able to get through your daily life. I feel like if you can't read, you really can't get anywhere. You're always gonna be improvising or making up stories about how come you can't read this. Or getting people to do things for you. Kinda cheating your way through life.

All through her interview, Michelle reiterated her commitment to ensuring that Randy had a bright future.

WHY RANDY NEEDED HELP WITH HIS READING DEVELOPMENT. According to Michelle, Randy's reading problems were identified early in his academic career. "His teacher just kept telling me that he was behind with his reading. But they never told me what was wrong," she explained.

> I kinda thought that it was because he was having a hard time sitting still. They would always tell me that too. But then, they never told me what to do about it, so I just thought that it would get better on its own.

Unfortunately, Randy's reading problem did not get better on its own. "He just got further and further behind," Michelle said. "I was really concerned because he was so upset about it. Like he was embarrassed because he knew that he could not read as well as everyone else."

Randy's attention span consistently came up in all of the interviews. In school, his teacher,

Ms. Sanders, commented, "Randy would do little distracting things. Like tapping his pencil on the table for long periods of time in a total daze." His teacher noticed his lack of attention was also having a negative impact on Randy's schoolwork. "He just wasn't completing any assignments." At the time the study was completed, Randy was not on medication.

THE FAMILY LEARNING INSTITUTE AND CHANGES AT HOME. Prior to enrolling Randy at the FLI, Michelle looked into several private tutors, but "the cost was just too much. I mean, I wanted him to learn how to read, but my goodness." Finally, she stated,

> His reading was really hindering his progress in school, so I decided that we would have to do without some things in order to improve his reading. So, that's when I started looking into [a for-profit tutoring center]. Their prices were high too, but I thought that it would be worth it.

On the same day she was going to call the for-profit tutoring center, Michelle saw the article about the FLI in the newspaper. She called the FLI and enrolled Randy in the program. Randy had been attending the FLI for the past year and a half.

When asked what she initially thought her responsibility was in helping Randy improve his literacy skills, Michelle stated, "I needed to get him to the Family Learning Institute and to make sure that he had all of his papers with him." Later on, after talking with Doris and working with other staff members at the FLI, Michelle realized she had to do much more than she initially thought, and made several changes at home. "First of all, I'm making him read more." To increase the amount of reading time that he is engaged in, Randy has been able to incorporate reading activities into other activities. "When I don't have anything to do in the car and I'm kinda bored, I start to read the signs and build-

ings around me," he said. "My mom now lets me keep books in our car so that I can read when we are going someplace so that I can read more."

Michelle stated that although she was pushing him to read more, she realized that she also needed to be positive and patient with his reading development. According to Michelle, it was initially frustrating because she felt Randy "should know how to read." However, she realized the need to approach the situation differently and to be more positive. Michelle found that Randy "doesn't get so frustrated [about struggling with reading]" and "he's more comfortable with it." According to Michelle, all of these changes have "made big differences in his reading. We're gonna keep it up until he is at grade level."

Another area that Michelle worked on was to make sure Randy was more responsible, saying,

> I know that they think that I am not doing everything I am supposed to do because he is always forgetting something. It's either his homework, his reading log, or that he isn't supposed to get on the bus and that he needs to go to the Family Learning Institute. But I am on him now and we are working on it.

In response, Randy stated, "I do get it [reading log] finished. I just don't get it turned in because sometimes I leave it on my desk." When asked what happened when he forgot his homework or his reading log, Randy replied, "She takes my stereo or I can't play video games. One time it was for a week and another time it was for two weeks." Randy then told me, "I haven't forgot it since."

Michelle went on to describe a total family effort to help improve Randy's reading skills:

> I think just talking to him, me, my mother, my sister, we're really close. His dad, his step-dad, we try to talk to him, we try to encourage him and I think it just kind of clicked in finally. OK, this is important. I think he's also reading more things that he enjoys too. They've all noticed that he reads like faster and they tell him.

According to Doris, Dr. Bob (Randy's tutor), and Ms. Sanders (Randy's classroom teacher) reading became a priority in Randy's home. Ms. Sanders stated, "I think that his mother is swamped with daily life stuff. But I feel like she is somehow committed to improving his reading." Dr. Bob said, "although he isn't bringing his reading log in all the time, I personally think that's him forgetting it, but I think that she is making him read more at home. That is so important and it shows."

His mother agreed that Randy's reading has improved, asserting,

> And he's more confident—he feels a lot better. Like, just now, he'll read anything. Now I can see that he feels more comfortable reading. Cause he'll just sit there and read something or when we're driving he'll say, "Oh this is that" or when we're sitting here and something is on TV, he'll read it whereas before, he would kinda shy away from it or run away from it. Now he'll read around people too. Whereas before, he would not do that at all.

Michelle also stated, "But, I know that he still has work to do. So, he will keep on doing this until he is above grade level. I will keep stressing to him that he needs to improve his reading and making him read more." Overall, Michelle felt that Randy would accomplish all of his dreams and goals "because we as a family are going to make sure that he does."

Discussion: Major Themes

Families and Staff Perceived Family Involvement Differently

Families in this study perceived family involvement as getting their children to tutoring every week and on time and encouraging them to behave during their tutoring sessions. The staff perceived family involvement as families reading with their children, asking students relevant questions after they've read, purchasing reading materials that interested the child, and requiring the children to read independently every night.

Families and Staff Perceived Family Level of Caring Differently

The families expressed that they wholeheartedly wanted their children to succeed. However, because they were not teachers they did not know how they could help their children with literacy skills. They perceived that the teaching should be done by those more knowledgeable. The staff perceived that because the families were not involved in the tutoring process and—given the families' views on how to best help their children—that they did not care as much as staff perceived they should in regard to their children's literacy development.

Families and Staff Both Benefited When the Lines of Communication Were Opened

When the staff initiated telephone calls to families, the staff members found out more information about the students (e.g., health histories, school histories, concerns), their family situations (e.g., socioeconomic status, culture), and other relevant information. This information was then used to support the families in the form of workshops, one-on-one sessions, home visits, and school visits. The families benefited by receiving support from staff members. Doris would join families at individualized educational plan conferences, help them with securing reading materials, and suggest strategy instruction to help their children with their literacy development.

Self-Efficacy Levels Increased

The families initially reported not knowing how to help their children with their reading development. Thus, according to Bandura (1997) one can surmise their self-efficacy levels were low in regard to this issue. However, with the assistance of the staff and improvement of their children's reading skills, the families' and their children's self-efficacy levels also began to improve.

Implications

According to Allington and Cunningham (2002) schools that have a higher success rate with struggling readers have a higher level of family and community support. Data from my study also suggest this is true for after-school community-based volunteer reading tutorial programs. Brittany's and Randy's mothers were committed to improving their children's reading skills, as suggested in their willingness to pay for tutoring, concerns about their children's futures if they had poor reading skills, enrollment of their children at the FLI, and commitment to getting them to the FLI weekly for their tutoring sessions. However, the data indicate a lack of communication between the staff at the FLI and the families caused confusion about how active a role each should take in the tutoring process and also reinforced incorrect preconceived notions about each group.

Both mothers initially had a different view of how to be actively involved in the tutoring process at the FLI than the staff. However, when they received assistance and support from the staff at the FLI, both mothers implemented techniques and strategies that proved beneficial to their children's reading development, and in Brittany's case, her other family members' reading skills improved as well. On the flip side, the staff at the FLI began to see the families differently—to see that they did care—but that some families may believe that they are not knowledgeable enough to help their children improve their reading skills. The staff began to recognize that some families might need extra support and guidance in assisting their children in the tutoring process.

The results of the study indicate that communication between families and staff at after-school community-based reading tutorial programs is key to having families actively involved in the tutoring process in meaningful ways. The data suggest that high levels or even increased levels of family support may help children and other family members improve their reading skills and boost their self-confidence and self-efficacy levels. Thus, getting children to their tutoring sessions, making sure they turn in their reading logs or homework, increasing reading time, encouraging family members to read together, placing a strong emphasis on reading, encouraging their children, and sharing their own struggles with their children all may show children that reading and being literate is important to their families, their daily lives, the community, and their future endeavors.

> Schools that have a higher success rate with struggling readers have a higher level of family and community support.

As a former classroom teacher and supervisor of student teachers, I can also see implications from my study for preservice teacher education programs and inservice teachers. I believe that my findings shed light on some of the unique circumstances, challenges, and potential solutions for preservice and inservice teachers who are trying to initiate better communication with their students' parents. It goes without saying that parental involvement is important, and through my study I found that a lack of communication caused confusion on both parts, as well as confirmed or disconfirmed preconceived notions by both parties.

For instance, I found that the staff viewed parents' absences as a sign that they did not care about their children. However, from the parents' point of view, their absence may not mean that they do not care, but may indicate that they may not know what to ask for, how to ask for help, or that they are too embarrassed to ask for help. I firmly believe that preservice and inservice teachers need to develop strong, long-lasting relationships with their students' parents, because the parents have been their students' first teachers and may have valuable information about the students' interests, family circumstances, and physical, social, and emotional development—all of which are relevant to teaching, lesson planning, assessment, classroom management, group formations, and so on. Thus, regardless of whether the teaching or tutoring is taking place in school or out of school, parents, teachers, tutors, and staff members need to work together to help our students best.

Words of Advice

Some families may need assistance in learning how to help their children achieve literacy success. Some possible areas on which to focus include the following:

- Letting them know what programs are available. Some of the families I interviewed said they did not know that there was help available for them.

- Showing them how to locate free or low-cost resources such as books, magazines, computers, and writing utensils.

- Assisting and assessing older children with their reading development.

- Locating tutoring programs for adults if family members feel they have limited literacy skills.

REFERENCES

Allington, R.L., & Cunningham, P. (2002). *Schools that work: Where all children read and write* (2nd ed.). Boston: Allyn & Bacon.

Baker, L., Serpell, R., & Sonnenschein, S. (1995). Opportunities for literacy learning in the homes of urban preschoolers. In L.M. Morrow (Ed.), *Family literacy: Connections in schools and communities* (pp. 236–252). Newark, DE: International Reading Association.

Baker, L., & Wigfield, A. (1999). Dimensions of children's motivation for reading and their relations to reading activity. *Reading Research Quarterly, 34*(4), 452–477. doi:10.1598/RRQ.34.4.4

Bandura, A. (1997). *Self-efficacy: The exercise of control.* New York: W.H. Freeman.

Cohen, P., Kulik, J.A., & Kulik, C.C. (1982). Educational outcomes of tutoring: A meta-analysis of findings. *American Educational Research Journal, 19*(2), 237–248. doi:10.3102/00028312019002237

Eccles, J.A., & Harold, R.D. (1993). Parent-school involvement during the early adolescent years. *Teachers College Record, 94*(3), 568–587.

Elbaum, B., Vaughn, S., Hughes, M.T., & Moody, S.W. (2000). How effective are one-to-one tutoring programs in reading for elementary students at risk for reading failure? A meta-analysis of the intervention research. *Journal of Educational Psychology, 92*(4), 605–619. doi:10.1037/0022-0663.92.4.605

Fitzgerald, J. (2001). Can minimally trained college student volunteers help young at-risk children to read better? *Reading Research Quarterly, 36*(1), 28–46. doi:10.1598/RRQ.36.1.2

Glaser, B.G., & Strauss, A.L. (1999). *The discovery of grounded theory: Strategies for qualitative research.* Chicago: Aldine.

Hoover-Dempsey, K.V., Bassler, O.C., & Burow, R. (1995). Parents' reported involvement in students' homework: Strategies and practices. *The Elementary School Journal, 95*(5), 435–450. doi:10.1086/461854

Invernizzi, M., Juel, C., & Rosemary, C.A. (1996). A community volunteer tutorial that works. *The Reading Teacher, 50*(4), 304–311.

Jayroe, T.B., & Brenner, D. (2005). Family members as partners in an after-school and summer literacy program. *Reading Horizons, 45*(4), 235–253.

Juel, C. (1996). What makes literacy tutoring effective? *Reading Research Quarterly, 31*(3), 268–289. doi:10.1598/RRQ.31.3.3

McLurkin, D. (2004). *"It's not gonna not be a struggle": An investigation into possible factors that may have contributed to some children's reading improving while others did not at the reading center.* Paper presented at the 2nd Annual Hawaii International Conference on Education, Honolulu, HI.

Morris, D., Shaw, B., & Perney, J. (1990). Helping low readers in grades 2 and 3: An after- school volunteer tutoring program. *The Elementary School Journal, 91*(2), 132–150. doi:10.1086/461642

Scales, A.M., Morris, G.A., & George, A.W. (1998). A church operated after-school tutorial enrichment program. *The Negro Educational Review, XLIX*(3–4), 153–164.

Shanahan, T. (1998). On the effectiveness and limitations of tutoring in reading. *Review of Research in Education, 23*(1), 217–234.

Strauss, A.L., & Corbin, J.M. (1990). *Basics of qualitative research: Grounded theory procedures and techniques.* Newbury Park, CA: Sage.

Vadasy, P.F., Jenkins, J.R., Antil, L.R., Wayne, S.K., & O'Connor, R.E. (1997). The effectiveness of one-to-one tutoring by community tutors for at-risk beginning readers. *Learning Disability Quarterly, 20*(2), 126–139. doi:10.2307/1511219

Wasik, B.A. (1998). Volunteer tutoring programs in reading: A review. *Reading Research Quarterly, 33*(3), 266–292. doi:10.1598/RRQ.33.3.2

Wasik, B.A., & Slavin, R.E. (1993). Preventing early reading failure with one-to-one tutoring: A review of five programs. *Reading Research Quarterly, 28*(2), 178–200. doi:10.2307/747888

Wigfield, A., & Guthrie, J.T. (1997). Relations of children's motivation for reading to the amount and breadth of their reading. *Journal of Educational Psychology, 89*(3), 420–432. doi:10.1037/0022-0663.89.3.420

ABOUT THE CONTRIBUTOR

Denise L. McLurkin *is an assistant professor at The City College of New York, New York, USA. She is a former classroom teacher who teaches literacy methods classes for undergraduate and graduate students. She has a B.A. in Psychology from the University of California, Irvine, an M.S. in Counseling Psychology from California Baptist University, and an M.A. in Literacy Education and a doctorate in Educational Studies from the University of Michigan. E-mail: dmclurkin@ ccny.cuny.edu*

CHAPTER 8

Everybody Wins: A School–Higher Education Partnership for Reading Improvement

Neva Ann Medcalf, Karen Bessette, and David Gibbs

A fifth grader at risk of failure on the state standardized tests arrived the first night of our tutoring program with a very negative attitude. "This is cruel and unusual punishment!" he said as he flopped down on the bench near the door to the school.

"Okay," I (Medcalf, first author) said, "but we really have a great time."

"I don't want to be here, and I'm not going to like it or do anything," he grumbled emphatically crossing his arms and setting his face in a frown.

"Well, let's see how it goes tonight; and then you can decide what you want to do," I replied with a smile. Secretly I worried that his attitude was going to be a real problem; perhaps he would not be able to be part of the program. He began work with an outgoing, enthusiastic graduate student, Megan, who had a wonderfully contagious grin. By the end of the second tutoring session, he participated with Megan and seemed to enjoy learning. After a few more weeks, he was the leader of his group. Megan often had to ask him to give other children a chance to answer and read aloud. When given a choice between the teacher reading to him or reading for himself, he always chose to do oral reading. When given a choice of waiting for the other members of his group to arrive or beginning without them, he always eagerly chose to get started.

The opening vignette represents a composite of students' attitudes and portrays an example of the positive results stemming from the partnership between the Master of Arts in Reading program of St. Mary's University and Randolph Elementary School in greater San Antonio, Texas. There are many other positive outcomes for the elementary children and the graduate students. As the principal of the school, Karen Bessette (second author), notes, "This is a program where everybody wins."

The Master of Arts in Reading is a state-approved program to prepare certified teachers for advanced certification as Reading Specialists and Master Reading Teachers. The program was expanded in the spring of 2002 to offer second-career professionals a path to initial early childhood through fourth-grade teacher certification.

Literacy Tutoring That Works: A Look at Successful In-School, After-School, and Summer Programs, edited by Janet C. Richards and Cynthia A. Lassonde. © 2009 International Reading Association.

Although students were successful in passing the state certification tests, in the fall of 2004 I identified a need to add field experience to provide connections between theory and practice. At that time, many graduate students seeking initial certification were military personnel approaching retirement. Therefore, each semester one eight-week course was taught at Randolph Air Force Base.

I contacted the elementary school on the base to recruit students for graduates to tutor from 6:00 to 7:00 P.M. on Monday and Wednesday evenings and asked to hold the graduate class at the school. At first, David Gibbs (third author), the vice-principal, was hesitant to allow use of the facilities because of the timing of the evening session, possible costs, and lack of available custodial personnel. However, after consultation and careful consideration, Karen and David determined the potential to assist at-risk children far outweighed the possible costs. Therefore, classes began to meet at Randolph Elementary School in the Early Childhood Center.

Even though graduate students are now predominantly civilian, the partnership with the school is such a strong, positive component of the Master of Arts in Reading program that we continue to hold classes at the school. Enrollment in graduate courses averages 20 students per semester. For certification as a Reading Specialist, the State of Texas approved 24 graduate credit hours in reading, which are offered on a rotating basis. Course content determines the age and grade level of the elementary students recruited for the tutoring sessions. Older children come for the Diagnosis and Remediation course; younger ones come for the Developmental Reading course. These are eight-week courses with the first two weeks focused on instruction for graduates and the remaining six weeks centered on a combination of tutoring and instruction. We recruit children for the tutoring sessions who are at risk of failure on the state-mandated standardized test (Texas Assessment of Knowledge and Skills, TAKS). Families transport children to the school for small-group work with the graduate students, who remain at the elementary school for class from 7:15 to 9:00 P.M.

> Although students were successful in passing the state certification tests, in the fall of 2004 I identified a need to add field experience to provide connections between theory and practice.

At the end of each semester, we have a celebration of accomplishments for all participants. We reward children's efforts, achievements, attendance, and enthusiasm with a pizza party, certificates, and individual recognition. We also give them information about the university and encourage them to think about attending college in the future. Support for the program comes from all over campus. The Graduate Dean pays for pizza; the Bookstore Manager supplies pencils and folders; ROTC, Campus Police, Athletics, and Admissions contribute goodies for gift bags. The children sign posters for these supporters, and the posters are displayed on campus with pride.

Questions Guiding the Research

Primarily, we wanted to know the following:

- How does the tutoring program affect children's reading abilities?

We also sought answers to the following secondary questions:

- What do families think about the program?

- What do teachers think about the program?

- Do children who participate in the program pass the state-mandated standardized test in reading?

- What impact does linking theory and practice have on graduate students' teaching practices and self-confidence in their teaching abilities?

Theoretical Background and Perspectives

We used both qualitative and quantitative data analyses. Because the majority of data were anecdotal, our study was informed by tenets of qualitative research methods. Much of the data collection took the form of "kidwatching" (Jaggar, 1985), which is "action research—jotting field notes, gathering data from close observation or interview, and interpreting the scene" (Zeni, 1996, p. 30). This is a well-established and effective method of learning about growth and development and is a valuable tool for researchers (Jaggar & Smith-Burke, 1985). Observing children in the classroom and in other natural settings reveals aspects of their learning we could discover in no other way. "We aren't outsiders… but insiders responsible to the students whose learning we document" (Zeni, 1996, p. 30).

> "We aren't outsiders…but insiders responsible to the students whose learning we document."

When testing young children, Fleischer and Belgredan (1990) state that informed and knowledgeable perceptions of those who have direct contact with children are vitally important in any comprehensive evaluation of them. Neisworth and Bagnato (1988) use the term "judgment-based assessment," which collects, structures, and quantifies the observations of professionals regarding the characteristics and performance of the child. This is descriptive ethnographic research (Garson, 2006). As Medcalf-Davenport (2003) states, careful analytical observations of the quality of a child's behaviors and responses in the context of the whole setting create a more valid, reliable picture of developmental stages and abilities. The main focus of the observations for this research is the effectiveness of the program to improve children's reading skills and motivation to read. It also measured the changes families observed in their children. Therefore, kidwatching and qualitative research data collection fit the design of this study.

Vandell, Reisner, and Pierce (2007) state, "(R)egular participation in high-quality after-school programs is linked to significant gains in standardized test scores and work habits" (p. 1). According to these researchers, high-quality programs are characterized by the following:

- Leaders who expect students to participate regularly

- Students who are highly engaged with one another and activities

- Teachers/tutors who structure age-appropriate activities to maximize learning and positive relationships

- Low student-to-adult ratios

- Teachers/tutors who are trained and feel satisfaction and a sense of accomplishment

- Strong connections with partner schools and with families

By intentional design, all of these qualities are in the partnership between St. Mary's University and Randolph Elementary School. In addition, instruction is intentionally designed to meet the needs, abilities, and learning styles of students. Activities are designed to increase motivation to learn, and content connects school lessons to the real-world applications. The benefits of the partnership extend to graduate students, who gain hands-on experience with children of various ages and abilities. They learn to plan and execute lessons and activities that are interesting and motivating. They learn to monitor and adjust their teaching "on the spot." This forces the graduate students to think beyond the textbook to the real world of teaching children.

Research shows college students who participated in such programs are more likely to have a higher grade-point average and an increased knowledge base (Collaborative After School Project, 2001; Lougee, 2007). Those seeking initial certification are paired with experienced teachers for the work with the children. As the professor, I am there to monitor and observe what they are doing with their students and can step in and model if needed. The graduate students write and execute lesson plans and then write reflections regarding the successes or weaknesses in the lesson following each session. I read and give constructive guidance on each and every one of these documents. During our class time, I instruct on strategies, assessment methods, and theoretical background for teaching reading.

Methodology

Participants

Study participants were elementary children considered at risk for failure on the state standardized reading tests. Teachers recommended children for the program and David contacted families. Each semester 20 to 30 students participated in the tutoring sessions. Graduate students from St. Mary's University enrolled in the Master of Arts in Reading program worked as tutors and were members of the study popula-

tion along with families and classroom teachers of children who participated.

Data Sources

Elementary children completed the Elementary Reading Attitude Survey (ERAS; McKenna & Kear, 1990) at the beginning and end of each semester. Using this instrument, in which Garfield the cat is pictured with various expressions to show mood, children rate their own attitudes about reading. We compared pre- and posttutoring results. At the end of each course, graduate students wrote brief descriptions of their learning about the reading process and their attitudes regarding their work with elementary children. They reflected on what they learned from the experience and what impact that learning would have on their future teaching. Graduate students also reported any changes they observed in the children they worked with and how those changes affected the child's self-esteem, motivation, and participation during the tutoring sessions.

We also examined formal course evaluations for comments regarding working with the elementary students. We surveyed families and teachers at the end of each semester regarding their perceptions of the program as well as any changes they noticed in the children's attitudes toward reading and changes in school achievement while participating in the program. (See sample surveys in Figures 8.1 and 8.2.) We used standardized reading test results for the school as a measure of effectiveness of the program because children who attend are those at risk for academic failure.

Data Analysis

Smith (2004) writes, "(T)he emotional response to reading…is the primary reason most readers read, and probably the primary reason most

Figure 8.1 Family Survey

1. How many semesters has your child participated in the program?
2. What are the strengths of this reading program?
3. What suggestions could you make for the improvement of the St. Mary's University tutoring program?
4. What did you like the most about the program?
5. Would you recommend our tutoring program to others?
6. How did your child feel about reading before the program?
7. How does your child feel about reading after the program?
8. Does he or she read for pleasure?
9. Does your child show greater motivation to read since being in the program?
10. What differences and/or improvements did you notice in your child's reading ability?
11. Did you see an improvement in your child's writing abilities?
12. List one way your child benefited from this program?
13. Have you noticed a change in attitude toward school in general since being in the St. Mary's University program?
14. Did your child look forward to attending our program?
15. What was your child's mood/attitude when you picked him/her up?
16. Does your child discuss any topics he or she may have learned during any of our lesson plans?
17. Were improvements made in subjects other than language arts? If yes, what were those changes?

nonreaders do not read" (p. 177). Lipson and Wixson (2003) explain that children's attitudes toward reading were the main factor affecting their reading achievement. Therefore, we employed the quantitative portion of data analysis with the ERAS (McKenna & Kear, 1990). It provides estimates of children's attitudes toward recreational and academic reading. McKenna and Kear's research showed value on a four-point scale to avoid a neutral, central category. They developed a scoring sheet that makes the results quick and easy to analyze. We also analyzed children's comments at the end of the program.

We analyzed the Family and Teacher Surveys for patterns of comments, suggestions for improvement, and strengths and weaknesses in the program. We were especially interested to find whether program participation had any effect on children's classroom attitudes and behaviors regarding the reading process and activities. We also analyzed the writing of the graduate students for patterns of comments and suggestions for improvements in the program.

We examined the TAKS results for the school for evidence of reading skill improvement. Individual scores for students are not available to the public, but the school has excellent passing rates. David was able to identify test results for program participants so we could compare pre- and posttutoring results.

Limitations

The program is of short duration. Therefore, we cannot directly attribute final results on the state reading tests to participation in the university reading program. However, Karen and David believe that the tutoring does contribute to the success their at-risk students have on these tests. The data are primarily qualitative. As Richards (2006) points out, "(R)esearcher subjectivity is a central component of the qualitative research process whether the data is visual, narrative, or a combination of both" (p. 46). However, our careful analyses revealed patterns and quantifiable evidence that the reading program is very effective in improving students' attitudes toward

Figure 8.2 Teacher Survey

1. How did student feel about reading before being in the Reading Program?

1	2	3	4	5
Very negative	Somewhat negative	Neutral	Somewhat positive	Very positive

2. How does student feel about reading after participation in the program?

1	2	3	4	5
Very negative	Somewhat negative	Neutral	Somewhat positive	Very positive

3. Did student read for pleasure before participation in the program?

1	2	3	4	5
Never	Rarely	Neutral	Sometimes	Often

4. Does student read for pleasure after participation in the program?

1	2	3	4	5
Never	Rarely	Neutral	Sometimes	Often

5. What improvements, if any, have you noticed in this student's **reading skills** since participation in the program?

6. What improvements, if any, have you noticed in this student's **writing abilities** since participation in the program?

7. What changes have you noticed in the student's attitude toward school in general?

8. What changes have you noticed in the student's classroom behavior?

9. Does student view him/herself as a reader since participation in the program?

1	2	3	4	5
Not at all	Very little	Neutral	Somewhat	Definitely

10. Please add any additional comments you feel would be helpful either in evaluating the Reading Program or in structuring the Program in future semesters.

---

reading. We also found improvement in their reading skills, decoding, comprehension, fluency, and vocabulary development.

Results and Discussion

Each semester, elementary school children completed the ERAS (McKenna and Kear, 1990) at the beginning of the reading program and again at the end of the six weeks. The scoring guide converts the pictures to a Likert scale, with the happiest Garfield image ranked 4, the angriest Garfield ranked 1, and the Garfields in between ranked 2 and 3. We analyzed the pre- and post-tutoring results for changes in attitude.

Although analysis of the surveys did not show changes in children's general attitude toward reading, we did discover some interesting phenomena. The lowest overall rating for any item on the survey was for reading workbook pages and worksheets. This was followed by reading instead of playing, reading during summer vacation, and taking a reading test. The highest overall rating was for reading different kinds of books, followed by learning from books and then by going to a bookstore.

When we analyzed the children's writings, we found all of them were positive regarding attending the tutoring sessions and working with the teachers. Many children gave specific examples of strategies they learned, such as the following:

> "I learned how to stretch out long words then smush them together to sound out words!"

> I was embarrassed to read before but now I can read in front of my class. I had a good time here. I want to come back again.

> I want to come back. I want to read more chapter books. My mommy is proud of me!

> I liked playing the matching and vocabulary card games.

> I like the sight word bingo.

> I liked when we read and we play games.

> I like the spider booke. I like evethang. YES! (written by a first grader with invented spelling)

> I learned how to stretch out long words then smush them together to sound out words!"

> I learned to use my finger to keep track.

One of the most encouraging comments came from a second grader who started the program discouraged and not wanting to participate because he struggled so much with reading: "Now I know 86 sight words, and I want to know them all!"

When we analyzed the Family Surveys, all of the families said they would recommend the tutoring program to others. Other positive aspects specified by parents included:

> Children gained confidence and became excited about reading.

> The small-group setting and/or one-on-one instruction with consistency and repetition made these changes possible.

> The variety in instructional approach enhanced fundamentals learned in the classroom with a very positive atmosphere and teachers who really cared about children.

Understandably, what parents liked most about the program related to the impact on their children:

> It helped my son to like reading and encouraged him to read more and to write his own comic, which made us so proud of him and his accomplishments.

> I appreciate the additional help for my child and the fact that the teachers and the Director was willing to take the time out to nurture and teach.

> The program encouraged my son to improve his reading skills. He has become a self-motivated reader and enjoys reading to his little sister.

> Getting feedback from the teachers about his progress and/or weakness and suggestions from teachers about different things you can do to help child become a better reader.

> When I picked him up, he had so much to talk about.

Twenty-eight percent of families said it was an excellent program, and they would not change anything. Thirty-six percent wanted both the individual sessions and the number of sessions each semester to increase. Many suggested 1½-to 2-hour sessions over 9 to 12 weeks. Twelve percent said they would like more feedback from the teachers about how to support and help their children with reading.

The responses to "How does your child *feel* about reading *after* the program?" were 100% positive, including the following:

> He is excited about reading.
> Projects a higher motivation to read at home.
> He loves it!
> He is now starting to enjoy reading.

> Very enthusiastic—more apt to sound out words.
>
> He wants to read a lot more.
>
> Tackles chapter books with more enthusiasm.
>
> He is confident in his reading ability and enjoying learning more.
>
> She loves to read and let us know what she is reading.

The comment that made the whole program worthwhile was the following: "His reading has improved. He doesn't *hate* it as before!"

Families observed positive attitudes and motivation in the children, whereas the children did not seem to perceive changes in themselves. When asked about improvements they had noticed in their children's reading abilities, families were clear. One hundred percent noted increased motivation, self-confidence, fluency, and comprehension. Fifty percent reported children choosing to read more. One parent stated, "I notice in her free time she would pick up books vs. watching TV." In response to whether or not the child looked forward to attending the program, 99% of families responded, "Yes." One parent said, "Not at first … after the first day he would remind us." Forty-five percent of families stated that their children reminded them of the tutoring program every Monday and Wednesday.

When we analyzed Teacher Surveys, teachers reported that 89% of the students participating had more positive attitudes about reading at the conclusion of the program. When asked whether the target children read for pleasure prior to participation in the program, teachers indicated that seven children rarely read for pleasure. Following the program, teachers reported that all seven increased their time spent reading for pleasure. At the end of the program, teachers indicated 89% of students saw themselves as readers. Teacher comments included, "J. has confidence and monitors his own mistakes while reading" and "M. is less shy about reading. She participates more in class discussions."

Participation in the program affected more than just children's reading skills. Teachers reported growth in written expression. Teachers told us things such as,

> He enjoys putting his ideas on paper and sharing them with others.
>
> He is growing in his confidence and ability to write.
>
> She no longer seems overwhelmed and enjoys sharing her stories with the class.
>
> She loves to write stories and can read them to others.

Teachers reported that individual children "plunge into all learning opportunities" and "she is surer of herself." And this statement summarizes the feelings: "S. loves school now. He was very shy and did not enjoy school when the year began. The program gave him a great jump-start to enjoy reading and school."

Changes in children's classroom behavior were described as "more outgoing and confident," "smiles more," "more on task," "raises her hand more," "developed a real take-charge approach," and "very sure of herself." Additionally teachers said, "The program really helps set the tone for a fun and successful school year!" "I credit the program with instilling a real 'can do' attitude in M. She believes in herself!" "The program let C. see that reading and learning are fun and you don't need to be afraid of failing. Just enjoy what you are able to do and you will keep growing." "The program was a wonderful way for J. to begin third grade. It really helped his confidence."

Table 8.1 displays the participant reading TAKS results since the inception of the partnership with St. Mary's University reading program. For the 2007–2008 school year, 100% of third graders passed the TAKS. Four who

Table 8.1 TAKS Results

School Year	2004–2005	2005–2006	2006–2007	2007–2008	Summary 2004–2008
Fall participants	15	23	45	22	105
Fall participants in non-TAKS grades	0	3	13	0	16
Spring participants	30	20	22	24	96
Spring participants in non-TAKS grades	0	0	22	24	46
Total participants	45	43	67	46	201
Number in both sessions	6	0	0	0	6
Number of test takers	35	19	26	22	102
Number who met standard	34 (97%)	19 (100%)	24 (92%)	21 (95%)	98 (96%)
Number commended	2	4	9	5	20
Number SDAA* takers	2	1	1	0	4
Number who withdrew from school	2	0	3	0	5

Note. *State Developed Alternative Assessment, the test for students with individualized education plans.

participated in the program scored at the commended level. All but one fifth grader passed the test. One who participated in the program scored at the commended level. The one fifth grader who failed the test had not attended the reading program even though his teacher recommended it to his family.

We examined test results for the school district and found 100% of eighth graders passed the TAKS tests. This class of eighth graders comprises children who were part of the reading program the very first semester of the partnership. One had failed the fifth-grade test on the first administration but passed it the second time after attending the tutoring sessions. One hundred percent passage of eighth graders indicates that the reading improvements made through the partnership reading program are permanent.

When we analyzed the writing of the graduate students, their professional growth was evident, as demonstrated in the following comments:

I was new to this program. I am a semi-experienced teacher and did not see the benefit of one hour for a few number of visits. Boy, was I wrong! I saw huge growth in attitude. My student started out a boy of few words and not wanting to read aloud to one who wouldn't stop talking and wouldn't let me read. He also became a leader when we worked with other groups. I can see the growth and speed of growth that is due to small-group and one-on-one connections. I could have done this in a classroom setting but it would have taken twice as long or longer. At the beginning my student would look for ways to get out of work and at the end, if given the choice, he would choose academic work.

Throughout the sessions, I worked on reading skills that would be assessed on the TAKS test while also concentrating on fluency and group participation. I saw improvement in both students' (fifth graders) ability to perform in a slightly larger group setting. The student having fluency difficulty showed overall improvement by actually slowing down her rate and using a place marker. I enjoyed both students immensely, and learned a great deal in constructing a usable lesson plan.

I received firsthand experience working with students in reading. This is especially beneficial for grad students like me who are going for initial certification and work with students in a classroom. It allowed me to apply what I was learning in class to real situations.

The program fosters a love of reading in the students. The children realize through the program that reading is not always boring and does not always have to be done only in school, but that it can also be enjoyable and interesting. One of our students gave up cheerleading practice for it. Another, last semester, came in with a fever, because she absolutely refused to miss 'reading practice.' It is simply a wonderful opportunity for them to work on reading skills in a comfortable and interesting environment.

Each semester we deal with different students with different ages and different backgrounds. It made me more confident in dealing with the students. We have a chance to create lesson plans with no restrictions and learn new strategies and ideas from other classmates.

My only regret was that we didn't get to spend the whole semester with the kids. I wish this course were of regular length, because I feel like I, and my students, could have learned and accomplished so much more. It seemed like we were just getting to know our students, and then it was over. But I learned a lot just by observing and applying what we've learned in class in a hands-on environment. I really hope this program continues to grow and provide a wonderful learning environment for everyone involved.

Implications

We believe there would be more evidence of children's self-reported changes in attitude between beginning ratings and ending ratings if the program were longer. The tutoring sessions occur for only six weeks with 12 one-hour sessions, the last of which is a celebration and awards ceremony. Therefore, there is not enough time for overall self-expressed attitude toward reading in various situations and with various types of text to be made more positive.

Family Survey comments evidenced a great deal of positive change in students' attitudes toward reading, as well as growth in reading skills. Although we cannot attribute all of the positive findings to our tutoring initiative, there is strong evidence that with this model, everybody wins. Elementary children receive one-on-one instruction, have opportunities to practice and strengthen reading skills, and receive immediate feedback. They are prepared to take and pass the TAKS test. Children's motivation to read in their free time in self-selected material increases. They feel positive about their improved abilities and accomplishments.

University graduate students implement the strategies they have learned about from textbooks and class sessions. Then they reflect upon their practice and implementation with the professor and colleagues. The graduate students gain confidence in their abilities as effective teachers. They understand and can implement differentiated instruction to meet the needs and abilities of their students.

This is a positive model for reading improvement that others can replicate. Public schools (and other organizations such as afterschool programs and summer camps) can seek partnerships with universities. For partnerships to be mutually beneficial, the parties must rely on combined strengths. Strong and lasting partnerships are built only when open communication is in place. Partners must learn to ask the right questions and must cultivate respect as a key to sustained collaboration, as noted by Noguera (1998):

> (I)n order for a partnership between a K–12 school and a university to be sustained over time, relationships between the parties involved

must be based upon mutual respect. From the outset, it is very important to make it clear who is going to benefit...and to be sure that expectations and roles are clearly defined.... Collaboration between schools and universities is essential because it allows for the strengths of the university and the schools to be matched for...problem solving and mutual benefit. (p. 4)

Trust and respect come from perseverance and dedication.

This program is a strong component of a graduate reading specialist program that helps ensure that teachers thoroughly understand and can implement theory into practice. They get hands-on experience working with children while they reflect upon their practice and work collaboratively to increase children's learning. Results on state-mandated tests reflect benefits for children's participation in the program, and families become more involved and committed to children's success. This in turn strengthens the home–school relationship. There was a positive impact on the affective domain for all stakeholders toward the teaching and learning of reading. Again, as Noguera (1998) proposes,

For those who are willing to invest the time in forging such relationships, trust will gradually develop, and from that trust can come a willingness to test out new ideas, to try things that we've never considered before and that can actually lead to lasting change. (p. 6)

We would tell everyone it is worth the effort because absolutely everybody wins.

Words of Advice

- Don't be apprehensive in seeking out locations for site-based instruction.
- Make sure families buy into the program and are committed to having their children participate on a regular basis.

- Ensure that everyone leaves facilities in good condition after each tutoring session.
- Express gratitude and appreciation to those involved in making the program possible (i.e., school administration, custodial staff, and families).

REFERENCES

Collaborative After School Project. (2001). *Rationale for K–16 after-school learning partnerships*. Irvine: University of California.

Fleischer, K.H., & Belgredan, J.H. (1990). An overview of judgment-based assessment. *Topics in Early Childhood Special Education, 10*(3), 13–23.

Garson, G.D. (2006). *Ethnographic research*. Raleigh: North Carolina State University. Retrieved June 6, 2006, from www2.chass.ncsu.edu/garson/PA765/ethno.htm

Jaggar, A. (1985). On observing the language learner: Introduction and overview. In A. Jaggar & M.T. Smith-Burke (Eds.), *Observing the language learner* (pp. 1–7). Newark, DE: International Reading Association; Urbana, IL: National Council of Teachers of English.

Jaggar, A., & Smith-Burke, M.T. (Eds.). (1985). *Observing the language learner*. Newark, DE: International Reading Association; Urbana. IL: National Council of Teachers of English.

Lipson, M.Y., & Wixson, K.K. (2003). *Assessment and instruction of reading and writing difficulty: An interactive approach*. Boston: Allyn & Bacon.

Lougee, A. (2007). *The SMILE program*. Retrieved July 23, 2007, from smile.oregonstate.edu/

McKenna, M.C., & Kear, D.J. (1990). Measuring attitude toward reading: A new tool for teachers. *The Reading Teacher, 43*(8), 626–639. doi:10.1598/RT.43.8.3

Medcalf-Davenport, N.A. (2003). Questions, answers and wait-time: Implications for readiness testing of young children. *International Journal of Early Years Education, 11*(3), 245–253. doi:10.1080/0966976032000147558

Neisworth, J.T., & Bagnato, S.J. (1988). Assessment in early childhood special education. In S.L. Odom & M.B. Karnes (Eds.), *Early intervention for infants and children with handicaps* (pp. 23–49). Baltimore: Paul H. Brookes.

Noguera, P.A. (1998, July 9). Toward the development of school and university partnerships based upon mutual benefit and respect. *In Motion Magazine*. Retrieved April 14, 2008 from www.inmotionmagazine.com/pnsup1 .html

Richards, J.C. (2006). Post modern image-based research: An innovative data collection method for illuminating preservice teachers' developing perceptions in field-based courses. *The Qualitative Report, 11*(1), 37–54. Retrieved April 30, 2008, from www.nova.edu/ssss/QR/QR11-1/ richards.pdf

Smith, F. (2004). *Understanding reading: A psycholinguistic analysis of reading and learning to read* (6th ed.). Hillsdale, NJ: Erlbaum.

Vandell, D.L., Reisner, E.R., & Pierce, K.M. (2007). *Outcomes linked to high-quality afterschool programs: Longitudinal findings from the study of promising afterschool programs.* Irvine: University of California Policy Studies Associates.

Zeni, J. (1996). A picaresque tale from the land of kidwatching: Teacher research and ethical dilemmas. *The Quarterly, 18*(1). Retrieved May 31, 2006, from www.writingproject.org/cs/nwpp/lpt/nwpr/279

ABOUT THE CONTRIBUTORS

Neva Ann Medcalf *is a professor of Education and director of the Master of Arts in Reading program at St. Mary's University in San Antonio, Texas, USA. She is the author of* Kidwatching in Josie's World: A Study of Children in Homelessness *as well as numerous articles regarding the language development of children, the testing of young children, and the uses of technology in training future teachers. E-mail: nmedcalf@stmarytx.edu*

Karen Bessette *has served as principal at Randolph Elementary School in San Antonio, Texas, USA, for 13 years. She was also a vice-principal and supervisor of special education programs for Northside Independent School District in San Antonio. Before moving to San Antonio, she taught second grade in Panama and in Heidelberg, Germany. Currently, she serves as Past President for Texas Elementary Principals and Supervisors Association (TEPSA), an organization of over 5,000 members. E-mail: bessette@rfisd.net*

David Gibbs *has worked in the Randolph Field Independent School District, Universal City, Texas, USA, as an assistant principal and school counselor for 19 years. He previously was a school counselor and first- and fourth-grade teacher in the Judson Independent School District, Converse, Texas, USA. Email: gibbs@rfisd.net*

CHAPTER 9

Teaching and Learning About Literacy Through Arts Infusion: Successes, Challenges, and Lessons Learned in an After-School Program

Nancy Rankie Shelton and Morna McDermott

It's 3:50 P.M., and Ronnie's students, Natalia and Nell, arrive and sit down. Nell smiles and says to no one in particular, "I got a Jolt. It's an energy drink."

Ronnie, the preservice teacher who has been working with the students Nell (age 12) and Natalia (age 13), smiles and says, "Did you bring an object?"

"I brought an object—my Jolt." Nell is smiling.

Natalia is not smiling and responds, "I brought me," to which Nell challenges, "That's not an object."

Ronnie redirects the girls to the poetry book they have been reading, *A Wreath for Emmitt Till* (Nelson, 2005). "Do you want to read a page each?" she asks.

The girls' disagreement continues when Nell says, "No," but Natalia agrees to read aloud. She begins to read the poem softly and tentatively. "'Would you bow your head in humility….'"

Natalia finishes the poem and pauses. Nell lifts her bottle and drinks noisily, then holds the book, just looking at it. She starts reading aloud. She reads fast and corrects herself when she recognizes her miscues. She hands the book to Natalia who says she can't read well. "You actin' childish. Just read," Nell says, and then corrects Natalia's mispronunciations and points out that Natalia skipped a "whole line." She also reads some parts for Natalia.

Ronnie asks Natalia what object she will write about today. "Something that means a lot to you. You don't have to write a poem today but I want you to write something." The conversation moves rapidly.

Natalia: We should both do a poem about the same object but different views. We could use the same topic ….

Nell: Lawn chair.

Literacy Tutoring That Works: A Look at Successful In-School, After-School, and Summer Programs, edited by Janet C. Richards and Cynthia A. Lassonde. © 2009 International Reading Association.

108

Natalia: I thought you were going to do something about your mom.

Nell: My real mom is cremated.

Natalia: Did she have a will?

Ronnie: My mom.... [Ronnie cuts her sentence short when Natalia butts in.]

Natalia: If they're young, they don't have a will. How old was your mother?

Nell: 32.

Ronnie: My mom was 62, and she didn't have a will.

Natalia: I'm gonna make a will when I'm 16.

Ronnie: [looking at Nell's drawing] You have a dog?

Nell: Her name is Smuggle.

Natalia: Are you for real? I have a cat.

Nell: I hate cats. They're evil.

Ronnie: Cats aren't evil.

Natalia: You have a cat?

This interaction led to Nell's decision to write a poem called "Evil Cats."

Efforts in our tutoring program focused on bridging content areas such as music, art, and physical education with more traditional notions of literacy, simultaneously providing tutors with authentic interactions with urban children and young adults. Beginning teachers often enter this profession with preconceived notions about students, assuming they are more likely to be behavior problems simply because they are black or come from low-income families. An overwhelming number of preservice teachers in the education program at Towson University grow up in middle-class, suburban communities where there is limited diversity in terms of race or class. In spite of this, they will become teachers in diverse educational settings where cultural sensitivity and critical awareness of life experiences different from their own are necessary for both student and teacher success. As beginning educators they are also unprepared to make the needed empathetic and personal connections with their students, which are vital to student success. Our goal was to report the success of a program to combat the these-kids-can't-(or-won't)-learn stereotype embraced by many. Our findings invite language arts educators to consider the vital role the arts can play in promoting meaningful literacy experiences for students.

This study and proposed method of infusing art and literacy in the content areas is applicable to educators in elementary, middle, and high school settings. The methods employed in teaching/tutoring and the materials used are all easily transferable to classrooms. Morna (second author), who served as the instructor of record for the tutors, has an interest in working with beginning and experienced educators developing democracy, social justice, and arts-informed inquiry in kindergarten through post-secondary educational settings. In an effort to work toward improving tutors' abilities to work successfully in challenging urban settings, we redesigned a traditional Literacy Across the Content Areas course into one taught off campus with students in kindergarten through grade 12. Nancy (first author), committed to helping preservice and inservice teachers hampered by restrictive literacy mandates find ways to provide meaningful literacy instruction, acted as the researcher.

We first held this course and its connected tutoring activities in the Sugar Hill neighborhood school in a large east coast city. Sugar Hill experiences high incidences of crime, poverty, and violence; yet is also a strong family-oriented neighborhood that prides itself on its history and sense of community. The combined elementary/middle school serves approximately 450 pre-kindergarten through grade 8 students. The project included 25 preservice teachers and 72 Sugar Hill students, and focused on using arts and literacy to depict beauty in the students and their community.

> "Motive, emotion, and identity are important aspects of our being in the world, and mediate what we know and how we know it."

The preservice teachers who participated in the Sugar Hill project began to transform initial negative assumptions about working in low-income, culturally diverse settings as they participated in the project. The arts created spaces for the Sugar Hill students to articulate their lived moments creatively and meaningfully (McDermott & Shelton, 2008). We learned that pre-service educators can engage in arts-infused activities as acts of critical pedagogy and bring children's voices and worlds to the foreground.

We offered a second redesigned project, entitled Safe Harbor Partners, at a shelter located less than one mile from the city line. Situated on a 44-acre campus, Safe Harbor expanded from its original function as an orphanage to include a diagnostic treatment center in addition to providing short- and long-term residential facilities for youth ages 8 to 21. Approximately 45 youth reside at Safe Harbor.

Safe Harbor Partners met weekly throughout the semester in the common building at the shelter. The first three weeks the preservice teachers studied course content materials, learned to write lesson plans, studied conflict resolution techniques, and designed a reading interviewing protocol to be used with their tutored residents. For the remainder of the semester (12 weeks), the first 60 minutes of class time continued the study of course content; preservice teachers tutored Safe Harbor residents for the remaining 90 minutes. The preservice teachers acted as tutors, and we refer to them as tutors throughout the chapter. Our tutor/resident partners migrated to self-selected areas on the grounds (cafeteria, computer room, lounge area, or outside on the picnic tables) to work.

Morna roamed from group to group offering support as needed while Nancy recorded field notes, took photographs, and minimally interacted with Safe Harbor residents and tutors. Because of legal aspects of guardianship, we did not have permission to use audio or video recording. The project culminated in a showcase where residents shared their work with the Safe Harbor community. The seven preservice teachers who registered for this special section of the course developed and taught lessons infused with literacy (reading, writing, speaking, and listening) and art (music, visual art, and dance) to either one or two Safe Harbor residents.

Questions Guiding the Research

Research questions for our study were the following:

- How do the arts combined with literacy engage students in critically and personally relevant learning?
- In what ways does using a nontraditional, off-campus, hands-on approach to learning about teaching arts and literacy generate meaningful experiences that offer insight on teacher/student interactions and the skills needed to be successful at teaching diverse students?

We define success by two guiding ideals.

1. Tutors would become aware of their own biases and perceptions in working with diverse populations and work toward self-reflection for change.
2. Tutors would develop an understanding of how to teach and how students learn in literacy-rich contexts.

We met these objectives through setting up the following structural guidelines. First, we created a hands-on, arts-infused (Mello, 2004) literacy learning experience that encourages K–12 participants to create arts- and language-infused products for personal meaning. Although arts-infused learning is not inherently a form of critical pedagogy, it provides an exemplary means for integrating social justice issues and teaching (Mello, 2004). In this instance, participating students rendered comprehension and personal meaning of texts through artistic applications (e.g., poetry, drama, painting).

Our goal was also to provide an experience with literacy learning that goes beyond scripted instruction. Maryland's education policy endorses scripted, phonics-based reading programs devoid of teacher input. Pressure to purchase identified core programs has resulted in the spread of these programs to schools across Maryland, even those not funded by Maryland Reading First (Grasmick, 2006).

Theoretical Background and Perspectives

The passage of No Child Left Behind (NCLB) legislation triggered an emphasis on standardized test achievement in the United States. Struggling students served in schools funded by Reading First receive a steady diet of phonics and reading rate and accuracy instruction that often ignores the roles communication and critical thinking play in language learning. Scripted, skills-based reading programs narrow the reading curriculum (Allington, 2002; Garan, 2002; Shannon, 1990; Shelton, 2005), reduce interactions between teachers and students to simple question/answer formats, and strip students of identity, voice, and motivation. Yet, "motive, emotion, and identity are important aspects of our being in the world, and mediate what we know and how we know it" (Roth, 2007, p. 40). Students, like all of us, are identified by the activities in which they participate, which is what drives motivation. In school environments where student activity is predetermined by strict reading programs, students' motivation is driven by the program. Repetitive programmatic instruction disconnected from students' lives fails to motivate students. This is actualized in our city's 25% graduation rates for black males (Foxworth, 2006), high teen pregnancy rates, and rising school violence.

On the other hand, Stevenson and Deasy (2005) found "the arts put students in active and meaningful roles in their classrooms and connected schools to students' lives and cultures"

(p. 17). Economically disadvantaged students play active roles as meaning makers when educated in schools with outstanding art programs. The complexity of the intellectual work in art-infused education contributes to "a desire to understand, master deeply, and use multiple forms of human communication to grasp matters deeply and to express personal meanings" (p. 63), in turn advancing literacy performance.

Carey (1998) suggested that "to understand art better, we should broaden our focus beyond aesthetic quality and aesthetic experience to include the complex spheres of social, political, and cultural functions art carries out in the human experience" (p. 53). School curricula must offer an entry point for students who personally experience violence, poverty, racism, drug and alcohol abuse, parental imprisonment or death, and homelessness. The arts can encourage students to speak out about experiences that would otherwise remain hidden, especially students who struggle with traditional forms of literacy as a means of personal expression.

Methodology

Participants

The lessons learned in the first semester of this effort conducted at Sugar Hill Elementary/Middle School led us to intentionally keep the Safe Harbor Partners project small. Unlike the previous semester when Morna advertised for and recruited students to participate in the project at Sugar Hill, the seven students enrolled in Safe Harbor sought the off-campus option on their own through the online course catalog.

Morna and Nancy proposed the after-school tutoring plan to the administrators of Safe Harbor who welcomed the opportunity for their residents. We organized a meeting to explain the program to the 45 residents of Safe Harbor, answer questions they might have, and invite them to participate. The assistant director acted as the liaison for the program, accepted requests from the residents, and conferred with Morna and Nancy to match potential Safe Harbor residents with tutors. The program began with 13 Safe Harbor residents, ranging in age from 8 to 18, who shared various books including fictional young adult (YA) novels and nonfiction books about musicians and professional athletes. Eleven students completed the program and created final projects.

Data Collection

We collected data throughout the planning period and implementation of the project. Our data included observation data, written reflections, interviews, questionnaires, and artifacts of the students' creative constructions. Table 9.1 summarizes how we collected this data.

Table 9.1 Participants' Roles in Data Collection

Data	Nancy	Morna	Tutors
Observations of teaching	Weekly field notes	Participant/observer: weekly reflective log	
Written reflections	Responded occasionally to posts	Responded to weekly posts	Posted weekly on electronic course site
Interviews		Tutors	Safe Harbor students
Questionnaires		Tutors	Safe Harbor students

Data Analysis

Spradley's (1980) thematic analysis guided our work. First, we independently identified patterns of interaction and instruction among the tutors and the K–12 students. We used students' and tutors' behaviors and language in the interactions as beginning codes. We compared major codes that emerged between the independent analyses we had conducted. Finally, we grouped the codes into themes that could be compared across tutors. Our findings blend the themes and our initial aims together like overlapping triangles. For example, arts-infused activities led to meaningful interactions where students and teachers got to know one another personally. The relationships that formed led to relevant literacy-rich learning experiences.

Limitations

Our study did have limitations. We had no concrete way to track the impact the program had on student residents' success. This limitation is directly related to another, which is the short time period of the project; the program participants met just once a week for a single semester. The difficulty collecting data about students and youth protected in a shelter home limits access to school files and personal records, which is compounded by the short time frame allowed in one semester.

Results and Discussion

We explain our findings as they relate to our overarching objectives and purposes. We share evidence from our data that does the following:

- Confirms the tutors' awareness of their own biases when working with diverse students

- Shows tutors made efforts to work toward self-reflection to change some of those biases
- Illustrates how the tutors developed an understanding of how to teach and how students learn in arts- and literacy-rich contexts

Becoming Aware of Biases and Preconceptions

The tutors explicitly stated that they expected Safe Harbor to be a difficult teaching environment. A number of reasons emerged for this expectation, including blaming K–12 students for their lack of motivation ("this is a problem with the student, not necessarily the system he is in"), blaming teachers for just giving up on difficult students, and blaming the community for not supporting schools.

At times, the tutors made biased statements out of frustration, when a lesson did not go well, or a student did not respond as expected. However, this was not always the case. First impressions shared before the tutors even met their students indicated two of the tutors equated being black with poor education:

> The biggest problems with the African American community are the high crime rate, the high poverty rate, and the low education rate. I don't doubt for a second that these three factors are linked.

> A lot of the problems that occur with the African American community are brought on by a low education rate.

Another preservice teacher, less willing to attach race to the low literacy rates of his students, blamed "urban cultures":

> I have heard throughout my life and throughout classes and news reports and such about the low level of literacy prevalent in urban cultures. When I found out that I would be working with urban kids on reading, I figured that the aforementioned problem is precisely what I would be working on.

Working Toward Self-Reflection for Change

Jason was the only preservice teacher who admittedly and openly lacked confidence in his teaching and said he didn't think he was reaching his student, Terrell. However, open-ended and unplanned dialogue between Jason and Terrell provoked a positive shift for the last three weeks of the program. Terrell was, once again, resisting Jason's requests to read or complete the planned lesson. In a moment of desperation, Jason took out his iPod and allowed Terrell to listen to music. They found a mutual interest in the music of blues musician Robert Johnson. Based on that, Jason began reading *Black Cat Bone* (Lewis, 2006), a picture book about Robert Johnson, with Terrell. They enjoyed reading the lyrics to music.

Terrell's interest in participating and Jason's confidence in teaching both began to increase:

> I definitely get the feeling that Terrell is more of a math and left-brained kind of person than he is an English kind of person. I wished I would have known this earlier in the program; perhaps I could have utilized it more to Terrell's advantage. I'm learning as well. We moved next to our song lyrics. We listened to a few Smokey Robinson songs and I asked Terrell to read the words aloud after each stanza.... his reading speed was even somewhat "conversational".... he complained a little about just wanting to listen to the songs and not read lyrics. I had to explain to him that the purpose I was there was so that he could improve his reading. I had hoped to work our way through two songs, and we did that a lot faster than I had anticipated.

Although evidence in the data indicates Jason and Terrell made progress, it was not enough for Jason. In his exit interview with Morna, Jason identified three important strategies he will use in future interactions with students. He stated he will do the following:

1. Use his "sheer passion" for music as strength to teach all content areas

2. Offer more choice in print materials and "try to read a different book" if his students are not responding and enjoying a text

3. Work on more ways to connect his students' interests with real-life experiences to build and retain information

Similarly, Ronnie's ability to connect with the younger generations' interests and her ability to view things through her students' eyes will help her "reach" her students. Ronnie had deeply personal connections with her students. When we paired students with teachers we only kept gender considerations in mind (girls with girls, boys with boys). Coincidentally, Ronnie had recently lost her mother to a terminal illness and her student, Nell, had also just lost her mother. This common experience enabled Ronnie to connect with Nell by sharing her personal grief. Their discussions led to a mutual desire to write poetry as a way to express their feelings.

Brian was one of the more aloof teachers in the group. He always seemed to remain distant from his students. But with two weeks left in the semester, he opened up, too:

> Damien was his usual self but, like I said, Avery was not; he was clamming up because of his suspension.... Then I said to Avery that I was suspended from school once when I was about his age. I think this was what cracked him. He then told me why he was suspended...and began to laugh and carry on with Damien and I even got him talking more about his interest, which is bugs! Sometimes I feel like my lessons are not as powerful when trying to reach out to these kids as me just being me and talking with them.

Megan found her strengths as a teacher in her ease in talking to and confronting her students. One of her students told her "she feels like she can talk to or ask Megan questions," which pleased Megan because she didn't "want to be seen as just their teacher, but also as a person to confide in or mentor." Each of the tutors developed a foundation to build on that will give them confidence to develop more strategies to provide meaningful instruction for all students.

Regardless of the reasons the tutors gave for their theories of why the Safe Harbor residents struggled, each resident made shifts in his or her perceptions. The tutors realized that appropriate, well-planned, yet flexible teaching could meet the needs of students entangled in difficult life situations.

Recognizing Positive Aspects of Diverse Cultures

Our findings indicate that the tutors also started to understand students from diverse cultures. Victor, for example, who had little previous experience working with youth from backgrounds different from his own, said,

> [I was] surprised to see how well the students responded to my lessons and it gave me confidence to be able to do it again on a larger level. This experience has shaped my outlook of working with diverse learners by allowing me to create lessons that are interesting to students of a different culture.

Myles worked to untangle the mystery hidden in his student, Kevin, including his interactions with other residents:

> I would sit and watch how these students interacted with one another and it is amazing the rules and laws that govern them within their society as students...they have a sense of rank and hierarchy. All of the students tend to respond to particular adults with the utmost respect and loyalty. These students also always look out for the younger kids in terms of not taking advantage of them, caring for them in words and action, and not being as rough as they would with the students their age or older.

Kevin was the youngest student in the project, and the student with the least ability to communicate. This did not discourage Myles's efforts. Each week Myles arrived with a new and exciting picture book for Kevin, and each week Kevin and Myles made progress.

Overall, we found strong evidence that involvement in the project increased the tutors' desire to work with special needs populations, as Derek explained:

> This experience reinforced my passion of wanting to work with disadvantaged students. I was very impressed with Wendel and Simone. I found that they both are very intelligent people but they have fallen through the cracks and haven't been dealt the greatest hand.

Developing an Understanding of Teaching and Learning in Literacy-Rich Contexts

The tutors intentionally planned opportunities for their students to express themselves and to make personal connections to their texts by providing choice and using the arts as the medium of expression. Some students indicated a passion for poetry while others enjoyed music or painting. The weekly lessons were developed out of the individual artistic interests of the resident students. The tutors crafted literacy activities that interwove the artistic forms of expressions with the selected readings or books.

> Overall, we found strong evidence that involvement in the project increased the tutors' desire to work with special needs populations.

These efforts lead naturally to increased literacy performance. For example, Victor wrote,

> In the book, the author explains that when the tapes were proven to be unaltered, R. Kelly tried to say it was his brother in the tapes instead of him. This led to a good conversation between us

about Umit's brothers and how their relationships were…. I asked if he'd ever try and blame one of his brothers for something he had done to get out of trouble and his reply was "Never."

This process is also illustrated well in Derek's interaction with his two students, Wendel and Simone. Derek used art to connect the book *Monster* (Meyers, 2001) to what was going on in Wendel and Simone's lives. In one of the lessons, Wendel replaced his inappropriate behavior with artistic expression. Derek described the lesson in his weekly reflection:

> "Aesthetic knowledge is dangerous knowledge" in that it "opens the knowledge process to the subjective qualities of lived experiences."

I asked Wendel if he had completed the picture of the "My Jail" activity that we worked on last week. He pulled out some color pencils and began drawing a picture of Safe Harbor. He even drew bars around the window of his room. He then drew hills to the side of Safe Harbor. I asked him what those hills represented and he said "They represent how far away I am from home." He also drew pictures of people around Safe Harbor dropping trash on the ground. He said this represents the disrespect and ignorance in his life….

In his final interview with Morna, Derek recognized the role art played in his students' comprehension of the text, in expressing events and difficulties in their lives, and in his own development as a teacher:

I found that students are able to learn literacy through art. Through art activities I was able to reinforce the ideas, themes, and concepts addressed in the book we were reading.

In addition to learning how to provide an environment for art-infused literacy learning to take place, the tutors learned a great deal about teaching literacy. Discovering Kevin could be such an energetic, intelligent student and yet still read so far below grade level shocked Myles, who had no prior experience tutoring. Myles developed an appreciation for the struggle teachers have when they are "faced with the obstacles around attention span and retention, while still working to build a relationship with a student." The tutors learned that patience, persistence, and planning engaging activities are paramount in teaching reading. They struggled with issues of dialect, selection of appropriate reading materials, and students who lack motivation. And they discovered how frequently and creatively students find ways to hide their failures.

Because the tutors shared books with their students, and because the culminating activity was a showcase performance, the tutors created multiple opportunities for their students to engage in meaningful oral readings. From this, they learned that readers have individual preferences and styles of reading. This led to increased understandings of teaching reading. As Victor explained, "I learned that different students have different behaviors when they read. For example, Umit preferred to read out loud, it seemed to help keep him reading at a fast pace." On the other hand, Terrell refused to read aloud and Jason had to develop silent reading lessons.

Implications

For our Safe Harbor Partners, arts and literacy became experiences with critical aesthetics, in which "aesthetic knowledge is dangerous knowledge" in that it "opens the knowledge process to the subjective qualities of lived experiences" (Carey, 1998, p. 303). We encouraged the tutors to continually ask themselves if their students could personally relate to the tasks they were being asked to perform (Sumara & Davis, 1998), and they responded.

The most significant learning for the tutors resulted from listening to their students, getting to know them, and beginning to transform their own ideas about self, teaching, and learning. In an effort to add meaning to the act of reading and writing, lessons required creative expression on the part of the Safe Harbor participants. Yet each lesson contained elements of choice for the tutors and their students. Together they determined the forms of artistic expression they liked best. Art media changed from week to week in response to the students' needs and interests. These elements of choice are vital components of successful classrooms.

Working with students in a one-on-one or small-group setting provided the tutors with the opportunity to develop strategies to use while working with larger groups of students. It allowed them time to learn about themselves as teachers. They learned how to see all students as individuals and approach their own pedagogy from a more personal foundation, one which does not follow a script or prejudge students but works to understand individuals and make personal connection within a group setting.

Arts-infused instruction can lead to transformative pedagogy, but it doesn't always. Much depends on the relationships between students and teachers as well as the teachers' own versatility in working with various art media and their personal level of risk taking. Findings suggest that a focus on students' identities and understanding students' lives can lead to effective teaching and learning. The tutors at Safe Harbor had challenging experiences, yet they related to and taught their students well.

We want to leave our readers with Jason's words. Jason started the program with few resources from which to draw when teaching students unlike himself, a strong predisposition that black families are overwhelmingly under-educated, and a belief that students should be self-motivated to learn. In his final interview, Jason stated,

> It surprised me that this group of African American students was so similar to my group of friends growing up. I've learned the race of the child does not alter the way they learn. We are all just people; I think any white kid could have had the same literacy problems as Terrell. Somewhere along the line that path has divided. Something happens to the student to create the negative low education image that so many blacks are imprisoned in. I want to know where this happens.

Words of Advice

Drawing directly from our experiences, we have three important recommendations:

- The tutors needed more time and opportunity for personal knowledge of the Safe Harbor students when setting up the program. This is true in all teaching environments—teachers must get to know their students. Before the tutor/student relationships are set, educators would benefit from an opportunity to work with smaller groups of students so that personal relationships can be formed.

- The tutors needed more instruction and support to learn how to capitalize on "teachable moments." We recommend explicitly teaching tutors how to develop reflective teaching skills. We required the tutors to engage in a reflective process but were not explicit enough for the tutors to respond to their students "in the moment" of teaching. These teachable moments need to be honored and protected in our classrooms; educators and policymakers need to recognize their prominent role in successful learning experiences for diverse students.

- We also needed to provide more instruction on authentic reading materials (children's and young adult literature) as well as arts-infused instructional approaches. Our initial interactions with the tutors before they were matched with Safe Harbor students included reviews of literature, but a more solid understanding of high-quality, contemporary texts is needed. In addition, the tutors need explicit instruction on how to allow instruction to be co-directed by the K–12 students involved.

REFERENCES

Allington, R.L. (2002). *Big brother and the national reading curriculum: How ideology trumped evidence*. Portsmouth, NH: Heinemann.

Carey, R. (1998). *Critical art pedagogy: Foundations for a postmodern art education*. New York: Garland.

Foxworth, R.D. (2006, November). Alone at the table: Growing up smart, ambitious, and black in Baltimore. *Urbanite Magazine*, (29). Retrieved December 23, 2008, from www.urbanitebaltimore.com/sub.cfm?ArticleID=543&IssueID=42&SectionID=4

Garan, E.M. (2002). *Resisting reading mandates: How to triumph with the truth*. Portsmouth, NH: Heinemann.

Grasmick, N.S. (2006, November 15). *Opening remarks*. Maryland Reading First Fall Leadership Conference, Cambridge, Maryland.

McDermott, M., & Shelton, N. (2008). A thing of beauty? Preservice teachers' experiences with cultural difference, literacy, and the arts. *The Arts and Learning Research Journal*, 24(1), 89–114.

Mello, R. (2004). When pedagogy meets practice: Combining arts integration and teacher education in the college classroom. *Arts and Learning Research Journal*, 20(1), 135–163.

Roth, W.M. (2007). Emotion at work: A contribution to third-generation cultural-historical activity theory. *Mind, Culture, and Activity*, 14(1 & 2), 40–63. doi:10.1080/10749030701307705

Shannon, P. (1990). *The struggle to continue: Progressive reading instruction in the United States*. Portsmouth, NH: Heinemann.

Shelton, N.R. (2005). First do no harm: Teachers' reactions to mandating Reading Mastery. In B. Altwerger (Ed.), *Reading for profit: How the bottom line leaves kids behind* (pp. 184–198). Portsmouth, NH: Heinemann.

Spradley, J.P. (1980). *Participant observation*. New York: Harcourt.

Stevenson, L.M., & Deasy, R.J. (2005). *Third space: When learning matters*. Washington, DC: Arts Education Partnership.

Sumara, L., & Davis, B. (1998). Underpainting. *Journal of Curriculum Theorizing*, 14(4), 1–5.

LITERATURE CITED

Lewis, J.P. (2006). *Black cat bone: The life of blues legend Robert Johnson*. Ill. by Gary Kelley. North Mankato, MN: Creative Editions.

Meyers, W.D. (2001). *Monster*. Ill. by Christopher Meyers. New York: Amistad.

Nelson, M. (2005). *A wreath for Emmett Till*. New York: Houghton Mifflin.

ABOUT THE CONTRIBUTORS

Nancy Rankie Shelton *is an assistant professor of literacy education at the University of Maryland, Baltimore County, Baltimore, Maryland, USA. She was a classroom teacher in Florida for 10 years. Her research focuses on writing in elementary classrooms, the effects of mandated reform on literacy education, and critical literacy. She is an active member of NCTE, NRC, and IRA, and is the current president of the Alliance of Maryland College Professors of Reading. Her son Conrad's experiences as a student whose voice was more often silenced than heard inspired her to become an educator. E-mail: nshelton@umbc.edu*

Morna McDermott *is an associate professor at Towson University, Towson, Maryland, USA, where she teaches various theory and methods courses in the College of Education. Her scholarship and research interests focus on democracy, social justice, and arts-informed inquiry in K–postsecondary educational settings and working with beginning and experienced educators. She explores how the arts serve as a form of literacy that challenges traditional classroom learning and dominant narratives. E-mail: mmcdermott@towson.edu*

CHAPTER 10

Endless Possibilities for Learning and Reflection: Lessons From Two After-School Urban Literacy Clinics

Sharon M. Peck

The buses are lined up outside of Wright City Middle School. In the library, 13 teachers eagerly await the afternoon announcements and dismissal. When the bell rings, chaos ensues in the hallway as middle school children slowly file into the library, sign in, and sit down with a snack. A boy in the hallway exclaims, "Oh, yeah. Today is Wednesday! Oh, we are reading today? Oh, boy!"

To begin the tutoring session, a graduate student welcomes children and shares a read-aloud. The room is filled with calm yet eager anticipation as adolescents enthusiastically wait for instructions and graduate students visit with the children they will tutor.

In another site, in the heart of the downtown area in a large northeastern city, graduate students wind their way upstairs in an old church remodeled into a community center. As they walk toward a makeshift classroom, young children pass them in the hallway and say, "Hey! Are we going to read today? Can I read to you? Is today our day?"

These two scenes illustrate the motivation of children and graduate student tutors who participate in two urban literacy clinics offered by our rural liberal arts college. Our Literacy master's degree program requires graduate students to engage in 50 hours of clinical tutoring. The college is located in a rural area, but it is within 30 minutes of a large city in the northeastern United States. However, most of our master's degree graduate students have little experience working with urban students. The majority of our students begin their master's course work immediately after completing their undergraduate studies, and few have taught in urban areas. The goal of our program is to prepare teachers to be effective literacy teachers of all students. To that end, we hold our literacy clinics away from the college campus at two different sites: an adolescent reading clinic at an urban middle school and a childhood reading clinic at an urban community center after-school program. Offering our reading clinics in authentic settings provides powerful experiences for our graduate students to become acquainted

Literacy Tutoring That Works: A Look at Successful In-School, After-School, and Summer Programs, edited by Janet C. Richards and Cynthia A. Lassonde. © 2009 International Reading Association.

with urban communities and encourages them to reflect not only upon the intricacies of literacy tutoring but also upon the added complexities of designing and carrying out instruction targeted for urban youth.

In addition, our graduate students can collaborate with reading professionals at the site, incorporate culturally relevant texts as well as books and materials available at the site, develop empathy for the learning context of urban students, and interact with families.

In my classes, graduate students employ Running Records (Johnston, 2000), Words Their Way assessments and instruction (Bear, Invernizzi, Templeton, & Johnston, 2007), and the 6+1 Traits of Writing (Culham, 2003) to develop assessment-based literacy instruction targeted to the individual needs of each child. They engage in detailed record keeping to support their assessment conclusions and lesson planning. Moreover, before and after tutoring sessions, graduate students engage in reflection and coaching to push one another's thinking about literacy learning and instruction. They also read and consider best practices for literacy instruction and model and evaluate instructional strategies in writing, fluency, comprehension, word work, and vocabulary development.

Throughout the projects, I nurture graduate students' reflections through daily observations in which I provide written feedback immediately following the tutoring session, written e-mail interactions, in-class coaching, and written response to assignments. Graduate students reflect weekly through an e-mail memo to me, as well as by completing two videotaped reflections on their tutoring, providing a videotaped presentation of their tutoring to receive coaching from their peers, and completing a written reflection on teachers' beliefs on literate development and instruction. At the beginning and end of each semester, graduate students write about their own beliefs and understandings about reading and writing development. They use this opportunity to recognize their growth as literacy professionals.

Questions Guiding the Research

The following questions guided my research:

- What aspects of literacy clinics support graduate students' understandings of literacy learning with youth from diverse backgrounds?

- What instructional methods affect the development of graduate students through the clinical tutoring experience?

- How does the experience of tutoring diverse youth in urban settings affect graduate students' perceptions of literate learning?

Theoretical Background and Perspectives

The clinical tutoring projects are grounded in research on literacy teacher preparation, reflective practice, and urban needs. Quick-fix and one-size-fits-all models of reading intervention for struggling readers fail to realize the multiple needs and strengths of individual learners and have not proven successful (Allington & Walmsley, 1995). Rather, clinical instruction focuses on using assessments to guide instructional planning to meet the individual needs of learners. This shift in thinking, from teaching skills to teaching children, provides a learning context for teachers to explore the effects of assessment-based instruction. The one-on-one setting is ideal for teachers to explore key aspects of literacy teaching, including engagement.

Cambourne (1995) suggests that certain conditions need to be in place in order for children to learn. One crucial component in changing reading outcomes includes scaffolding instruction so the responsibility for strategy application is gradually released to the learner. Ruddell (2004) suggests that

> increasing teaching competency is found in three areas: (1) our understanding of the nature of high-quality teaching—and influential teacher research sheds light in this area; (2) increasing the effectiveness of our preservice teacher preparation and inservice graduate programs through partnerships between universities and schools; and (3) implementing carefully planned ongoing inservice teacher education programs in our schools that utilize the latest knowledge on literacy development and effective teaching. (p. 980)

Reading clinic internships often provide the context to study and understand how to develop reading teachers with the instructional understandings that this type of teaching requires.

One way that graduates make sense of clinical experiences is through reflective practice. Schön's (1987) work provides a model of how reflective teachers think and some goals for teacher educators, but it may not provide enough support for the reflection of graduate students who are learning to be literacy tutors. Without a concrete teaching experience upon which to reflect, prospective educators may not be able to engage in the critical pedagogy-informing-pedagogy approach discussed by Schön. Literature suggests that teachers engage in predominantly low-level, factual reflections (Risko, Roskos, & Vukelich, 1999; Zeichner & Liston, 1996) as opposed to critical reflection.

This critical reflection is particularly important to support graduates in dealing with the complexities of urban teaching, including issues of race, class, language, and culture.

Bartoli (2001) asserts, "Cultural assumptions about low-income urban communities, as well as racial and ethnic stereotypes, fuel the negative generalizations about city schools, teachers, families and communities. And, political, social, historic, economic, and corporate practices maintain them" (p. 8). Holding literacy clinics in urban communities can help teacher graduates to counter negative stereotypes and assumptions.

Research on urban literacy instruction suggests inclusion of key instructional strategies including structure, repetition, engagement, and relevance. Further, literature points out that like it or not, we all hold biases. To best teach urban children and those at risk, teachers must recognize the biases they hold and work to challenge them (Perkins, 2004). Compton-Lilly (2004) asks teachers to address and challenge assumptions they hold about urban children and literacy instruction. My focus brings together perspectives on clinical instruction, reflective practice, and urban literacy instruction and seeks to explore the interplay of factors on the experience of graduate students in offsite literacy clinics.

> Literature suggests that teachers engage in predominantly low-level, factual reflections as opposed to critical reflection.

Methodology

Participants

Participants were 13 graduate students seeking professional certification in literacy who tutored middle school children in an urban area and 7 graduate students seeking professional certification who tutored elementary children in an after-school community program, City Center for Community. All names and locations are pseudonyms to protect the identities of participants.

WRIGHT CITY MIDDLE SCHOOL. Wright City Middle School is a large semi-urban school in a district adjacent to a larger urban district. Participants included 13 sixth-, seventh-, and eighth-grade struggling readers who scored in the lowest two levels on the state English Language Arts assessment, including six African Americans, two Hispanic students, one Middle Eastern student, and four Caucasian students.

We began running our tutoring program off campus when a graduate of our literacy master's program invited our college to hold the literacy clinic at her school. As a component of her course work for administrative certification, we designed the program, titling the clinic Endless Possibilities in Literacy. Middle school students met in the library after school each Wednesday. They first enjoyed a read-aloud and a snack, which provided sufficient time for graduate students to travel to the site from their teaching locations. Tutoring took place in the library and in various classrooms from 4 to 5 P.M. At 5:05 children and graduate students gathered to walk students to three district-provided buses to travel home. Following tutoring, graduate students met with me for an hour of class instruction and debriefing.

CITY CENTER FOR COMMUNITY. The City Center is a community resource program supported by the city school district and the United Way. Students take the school bus there after school and engage in academic and extracurricular activities until 6:15 P.M. each day. The program supports children in kindergarten through grade 12 and our literacy clinic focused on students in grades 2 through 5. Students are selected based on their academic need and their regular attendance at the City Center. Students in the study reported in this chapter included five African American and one Hispanic student.

During the study, children arrived at the community center after school and enjoyed some snacks before meeting with their graduate student tutors from 4:30 to 5:30 P.M. Following tutoring, children returned to center programs and families usually arrived to pick them up between 6 and 6:30 P.M. The graduate students arrived at the center at 3:45 allowing for 45 minutes of class time for an assessment discussion prior to tutoring and a 45-minute class session following tutoring.

Data Sources

Data sources in my study included course syllabi, class readings, graduate students' written reflections, my reflective memos and field notes, graduate students' lesson plans and clinical case studies, as well as audio and videotapes of participating graduates as they taught and led coaching sessions. I also drew upon my experiences as the professor directing the clinics in both settings.

Data Analysis

I was guided in my data analysis by grounded theory (Strauss & Corbin, 1990) and narrative ontology (Polkinghorne, 1988). I compared reflective data from graduate students at both sites with my field notes and course reflections. In particular, I looked at areas of congruence and dissonance. Content analysis (Krippendorff, 2004) supported identification of instances of instruction and reflection upon instruction noted by graduate students and by me. Coding and a close review of course documents, student reflections, my responses to reflections, and video and audio excerpts of instruction led to themes that affected the urban tutoring experience. This lens led me to identify three key aspects of the literacy clinic that support graduate students' understandings of literacy learning with diverse children: literature as catalyst, rapport, and coaching from peers.

Limitations

Although this chapter explores the possibilities that holding graduate literacy clinics in urban settings offers, there are limitations. First, although the graduate students never missed a tutoring session, at times urban youth were absent repeatedly. In addition, although I did observe a segment of each of the tutoring sessions, I was not able to view each entire tutoring session. However, through the use of the videotape assignment, I was able to view two complete sessions for each graduate student, which represented growth over time. Finally, due to the nature of my own role in the study, I strove to keep field notes after each class session and to build in many opportunities for written and spoken reflections of graduate students to ensure an equal representation in the data.

Results and Discussion

I identified three issues central to the support graduate students felt they needed in order to work with urban children. First, critical literature served as an effective catalyst for discussion of topics that are difficult or challenging to graduate students. Second, such literature illuminated the importance of building rapport between graduate student tutors and children. Third, analysis led me to consider the ways in which dialogue and peer coaching affected the experience of the tutors.

Of course, holding a literacy clinic off site does not alleviate the common disruptions associated with literacy clinics. Graduate students were reluctant to believe that tutoring for an hour once a week for 14 weeks might lead to significant gains in reading ability. Graduate students still grappled with assessment-based instruction that differs greatly from the scripted activities they often must use as teachers. Graduate students continued to explore the balance of power as they came to assert their voices as teachers while working to support their students to become independent readers. They were challenged to employ wait time, to offer prompts not answers, and to focus on building meaning at all times.

> Analysis revealed that using critical literature for graduate students to read and respond to provided a catalyst for thinking and learning.

Literature as Catalyst

Analysis revealed that using critical literature for graduate students to read and respond to provided a catalyst for thinking and learning. Drawing on initial data noting graduate students' lack of preparation for working with urban youth, critical readings were added. The success of initial readings led me to use this model to support exploration of both urban youth and aspects of literacy, including comprehension, word work, fluency, and writing.

Graduate students' responses to questionnaires at the onset of the clinic and their initial reflections revealed that they did not feel prepared to teach urban children. This lack of preparation was evident in their views on literacy instruction, and their repeated statements conveying their discomfort, fear, and nervousness in working with an urban population. During intake surveys and initial classes graduate students admitted they were often nervous about working with a student one on one, and their discomfort in working with adolescents and children of different cultures detracted at times from their ability to build on their knowledge of literacy development and learning.

This led me to explore with graduate students the ways in which they were prepared to work in urban settings and with middle school children. They openly discussed their worries, sharing that they didn't know if they could relate to children from backgrounds so different from their own. Graduate students grappled with learning how to engage older children who had a history of low literacy achievement, and then explored how race and ethnicity played into literacy instruction for those learners.

To respond to the discomfort of my graduate students, I chose to use literature as a catalyst for learning and discussion. Analysis of class discussions and graduate student reflections suggested that critical exploration of literature provided a space for graduate students to learn new practices, critique accepted practices, and simply respond to and discuss ideas that were difficult and uncomfortable to explore. One graduate student was shocked when she saw the number of books on the syllabus, but admitted at the culmination of the class that she was even more surprised by how much she learned. This particular student was eager to apply her new knowledge in her own classroom. Another graduate student shared that she learned the most from talking things out. She really appreciated having time and space to argue about the course texts. She went on to admit that she didn't realize that her classmates held such different perspectives.

Drawing on work focused on urban literacy development and identity, graduate students read, reflected on, and discussed two key texts, Compton-Lilly's (2004) *Confronting Racism, Poverty, and Power: Classroom Strategies to Change the World* and Johnston's (2004) *Choice Words: How Our Language Affects Children's Learning.*

Compton-Lilly's (2004) work provides an opportunity to explore the complexities of urban literacy contexts. Based on her study of the literate lives of the families of her urban students, Compton-Lilly debunks myths and assumptions that some teachers hold about urban children. She then shares critical literacy projects to support teachers in drawing on students' cultural knowledge and experiences to make meaningful connections between in-school and out-of-school learning.

This critical text was not always well received by graduate students, who continually questioned the relevance to their setting. Our literacy clinics, though, were held in an urban environment not at all different from the location of Compton-Lilly's (2004) studies. Although teachers found it difficult to reconcile their beliefs with Compton-Lilly's provocative arguments, they felt comfortable challenging her book and one another. This discussion was rich and led to powerful realizations about assumptions they held about urban children. In particular, graduate students shared their frustrations with the lack of response and participation of urban parents. Compton-Lilly's narratives did not fully convince them to reconsider their views of urban parents, but the narratives did challenge them to closely explore their own assumptions.

Johnston's (2004) seminal text addresses the specific language used by effective teachers and how aspects of language position children and teachers. Johnston uses discourse analysis to explore the ways in which teachers' words position student learning and identity. In particular he examines teacher talk which focuses on, among other things, identity, agency, transfer, and support for learning. This language ultimately affects graduate students' notions of identity, reading, and their roles in their own learning. Graduate students studied *Choice Words* (Johnston, 2004) and endeavored to employ specific language for their clinical instruction. They focused on promoting identity and independence as they struggled to be cognizant of the impact that their language has on student learning. This text challenged conceptions of their roles as teachers and further reinforced the importance of questioning rather than telling.

These texts provided additional voices, real classroom and community experiences to which teachers could relate. Graduate students shared their honest reactions, which were both positive and negative. For instance, in responding to the language phrases presented in *Choice Words* (Johnston, 2004), they shared their dissention and disbelief that language could really make such a difference. One graduate student reflected that the ideas presented in Johnston's book were great ideas, but she just couldn't see it working in her classroom. Many graduate students echoed the notion that so-called "choice words" aren't realistic with urban children.

The ability to share their dissention significantly added to their experiences over the course of the literacy clinic. As they shared, the class listened to others' viewpoints and added their own. Later, as the clinic progressed, graduate students reflected and noted ways in which using choice words was helpful to their tutoring of urban children. One graduate student reflected that when her student, Jamila, was having an off day, she refocused her to the text by commenting on how she was thinking like a writer, and her attitude completely changed.

With such valuable responses to the two key texts, I continued this method of using the authority of outside authors to explore other key aspects of literacy instruction. To ensure that graduate students were well prepared for supporting all aspects of literacy development, we read and discussed texts focused on word work, fluency, comprehension, and writing.

To support word development we read and discussed Cunningham's *Phonics They Use* (2000). This text provided meaningful models for incorporating word work into the tutoring cycle. Graduate students are required to use a word wall in their instruction, and many struggled with this best practice. Using word walls represented another shift in thinking as graduate students explored the value of repeated readings of words and the use of visual prompts. Many struggled to apply Cunningham's notion of transfer words; others believed visual reminders were not effective for children.

> One shortcoming in our program is that our graduate students need additional understandings of how to teach and assess writing.

Graduate students also explored *Words Their Way* (Bear, Invernizzi, Templeton, & Johnston, 2007). They used spelling assessments to guide word work instruction, and many experimented with *Words Their Way* instructional strategies. To support reading comprehension, graduate students in the adolescent literacy clinic read *Strategies That Work* (Harvey & Goudvis, 2007), and in the childhood clinic we read *The Super Six Comprehension Strategies* (Oczkus, 2004). Graduate students chose relevant strategies to explore within their tutoring. This review of strategies, along with their critique, provided a means for graduate students to reconsider the challenges of supporting children to make meaning from texts.

One shortcoming in our program is that our graduate students need additional understandings of how to teach and assess writing. To this end I have worked to ensure that graduate students incorporate writing instruction within their tutoring sessions. Guided by *6+1 Traits of Writing* (Culham, 2003), graduate students explored notions of ideas, organization, voice, word choice, sentence fluency, presentation, and conventions. This shift—focusing on the craft of writing separately from the mechanics of language—led graduate students to view children's writing in a different light. For many it changed their conception of what writing is and how it connects with reading development. This focus on writing was particularly helpful as the majority of the urban children were below grade level in writing, even those who were on grade level for oral reading. Most children also struggled with spelling, so exploring the connection between spelling and writing was helpful, too. For instance, one third grader limited her writing to the words she could spell. She would think aloud to plan her writing. As she began writing a word that she could not spell, she orally listed synonyms until she came to a word that she could spell.

> Focusing on the craft of writing separately from the mechanics of language…led graduate students to view children's writing in a different light.

The final text discussed was *Good-Bye Round Robin: 25 Effective Oral Reading Strategies* (Opitz & Rasinski, 1998). This text on fluency development challenged graduate student views on oral reading. They appreciated learning other effective strategies beyond the very popular Readers Theatre, and many came to value the notion of avoiding "cold readings" that do not support readers' success in oral reading performance.

Graduate students embraced the texts. Reflections showed that we all believed our goals were met: I was happy they were critically reviewing relevant pedagogy and literacy theory, and they were happy to have ready teaching ideas and strategies to explore with their students. I also wanted to ensure the wide scope of literacy components was addressed. Our graduate program is strong, but faces issues that include a lack of literacy electives and an ever-changing faculty. I wanted to ensure that our graduates were prepared to support all aspects of student literacy development. Reading and discussing the texts strengthened all of our understandings and challenged our convictions.

Even more helpful was modeling. Graduate students chose strategies to model with the graduate class and strategies to engage in with their students. This active pedagogy led graduate students to reconsider the applicability of literacy strategies for their own students. Graduate students frequently admitted in their reflections that when they first read about strategies they didn't see the value of using them within instruction. After trying out strategies with their students, however, they came to a deeper understanding of the relevance of strategies for supporting literacy development. Using key texts provided a means for graduate students to grapple with key issues surrounding urban children and literacy development. I believe that it was more effective for graduate students to argue with the author as they came to understand the strategies than for me to present each strategy in succession. The ability to reject the ideas initially allowed graduate students to take ownership of their own growing understandings of literacy development.

Rapport

A close analysis of graduate students' instruction and reflections revealed that rapport played a critical role in the tutoring process. Literature on urban learners highlights the importance of developing rapport between teachers and children. Graduate students experienced different levels of success in developing sincere connections with their students. Additionally, I learned that taking time to build community within the class supported learning, and in particular, supported graduate students as they took on the role of literacy coaches. For graduate students to stay focused on assessment-based literacy instruction within this off-campus setting, the need for building rapport between classmates and with me was as important as developing rapport between tutor and student.

The graduate students who were able to connect with the students and who were not overwhelmed by cultural differences were able to grapple sincerely with key issues of literacy instruction. Establishing rapport allowed graduate students to identify specific needs and to motivate children to take responsibility for their learning. Conversely, graduate students who did not achieve rapport with their students spent more time questioning the effectiveness of their instruction and the behavior of the child rather than designing assessment-based literacy instruction.

Analysis of the data also suggests that rapport among graduate students is integral to the tutoring experience. Providing a safe space for graduate students to explore their relationships with the children was important, especially as they endeavored to develop dynamic working relationships with the children. For instance, one graduate student continually sought input from the class as she worked to connect with a particularly shy seventh-grade African American girl. Maya was a very quiet child who was timid and limited her interactions with adults. She had attended several different schools and had an unstable home life. Her tutor, Ashley, found it difficult to not take Maya's shyness personally. Ashley suggested several times that it was her whiteness that kept Maya from interacting with her, and her reflections focused more on their strained rapport than on assessment-based in-

struction. With the support of her peers, Ashley was able to develop a working rapport with Maya by the end of the clinical semester.

Graduate students used many strategies to develop rapport with the children. In particular, they focused instruction on children's interests. For instance, one child wanted to be a fashion designer. Therefore, she and her tutor engaged in reading clothing patterns, studying fashion trends, and developing vocabularies of words pertinent to fashion design. Other graduate students increased student choices, and used games, interactive writing, and technology to build rapport and motivation.

Building rapport with the children's families was not as successful. Graduate students endeavored to communicate with parents and families. They developed engaging home literacy activities for children to share with family members. They interviewed parents and met with parents on the final day of the clinic session. However, many graduate students were not successful in establishing weekly communications with families and were continually frustrated when children did not bring home literacy activities back to the clinic. This served to reinforce graduate students' views of families, rather than broaden them.

A final area of rapport affecting the experience is my interaction with graduate students. I worked to build open lines of communication and engaged in regular dialogue through one-on-one, whole class, and e-mail modes. During each tutoring session I observed and recorded on an assessment memo what I noticed, what I wondered about, and something of which the tutor should be proud. This immediate feedback was helpful to graduate students, and it provided a means for me to acknowledge and challenge them. Often I simply recorded the language used and asked what they noticed about it. Graduate students completed written reflections daily and sent reflective memos to me by e-mail every other week. All of these connections helped to strengthen our rapport.

At times I felt challenged in finding sincere and constructive ways to provide necessary feedback. In particular, close analysis of my field notes following each session led me to see the many ways in which I grappled with offering feedback. During class discussions, I learned to withhold my views until after all class members had shared their own thoughts. I learned to respond with questions such as, "Have you thought about…?" or "Can you tell me more about what you are thinking?" rather than with answers. I also learned that offering too many suggestions was overwhelming, and that a few powerful questions or directions to explore are more effective than providing many suggestions. This led me to value coaching and assessment discussions as learning tools.

Coaching From Peers

Analysis of the tutoring artifacts revealed coaching from peers was critical to the graduates' learning both in terms of diversity awareness and literacy learning. As graduate students grappled with how to really base instruction on the literacy assessments—a formidable challenge—they led whole-group discussions with their peers. Although this discussion seemed limited, the structures of What do you notice? What do you wonder about? and What could the tutor think about? provided language for graduate students to share their views. Graduate students prepared copies of a running record or other assessment data. They described the assessment and then asked for notices and wonders. This discussion was helpful to the graduate students and revealed their levels of thinking. Sincere coaching is a difficult skill to develop (Rodgers & Rodgers, 2007) so providing a safe place to

explore ways of giving feedback was useful. It took time for graduate students to develop comfort in participating in making suggestions and accepting feedback from others.

I required graduate students to videotape an initial session and a culminating session and provide detailed reflections of their growth noting physical stance, teacher and student talk, turn taking, and specific responses. Additionally, graduate students presented a 5- to 10-minute video excerpt of their instruction to the class. The selected segment was not intended to represent their best teaching but rather an instance in which they were challenged and would welcome feedback from their peers.

Following presentation of video excerpts, the class took on the role of literacy coaches and shared what they noticed about the interaction, asked questions of the tutor, and offered possible actions to consider. This coaching dialogue, along with the sincere reflection upon the videos, supported graduates to notice key factors within the tutoring dynamic. For instance, one graduate student did not recognize how disengaged her student was until she reviewed the videotape and noticed her student hunched over, holding her coat in her lap. She then looked at her own physical stance and realized that she was so intent on the word work activity that she did not focus on the student. In another case, a graduate student who had developed a strong rapport with a Hispanic eighth grader recognized in her attempt to discuss the chapter they had just read that she provided all the information necessary, so that the eighth grader could only agree, not elaborate.

During these dialogic sessions, I was continually impressed by the suggestions offered by the class. The sharing of ideas between graduate students was honest and sincere and provided ideas to consider and explore. I learned during these sessions to keep the dialogue flowing between graduate students, rather than using it as a platform for my views. Following Johnston's (2004) model, I used questions and choice words to further the dialogue.

Implications

My findings offer insights for others who run or hope to hold literacy clinics in off-site settings and to those who work to prepare teachers to support the literacy development of urban children. Offering clinics in urban settings provides endless possibilities for learning and reflection. Timely and provocative literature can be a powerful catalyst for critical dialogue. Developing rapport and providing regular reflection and communication improve the clinical learning for all participants, and dialogue provides a meaningful way for graduate students to offer and receive important feedback on their learning and instruction. These findings are aligned with the current models of coaching (Rodgers & Rodgers, 2007) that highlight constructivist dialogue.

Additionally, it is important to remember the possibilities that reading clinics hold for developing teachers. My graduate students have commented on the value of one-on-one instruction. They are impressed by the gains that the children make and by how targeted they are able to be in such an individualized setting. They complain that they would not be able to do this within their classrooms. However, it is my belief that what they take from the value of this teaching will help them find more ways to individualize their classroom instruction.

Another key consideration of this type of teaching is the focus on assessment-based instruction rather than curriculum-based instruction. For my graduate students, this shift is difficult. They are eager to try out lessons that they have read about and think would be fun even if they are not targeted for the children they are tutoring. The shift to analyzing assessment data to plan instruction based on student strengths and needs is new. It often takes the entire semester to fully realize this need. Overall, taking time to reflect upon what works in urban literacy instruction is worthwhile and holds many implications for teaching and learning.

> Offering clinics in urban settings provides endless possibilities for learning and reflection.

This work speaks to the need for more critical reflection by university clinical professors to take time to reflect upon and evaluate the methods they use to support graduate students' learning. The conclusions will also have an impact on my future teaching as I work to support the understandings of my graduate students and interact in the educational communities where the literacy clinics are located.

The inquiry also highlights the importance of preparing graduate students to meet the needs of diverse learners by taking time to explore the complex factors at play in urban settings. It underscores the need for building rapport both between tutor and student, and between professor and tutor. Furthermore, the study suggests that in on-site settings that do not have the benefit of behind-the-glass opportunities, where other tutors observe sessions through a two-way mirror, videotapes can provide a means for helping graduate students notice their teaching actions and explore the implications of such actions. Finally, the inquiry illuminates how powerful it can be to hold clinics in off-site settings where graduate students can become part of urban communities and understand what supports are in place for working with urban learners. Urban literacy clinics can provide endless possibilities for learning, for children as well as graduate students.

Words of Advice

- Off-site clinics can be powerful. Take advantage of any opportunity to try them!

- Don't assume graduate students are prepared to work in urban clinics. Explore their comfort levels and where their current understandings lie. Provide powerful texts on race and class as lenses for dealing with uncomfortable issues. This will inspire discussion and develop an authority from which to learn.

- Make critical talk and reflection the norm, and share models of instruction and assessment. Also engage graduate students in exploring how to establish rapport.

- Keep response to graduate students positive, short, and focused. Share the power by providing support while keeping them in control of their learning. Build in reflection and regular dialogue points through assessment dialogue and peer coaching.

- Take time as the clinic director to learn from the graduate students and the urban community.

- Don't overlook the value of protocols for establishing structure and support dialogue.

REFERENCES

Allington, R.L., & Walmsley, S.A. (1995). *No quick fix: Rethinking literacy programs in America's elementary schools.* New York: Teachers College Press.

Bartoli, J.S. (2001). *Celebrating city teachers: How to make a difference in urban schools.* Portsmouth, NH: Heinemann.

Bear, D.R., Invernizzi, M., Templeton, S., & Johnston, F. (2007). *Words their way: Word study for phonics, vocabulary, and spelling instruction* (4th ed.). Upper Saddle River, NJ: Pearson.

Cambourne, B. (1995). Toward an educationally relevant theory of literacy learning: Twenty years of inquiry. *The Reading Teacher, 49*(3), 182–190. doi:10.1598/RT.49.3.1

Compton-Lilly, C. (2004). *Confronting racism, poverty, and power: Classroom strategies to change the world.* Portsmouth, NH: Heinemann.

Culham, R. (2003). *6+1 traits of writing: The complete guide grades 3 and up.* New York: Scholastic.

Cunningham, P.M. (2000). *Phonics they use: Words for reading and writing* (3rd ed.). Boston: Addison-Wesley.

Harvey, S., & Goudvis, A. (2007). *Strategies that work: Teaching comprehension for understanding and engagement* (2nd ed). York, ME: Stenhouse.

Johnston, P.H. (2000). *Running records: A self-tutoring guide.* York, ME: Stenhouse.

Johnston, P.H. (2004). *Choice words: How our language affects children's learning.* York, ME: Stenhouse.

Krippendorff, K. (2004). *Content analysis: An introduction to its methodology* (2nd ed.). Thousand Oaks, CA: Sage.

Oczkus, L. (2004). *Super 6 comprehension strategies: 35 lessons and more for reading success.* Norwood, MA: Christopher Gordon.

Opitz, M., & Rasinski, T.A. (1998). *Good-bye round robin: 25 effective oral reading strategies.* Portsmouth, NH: Heinemann.

Perkins, J.H. (2004). Addressing the literacy needs of African-American students and their teachers. In R.B. Cooter Jr. (Ed.), *Perspectives on rescuing urban literacy education: Spies, saboteurs, & saints* (pp. 235–245). Mahwah, NJ: Erlbaum.

Polkinghorne, D.E. (1988). *Narrative knowing and the human sciences.* Albany: State University of New York Press.

Risko, V.J., Roskos, K., & Vukelich, C. (1999). Preparing teachers for reflective practice: Intentions, contradictions, and possibilities. *Language Arts, 80*(2), 134–144.

Rodgers, A., & Rodgers, E.M. (2007). *The effective literacy coach: Using inquiry to support teaching & learning.* New York: Teachers College Press.

Ruddell, R.B. (2004). Researching the influential literacy teacher: Characteristics, beliefs, strategies, and new research directions. In R.B. Ruddell & N.J. Unrau (Eds.), *Theoretical models and processes of reading* (5th ed., pp. 979–997). Newark, DE: International Reading Association.

Schön, D.A. (1987). *Educating the reflective practitioner: Toward a new design for teaching and learning in the professions.* San Francisco: Jossey-Bass.

Strauss, A., & Corbin, J. (1990). *Basics of qualitative research: Grounded theory procedures and techniques.* Newbury Park, CA: Sage.

Zeichner, K.M., & Liston, D.P. (1996). *Reflective teaching: An introduction.* Mahwah, NJ: Erlbaum.

ABOUT THE CONTRIBUTOR

Sharon M. Peck *is an assistant professor of literacy at the State University of New York at Geneseo in western New York State, USA. She teaches graduate courses and directs a professional development initiative, Reading and Writing the*

Community, where she works closely with urban teachers to support literacy instruction to meet the needs of urban learners. For the past five years, she has led off-site clinics for master's degree students. She also supports undergraduate students in informal tutoring in urban schools, and she studies urban teacher change, adolescent motivation to read, reflective practice, and uses of puppetry in literacy education. E-mail: peck@ geneseo.edu

Professional Development and the After-School Literacy Program: A Partnership for Overall Academic Improvement

Kathleen B. Quinn

Imagine me—walking in a very old school building in a run-down, urban neighborhood feeling afraid because of where I parked my car. But then I meet a group of caring, enthusiastic teachers and a young child runs up to me while I wait outside the school office. She gives me a big smile, a loving greeting, and a tight hug; my apprehension dissolves.

Three years later I can't wait to arrive to see the children's work decorating the halls and classroom walls, to hear them read and discuss the stories and plays and to coach and collaborate with a dedicated group of professionals who will soon be certified reading specialists. And, yes, my car is still OK. This is a story about what happened to me as a result of my participation in a partnership that included the after-school program.

Many urban school districts are faced with challenges to meet the adequate yearly progress (AYP) requirements of the No Child Left Behind Act of 2001. Philadelphia schools are no exception to this problem. In fact, in 2003, over 30 schools in Philadelphia were in corrective action. P.H. Bank Elementary School (a pseudonym) was one of these schools; however, as of 2006, it is no longer.

Since 1992, Holy Family University has held reading and writing clinics (called The Reading & Writing Connection), both on campus during the summer and in various public and charter schools in the Philadelphia region. So, running a clinic at an off-campus location was nothing new

for me. However, the magnitude of the commitment to holding all graduate classes for the teachers at the school along with conducting literacy events there, coaching the graduate students (the teachers at the school), and working in the classrooms during the school day would be a much more significant and unusual process than my prior experiences.

Naturally, when I was approached about this new project, I was skeptical. When I attended an organizational meeting at the school district's administration building, I voiced many of my concerns about the bureaucracy and corner-cutting that the school district administration had demonstrated in the past.

Literacy Tutoring That Works: A Look at Successful In-School, After-School, and Summer Programs, edited by Janet C. Richards and Cynthia A. Lassonde. © 2009 International Reading Association.

We had our initial meeting at the school to announce this new opportunity for teachers and had an overwhelmingly positive response with over 38 teachers applying for the 24 possible slots. However, once it was determined that the teachers would also have to commit to teaching after school along with taking a graduate course, 6 of the 24 teachers who were selected chose not to continue.

In the first course, held in the fall of 2003, the partnership included teachers from two elementary schools who applied to participate. The school district would pay for up to 27 credits of graduate work leading to a Reading Specialist Certification. All courses would be offered on site at the one elementary school during the regular school year, and faculty from the University would teach onsite as well. As part of the commitment from teachers, the first principal required that teachers teach reading in the after-school program, called Power Hour, two afternoons per week. In the first year of the partnership, the teachers used the school district's designated reading program, *Voyager Passport* (Voyager Expanded Learning, 2004). Part of the responsibility of university faculty members would be to monitor the after-school instruction of these teachers and include relevant topics and research in the courses so there would be a direct application for both classroom reading instruction and after-school reading instruction. I was asked to direct the program and to provide leadership to any other faculty who participated.

Starting in the fall of 2003 through the spring of 2006, the after-school program was part of the course requirements. This chapter focuses on the after-school clinical experience that took place in the spring of 2006 and provides some background information as to how the program took shape.

Both of the classes for the teachers and the literacy tutoring took place after school, at the school. Children from the P.H. Bank Elementary School and children from the middle school affiliated with the school attended. Teachers participated in graduate courses once or twice a week from 4:30 to 6:30 P.M. and taught reading and writing in the after-school program twice a week to small groups or individuals (depending on the semester) from 3:15 to 4:15 P.M. The after-school program started in early October and continued until the beginning of April each year (except the year in which it was part of the clinical preparation, when it continued until the beginning of May 2006).

Faculty from Holy Family University taught all the courses and supervised the after-school program for those teachers who participated in the graduate program. As part of this supervision, faculty planned with the teachers after a full assessment of each child was conducted. Assessment included the administration of the Slosson Intelligence Test-R (SIT-R, 1998) and Profile Analysis (1998), the Critical Reading Inventory (2004), the Elementary Reading Attitude Survey (1990), and, if needed, the Yopp–Singer Test of Phonemic Awareness (1995) and the Observation Survey of Literate Behavior (1993) along with a writing sample that was analyzed using both the school district's and the State of Pennsylvania's writing rubric. In addition, running records, retellings, and writing samples were collected throughout the after-school program. Teachers kept logs with anecdotal notes and personal reflections of their own improvement.

The initial after-school program used *Voyager Passport* (Voyager Expanded Learning, 2004), a published workbook approach that all teachers followed. As that year progressed, the teachers in the graduate program began to make modifications to this program, including adding more authentic children's literature, picking and choosing skills based on their assessments and observations, and including writing workshop one day per week for one half hour from January until April.

In the remaining years of the partnership, teachers who were in the graduate program abandoned *Voyager Passport* (Voyager Expanded Learning, 2004) entirely and created their own curriculum that included writers' and readers' workshop, literature circles, and Readers Theatre using children's literature selections based on the needs, interests, and strengths of the students with whom they were working.

> "A good first step in developing more effective instructional programs for struggling readers is developing a plan for continually upgrading each teacher's expertise."

Questions Guiding the Research

I addressed the following research questions:

- What impact does a professional development partnership have on the teachers who participate in the partnership?

- What impact does a professional development partnership have on the students who participate in the after-school program affiliated with the partnership?

To answer these questions, I decided to collect both qualitative and quantitative data about the teachers and the students who participated. I wanted to find out if this partnership had a positive effect on teaching as well as student achievement. I knew that this was a complex endeavor and that variables could not really be isolated. I do not consider this research experimental in nature; however, I did want to see if there were trends that appeared during the implementation of the after-school program that were not apparent prior to it.

Theoretical Background and Perspectives

The National Reading Panel and the No Child Left Behind Act of 2001 emphasize the importance of professional development in the achievement of schools and students. This partnership is a direct result of the recommendations found in these sources.

According to Allington (2001), "a good first step in developing more effective instructional programs for struggling readers is developing a plan for continually upgrading each teacher's expertise" (p. 112). This partnership is based on that premise along with Allington's emphasis on the use of the extended day or after-school programs which should be supplementary to high-quality regular day programs and fit into one of the following four categories:

1. School-based remedial assistance with expert instruction

2. School-based tutoring from trained community volunteers, high school, or college students

3. School-based homework help/child care/recreation with paraprofessional or volunteer support

4. Community-based homework help/child care/recreation

The program described herein fit the first category, school-based remedial assistance with expert instruction. Further, because the teachers were all also graduate students who had taken 15 graduate credits in reading that led up to the course work in the clinic and had also been participating in school district workshops, as well as receiving in-class coaching and after-school coaching prior to the clinic, this program should accelerate the students' reading growth as intended.

Rather than pulling children out during the regular day when they often miss important instruction and social opportunities, this program was meant to enhance and supplement the school's current reading and writing curriculum (Allington & Cunningham, 2002). In addition, the International Reading Association's (2000) position statement on Excellent Reading Teachers recommends that extensive professional development and powerful teaching are the keys to making a difference in children's achievement. Lyons and Pinnell (2001) and McAndrew (2005) emphasize the importance of staff training and leadership skills along with collaboration, which are all key components of our program. Friend and Cook (1999) show that teachers working together can enhance significantly the effectiveness of classroom instruction. I applied these key ideas to the development of the clinical experience for the teachers who participated in this after-school program.

Methodology

Participants

The participants included 12 teachers at a small urban elementary school in Philadelphia, 24 students at that same school, and three faculty members (the author and two others). The data collection and analysis are based on this clinical experience in 2006.

The teachers were all female ranging in age from late 20s to early 50s with a median age of 38. All were certified in elementary education, with three also certified in special education and one

certified in English as a Second Language. All had at least four years' teaching experience with most having more than five years of experience. All had been at this school for two years or more.

The children ranged in age from 6 to 10 with the median age being 8.5. There were 16 girls and 8 boys who participated—7% Caucasian, 34% African American, 55% Latino, and 4% Asian, which follows the ethnic make-up of the school. All qualified for free or reduced-cost lunches.

The School

This neighborhood school is located in a high-crime, high-poverty area of Philadelphia. At the start of the partnership, the school had high teacher turnover, with 40% of the teaching staff requesting transfers in 2002 (the year of the district takeover by the state), as well as high student mobility and low test scores. In 2003, 93% of the school's third graders were considered either at basic level (16%) or below basic (76%) on the Pennsylvania State System of Assessment's (PSSA) reading subtest. As a result of Tier II Corrective Action, the school had been under a private, for-profit management company with little success, and had just reverted back to being under the auspices of the School District of Philadelphia in partnership with the State of Pennsylvania and The School Reform Commission, which oversaw operations, budget, and academic progress. But Bank was still struggling to meet its goals. A new principal had been appointed and a regional superintendent was in place.

The Program and Procedures

After two years of making modifications to the district's after-school program, Power Hour, and after five initial courses, the after-school program was in place in spring 2006. This was a culmination of efforts to increase teacher understanding of the reading and writing process through their ability to assess, evaluate, and reflect during assessment and instruction of children. Teachers worked collaboratively with one another (groups of two to four) along with a faculty mentor/supervisor/coach assigned to them. The program began with an initial assessment in December prior to the start of the after-school program. Children were selected based on need, interest, and their families' willingness to allow them to attend. Most children were recruited by the teachers and participated enthusiastically. No fees were charged.

On Monday and Wednesday afternoons from 3:15 until 4:30, teachers worked in small groups with two children assigned to each teacher. In addition to instruction for the children, teachers conducted a pre- and postprogram assessment of each child. Teachers participated in a professional book club three times during the semester, discussing a self-selected book. Every week teachers wrote in a log reflecting on each child's progress and on what they were learning not only about the children but also about the reading and writing process and collaborating with peers.

Each group selected a topic related to their book club and their students' needs and researched a specific aspect of it further and then developed, planned, and conducted a staff development or family workshop based on it (Table 11.1 shows some of the workshop themes). At the end of the course, teachers created a portfolio that included their personal literacy and teaching history, their philosophy of reading instruction, evidence for and reflection on how they have met the Pennsylvania Standards for Reading Specialists, and a self-evaluation. Each teacher had to write detailed lesson plans for each afternoon session and one of these lessons had to follow the format of a ReadWriteThink plan (see www.readwritethink.org). These lessons helped teachers become very aware of how to connect theory to practice, integrate technology, and meet standards. Though much more detailed than what the teacher is expected to turn in, this format encourages teachers to think deeply about the details of planning.

For example, in one classroom, three teachers worked with six first graders and based their instruction on the Writing Workshop model to focus on phonemic awareness and reading improvement through writing development. To complement the instruction, the teachers focused their study on *About the Authors* (Ray, 2004). In addition, teachers developed a workshop to focus on how families can help their children with phonemic awareness and decoding at home while making reading fun. They presented this to the children's families one evening during the clinic.

Another group comprised two teachers working with four second and third graders, all English-language learners. Along with their book club selection, *When Kids Can't Read: What Teachers Can Do* (Beers, 2002), they also researched strategies for reading and writing for ELLs and developed and presented a workshop to the rest of the class and the faculty at the school demonstrating these strategies and helping their colleagues learn how to apply them. Based on the needs and interests of their students, each group's format revolved around thematic instruction and vocabulary development while integrating multicultural literature and world geography. Table 11.2 includes sample schedules from the after-school program classrooms.

Various literacy events and celebrations were also part of the after-school program, including the following:

- Readers Theatre performances
- Original writing with author's performances
- Poetry performances

Table 11.1 Workshop Topics

Workshop Title	Description
Strategies to Help English-Language Learners Improve in Reading and Writing	The graduate student teachers provided a variety of strategies, techniques, and materials that would help the other teachers in the school who have children who are English-language learners in their classrooms. For example, specific vocabulary techniques and decoding strategies were demonstrated and then the teachers had the opportunity to try them out and come back to the leaders of the workshop for advice and coaching.
Comprehension Strategies for Narrative and Informational Texts	The graduate student teachers provided specific comprehension strategies that they had used successfully with the students in both the after school program and their classrooms such as KWL, Text Connections, and Venn diagrams. They also provided a variety of texts that could be paired successfully while still meeting the standards and following the curriculum guidelines for the upper elementary grades.
How to Implement Reading and Writing Workshop in an After-School Program	The graduate student teachers provided a variety of schedules and lessons that they had successfully used during the after-school program and demonstrated how these could be applied in other programs based on the students' needs, levels, interests, and strengths. A variety of minilessons related to topic selection, book selection, and specific skills such as spelling, grammar, and revision were also included.
Helping Families Work With Their Emergent Readers and Writers	The graduate student teachers provided families with a wide range of word learning activities such as making words along with the materials to do so at home. Families appreciated being shown how to do these activities with their children as well as having the materials to take home and use with them. Opportunities were also provided for families to come back to school and receive further assistance so they could feel comfortable and successful. There was an open-door policy for all families to visit the after-school program at any time. Several families took consistent advantage of this option.

Table 11.2 Typical Schedules for the After-School Program

Classroom	Time	Format	Procedure	Activity
Grades 2 & 3	3:15–4:00	Reading workshop	Readers Theatre: Fairy tales	Spotlight on me
Grades 2 & 3	4:00–4:30	Writing workshop	Writing, conferences, and sharing	Script writing
Grades 4 & 5	3:15–3:45	Balanced literacy	Guided reading	Nonfiction
Grades 4 & 5	3:45–4:30	Writing workshop	Writing, conferences, and sharing	Informational writing

- Theater attendance, including discussion with the playwright and lunch
- Pizza party with award ceremony for children to celebrate success
- Family Literacy Night with workshops for families
- Fairy Tale Festival with performances
- Dinners and awards for teachers

Data Sources

To investigate the possible answers to the research questions, I analyzed both qualitative and quantitative data. I collected and analyzed teachers' logs, lesson plans, and portfolios using the constant comparison method (Savenye & Robinson, 2004). I also analyzed pre- and postprogram reading levels using descriptive and inferential statistics, as well as PSSA scores from the start of the partnership through the years of the after-school program including the clinical year, 2006.

Data Analysis

To determine the effectiveness of the program, I analyzed pre- and postprogram data. The teachers used the Critical Reading Inventory (2004) to determine the students' reading levels in January and April. I also examined all teacher writing for trends in data. All materials were read separately and more than once, by me and a colleague.

Limitations

Although specific variables could not be isolated and this was not a true experimental design, there were trends both in the teachers' perspectives and in the children's test results that indicate that during the time of this partnership positive effects were taking place. Having no comparison group is always a problem in the in-

terpretation of results. Yet if you believe as I do that each situation is unique, then finding an upward movement in measurable reading ability and a qualitative difference in teachers' response to instruction and professional development—especially in the areas of collaboration, cultural understanding, and differentiation of instruction—is noteworthy. As a result, though not easy to generalize, the findings may help us think about what worked here and what might be something others could try for their situation.

Results and Discussion

The postprogram Critical Reading Inventory (2004) levels were significantly different ($p < 0.001$, $t = 7.347$, 23 df) from the preprogram mean of 1.2417 ($SD = 1.10490$) and the posttest mean of 2.0292 ($SD = 1.35309$). This indicates that the majority of children improved by at least 0.25 reading level over the course of the program, with many seeing improvement of almost one year. Not only did the teachers verbally indicate positive changes in their teaching but also the children benefited in a measurable way from their teachers' efforts.

Further, the school also saw some improvements in PSSA scores, starting with 12% of the third graders falling into the *proficient* and *advanced* categories in 2003 at the start of the partnership and ending with 40% of the third graders in the *proficient* and *advanced* categories of reading in 2007 at the end of the partnership. While the partnership was in place, I also noted that there were changes in teacher attendance (90% in 2004 and 96% in 2007), teacher transfer requests (14 in 2004 and 2 in 2007), student attendance (86% in 2004 and 90% in 2007), and in serious incidents (from 50 in 2004 to 10 in 2007) and suspensions (from 240 in 2004 to 50 in 2007). Although these results cannot be attributed to the partnership alone, they did occur during this time period when the partnership was in place.

Initially, two broad categories emerged: teaching and students. Once agreed upon, the following themes became evident:

1. Teaching: (a) The need to individualize through careful observation and assessment and (b) the importance and influence of collaboration with colleagues and faculty

2. Students: (a) The importance of instilling a love of reading and writing in students and integrating cultural understanding and (b) the importance of comprehension for students

Some examples from the teachers' self-evaluations about their teaching follow:

> One of the major benefits of having the partnership was that we had many discussions of how things we learned could be implemented in our school instead of just in broad terms. Also, projects that we completed in class all directly impacted the achievement of our own students. For example, during the after-school clinic we had opportunities to work with very small groups of children that we knew were struggling. We knew their strengths and weaknesses and were able to use what we know to help them after school. We were able to continue this instruction during the day. I can only speak for myself but my two students were on grade level when they left the after-school program and continue to do well in third grade. (Carmelina, 2/28/06)

> I feel that the after-school program helped me develop positive relationships with my peers. By planning and team teaching we gained a new appreciation for our own abilities and professionalism. I had the opportunity to discuss problems and concerns that I would not have had if this program never existed. We all worked as a team to come up with ideas that would effectively help the children we were working with this year. (Martina, 4/12/06)

Implications

A positive impact occurred by preparing a cohort of teachers from a single school to become reading professionals and by implementing an after-school program that took place at that school and served the school's neediest students. Instead of using a particular program or curriculum, teacher education, staff development, coaching, and collaboration made the difference. Based on these results, it may be worthwhile to include more professional development that includes supervised clinical experiences directly related to the needs of the school and faculty it serves. Neither generic instructional programs for children nor those for teachers will have the same positive impact as ones that are developed specifically for the schools they serve.

> Reading is a complex process that is affected by culture, language, cognitive, psychological, structural, and social variables.

No one variable that has been discussed here can be seen as *the* solution to a school's difficulties, but a combination of factors and a specific group of teachers did make a difference in helping the children at Bank School improve in their literacy achievement. Reading is a complex process that is affected by culture, language, cognitive, psychological, structural, and social variables (Lapp et al., 2004) and the preparation of teachers and their ability to apply their knowledge to teaching. There is no quick fix (Allington & Walmsley, 2007), but there is much research that supports the preparation and importance of teachers of reading in making a difference in children's lives (International Reading Association, 2000).

To make a real difference for the children that participated in our after-school program, we had to focus on the best practices that also matched the children's needs, interests, levels, ages, and strengths. To do that, the teachers had to fully assess each child and then keep accurate records, reflect, keep up-to-date with current research and practice, collaborate with one another, and use a variety of resources, methods, materials, and strategies. I had to provide ongoing professional development, feedback, and coaching. I had to work closely with the teachers and the principal, carefully observe instruction, and collaborate with everyone. I believe that all of these things along with the dedication of the staff and the involvement of the families helped to make our program successful. The biggest lesson I can take away from this is that differentiation is important at all levels of education; if you differentiate and individualize for your school and your program, you will see positive results.

Words of Advice

This was a unique opportunity that may not be possible for most universities; however, if grant opportunities arise and you can build a long-term relationship with a school in preparing their teachers to become reading professionals, I would highly recommend it. The teachers, the students, the school, and the university all benefit. I recommend that you keep the following in mind:

- Be open to change.
- Don't judge a school by its appearance, age, or test scores.
- Focus on the children's needs, strengths, interests, and culture to help make a difference in their literacy achievement.
- Remember that teachers and children are more important than any program or curriculum.

REFERENCES

Allington, R.L. (2001). *What really matters for struggling readers: Designing research-based programs.* New York: Longman.

Allington, R.L., & Cunningham, P.M. (2002). *Schools that work: Where all children read and write* (2nd ed.). Boston: Allyn & Bacon.

Allington, R.L., & Walmsley, S. (Eds.). (2007). *No quick fix, the RTI edition: Rethinking literacy programs in America's elementary schools.* Newark, DE: International Reading Association; New York: Teachers College Press.

Beers, K. (2002). *When kids can't read: What teachers can do.* Portsmouth, NH: Heinemann.

Friend, M., & Cook, L. (1999). *Interactions: Collaboration skills for school professionals* (3rd ed.). New York: Longman.

International Reading Association. (2000). *Excellent reading teachers* (Position statement). Newark, DE: Author.

Lapp, D., Block, C.C., Cooper, E.J., Flood, J., Roser, N., & Tinajero, J.V. (Eds.). (2004). *Teaching all the children: Strategies for developing literacy in an urban setting.* New York: Guilford.

Lyons, C.A., & Pinnell, G.S. (2001). *Systems for change in literacy education.* Portsmouth, NH: Heinemann.

McAndrew, D.A. (2005). *Literacy leadership.* Newark, DE: International Reading Association.

Ray, K.W. (with L. Cleaveland) (2004). *About the authors: Writing workshop with our youngest writers.* Portsmouth, NH: Heinemann.

Savenye, W.C., & Robinson, R.S. (2004). Qualitative research issues and methods: An introduction for educational technologists. In D.H. Jonassen (Ed.), *Handbook of research on educational communications and technology* (2nd ed., pp. 1045–1071). Mahwah, NJ: Erlbaum. Retrieved April 5, 2006, from www.aect.org/edtech/39.pdf.

Voyager Expanded Learning. (2004). *Voyager passport.* Dallas, TX: Author.

ABOUT THE CONTRIBUTOR

Kathleen B. Quinn *is a professor of reading in the School of Education at Holy Family University in Philadelphia, Pennsylvania, USA. She has been a classroom teacher, a reading specialist, and a consultant in the Philadelphia region and has initiated several partnerships with local public school districts as well as with private and charter schools. Her main areas of interest include preparing reading specialists and the assessment and remediation of students who struggle with reading and writing. E-mail: kquinn@ holyfamily.edu*

CHAPTER 12

The Professional Development of Three Graduate Student Mentors in a University-Based After-School Program for Struggling Readers

Nina L. Nilsson

I'm attempting to be a positive mentor without seeming too "hawkish."

Instead of walking around and doing the "looking over the shoulder" the whole time, I decided to hang back and wait for them to approach me if they needed help. They seem like a group very willing to seek out help as needed.

My group has been very inquisitive, and I have plenty of questions to answer!

I think our first few meetings I scared them or something like that because they wouldn't talk.

My ideal role seems to be more of a guide. The teachers are knowledgeable and know what they need from us.

I am fine with observing…. My only problem is being an outside observer; at times last week, I just wanted to "jump in" and be involved.

The comments in the opening vignette portray how graduate students in an advanced literacy practicum course reflected on their initial experiences mentoring small groups of tutors. The tutors worked in an after-school, university-based literacy center with children who struggle with reading. The three mentors ranged in prior teaching experiences and are representative of students enrolled in our graduate reading programs. Although the challenges they faced as mentors differed, there are discernible patterns to their struggles and celebrations. This chapter tracks the professional development of the three mentors over the course of a 15-week semester during which each mentor offered support to a group of four or five tutors in their work with struggling readers. The mentors and the tutors were all graduate students in literacy education; however, the mentors were at an advanced stage in the literacy program and the tutors were at the beginning of their graduate studies.

Driven by the evolving role of reading professionals in public schools today, many graduate literacy programs are undergoing change. Although some reading professionals continue to work with children in school settings, many undertake leadership and professional development roles. Additionally, many are expected to serve as a resource to classroom teachers (Bean, Swan, & Knaub, 2003; International Reading Association, 2004a). Given the range of duties literacy professionals are expected to perform in the field today, graduate literacy programs face challenges in adequately preparing their candidates.

To learn what other institutions are doing to meet these challenges, I recently visited some exemplary literacy centers for struggling readers at other universities. When I returned, I drew upon what I'd learned and made modifications to fit the needs of our particular program. I implemented a community-of-practice framework within our literacy center because this framework embedded opportunities for graduate students in literacy education to gain an introductory experience coaching or serving as a resource to other graduate students in their role as tutors. Currently, plans are underway to extend the framework to a school site where graduate student mentors will have opportunities to help teachers in school contexts.

Situated on the campus of a large public university in an urban area in the southern United States, The Literacy Center provides after-school literacy support services to struggling readers and writers in first grade through high school. During the fall semester, in conjunction with the graduate literacy program's assessment course, graduate students tutored children attending the center, focusing primarily on assessing the children's literacy strengths and needs. At the conclusion of the fall program, children reading below grade level—as determined by their performance on literacy assessments and interviews with parents and teachers—are usually invited to attend the spring program for instructional intervention. In the spring, the graduate students enroll in a subsequent course on reading intervention instruction and provide the after-school tutorial services on a weekly basis.

The context for this inquiry was the fall session of The Literacy Center with a new community-of-practice framework in place. According to Lave and Wenger (1991), communities of practice allow apprentices within a community to develop new understandings and skills by directly engaging in activities with others. The community-of-practice framework of The Literacy Center provided advanced graduate students in literacy with introductory experiences pertinent to serving as literacy specialists or coaches in public schools. The advanced graduate students served as mentors in supportive roles to the tutors and received graduate credit for their roles; the other graduate students who were at the early stages of the literacy program did the actual tutoring of children. In this way, the university's Literacy Center provided a supportive initial coaching experience for the advanced graduate students prior to the next step, which was a scaffolded coaching experience in an authentic school context. For most of the advanced graduate students, this was the first time they had worked with adults.

In the fall, children attended one-and-a-half-hour sessions one day every other week. After the sessions ended and during the alternate weeks when The Literacy Center did not meet, the 13 graduate students met with the course instructor and three assisting mentors. During class time, the students learned about

> The Literacy Center provides after-school literacy support services to struggling readers and writers in first grade through high school.

various reading and writing assessments and other related topics.

Throughout the fall session of The Literacy Center, each mentor provided support to four or five tutors in a number of ways. First, each mentor met with a small group of tutors prior to their sessions with children to assist with procedures for various literacy assessments. Afterward, they helped with the interpretation of results. At times, the mentors recommended or selected books and other materials. Guided by interests that emerged in class, mentors periodically conducted brief presentations on additional assessments or assessment-related topics. Mentors also observed and took extensive notes while tutors met with the children. They shared these notes afterward when they met in small-group reflective debriefing sessions. In these capacities and others, mentors assumed many of the roles outlined in the revised Standards for Reading Professionals developed by the International Reading Association (2004b).

Questions Guiding the Research

The purpose of this study was to employ a sociocultural framework (Rogoff, Baker-Sennett, Lacasa, & Goldsmith, 1995) to examine the professional development of three graduate student mentors who tutored in a literacy center. Although important traits of effective mentors have been proposed, such as leadership skills (Bean et al., 2003), strong communication skills, public speaking and presentation skills (Fisher, n.d.), and knowledge about working with adults including issues related to power and positioning (Rainville, 2007), there is a dearth of research on effective ways to foster these traits in literacy training programs (Rainville, 2007).

Although definitions of the literacy mentor, or coach, vary across contexts (Rainville, 2007), most recognize that the literacy coach "helps teachers recognize what they know and can do, assists teachers as they strengthen their ability to make more effective use of what they know and do, and supports teachers as they learn more and do more" (Toll, 2005, p. 4). I used Rogoff's (1995) personal, interpersonal, and community planes of analysis or perspectives to examine the three mentors' professional development. Accordingly, from the personal perspective, I wanted to know what changes occurred in the graduate student mentors' professional development as shown by their weekly written self-reflections about their participation in activities with the tutors they mentored. From the interpersonal perspective, I wanted to see how their professional development was constructed through their communications with those mentored and their coordination of efforts interacting with those they mentored. From the community perspective, I wanted to know how their professional development grew through their contributions to practices and traditions linked to The Literacy Center and the graduate-level assessment course associated with The Literacy Center.

I also examined the similarities and differences across all three cases in terms of the mentors' transformations with respect to their personal professional development, interpersonal professional development, and professional development in connection with practices and values portrayed by The Literacy Center and classroom community.

Theoretical Background and Perspectives

My study was informed by notions implicit in sociocultural theories as they relate to communities of practice. Consistent with this perspective, rich opportunities for learning are possible when novices and more expert others come together to solve problems of mutual interest with language serving a key role in helping to identify problems and clarify issues. Through participation in authentic activities with other more experienced members, novices are able to gain access to professional knowledge and cognitive tools (Lave & Wenger, 1991; Rogoff, 1990, 1995, 1997; Rogoff & Topping, 2002; Vygotsky, 1978).

> Through participation in authentic activities with other more experienced members, novices are able to gain access to professional knowledge and cognitive tools.

Given the broad nature of context, Rogoff (1995, 1997, 2003) proposed considering the personal, interpersonal, and community planes of context to allow for more specific focus in analyses. Of note, others studying the professional development of teachers and preservice teachers in online and traditional offline cultural settings have used this framework for research and found it useful (e.g., Gray & Tatar, 2004; Richards, 2006). For this reason, I adopted the framework to analyze the professional development of graduate student mentors in this study.

Methodology

Participants

This research is a multiple case study (Merriam, 1998). It consists of an in-depth exploration of the professional development of three graduate students selected for study due to their contrasting backgrounds representing diversity typical of graduate students enrolled in literacy programs today. Ellen and Barbara were pursuing master's degrees, and Susan was engaged in doctoral studies. (All names are pseudonyms.) Ellen and Susan were experienced classroom teachers (a middle school language arts teacher

and a kindergarten teacher, respectively), and Barbara, who had graduated with a bachelor's degree in elementary education just a few years earlier, had no full-time classroom teaching experience.

It should be noted that in the position statement *The Role and Qualifications of the Reading Coach*, the International Reading Association (2004a) suggests that ordinarily teachers cannot meet the minimum qualifications for the position without having completed several years of outstanding teaching; however, due to the immediate need for coaches, some school districts may select candidates to serve in this capacity who do not meet the criteria but who have other qualifications that make them strong candidates for the position. Thus, it was of interest to include in the study mentors with, as well as without, prior teaching experience. The mentors offered support to 13 graduate students—9 of whom were experienced teachers—all enrolled in a reading practicum course, one of the required courses in the university's graduate literacy program. Most were pursuing master's degrees; a few of the 13 students were working toward doctoral degrees.

Data Sources

With the graduate students' permission and Institutional Review Board (IRB) approval, data sources employed at the end of the semester included e-mail correspondence, weekly written reflections, class listserv postings and exchanges, and field notes supplemented by an artifact collection.

Data Analysis

For data analysis, I adapted the Functional Pattern Analysis method used by Rogoff and Topping (2002) in their study of the personal, interpersonal, and community contributions of

Girl Scouts and others as participants in complex activities related to cookie sales and deliveries. First, I conducted multiple, in-depth readings of all data collected for each participant, making note of the various categories of information covered in the data for each mentor to identify overlapping information across cases. Then I reviewed and collapsed related categories, as appropriate, for purposes of manageability. This process resulted in a total of four categories, or tasks, related to mentoring that applied across all cases:

1. Fostering collegiality
2. Defining the mentoring role
3. Developing expertise related to mentoring
4. Gaining leadership experiences

Next, I noted the contributions of each mentor to each of the four tasks. For each contribution noted, I employed content analysis techniques and underlined keywords as identifiers for each plane of analysis. I coded references to the self (e.g., "I realize," "I recognize," "I learned that") as *personal*. I coded language related to coordination of efforts (e.g., "led a debriefing session"), promoting activity involvement (e.g., "encourage," "ask," "offer," "let me know," "e-mail me"), or restricting activity involvement (e.g., "refrained," "hung back") as *interpersonal*. Finally, I coded language that referred to "Literacy Center," "class," or "course" as indicators of the *community*.

Last, to identify mentors' transformative changes in all four areas noted, I drew from Rogoff's (1995) research related to transformations in participation patterns. Specifically, I color-coded the data for four categories of transformative change:

1. Taking on more responsibility
2. Becoming more familiar with an aspect of mentoring

3. Participating in new ways of teaching following the structure of The Literacy Center or classroom
4. Making use of or extending cognitive tools related to The Literacy Center or classroom community

Limitations

Given the nature of multiple case studies (Merriam, 1998), the results of this study cannot be generalized to other teaching and learning contexts (Gall, Gall, & Borg, 2007). In drawing comparisons between the cases in this study and other contexts, readers must consider my perspective in my dual role as researcher and course instructor and decide if it is compatible with their own perspectives. Another limitation to consider is the possibility that the context of the study, a graduate course for which each mentor received a grade, may have influenced the mentors' reflections and other self-reported data.

Results and Discussion

In the following sections, I discuss the mentors' transformative changes from the personal, interpersonal, and community perspectives.

A Personal Focus

In connection with their personal experiences and self-reflections, the mentors exhibited transformative changes. Specifically, they grew to define their roles in similar but different ways that varied by mentor and characteristics of the group mentored, exhibited a growing sense of responsibility for addressing the needs of an ever-widening circle of individuals, and became increasingly familiar with various aspects of mentoring, including familiarity with ways to build collegiality, with the content and cognitive tools essential to the work of The Literacy Center and classroom, and with a growing awareness of the tentative nature of boundaries between experts and novices. What follows is a description of each mentor's transformative changes from the personal perspective.

BARBARA. Barbara negotiated a mentoring role that blended her graduate students' preferences with her own and positioned her as a guide and observer in the background during assessment sessions. Barbara's reflections also suggest a developing awareness of factors relevant to establishing rapport with group members. Nearly from the start, there was a flurry of e-mail and other out-of class communications among Barbara and the individual students in her group, particularly early in the semester. All were novices to the field of education and lacked the background knowledge of students in the other groups, who were all experienced teachers. As Barbara noted in her Week 8 reflections, "The graduate students in my group have never taught in the classroom, and neither have I, so I feel they are comfortable around me and feel confident to ask questions and be open about their concerns." Barbara also recognized the important role her meetings outside of The Literacy Center and graduate class played in building relationships, as she noted in her reflections:

> "The graduate students in my group have never taught in the classroom, and neither have I, so I feel they are comfortable around me and feel confident to ask questions and be open about their concerns."

> My group has been very diligent about contacting me through e-mails and meeting with me in my office to discuss their questions about The Literacy Center sessions, as well as technical aspects of assignments. I feel these have been great ways for me to build rapport.

In addition to negotiating her role as mentor and learning ways to develop rapport, a third area of transformation for Barbara encompassed assuming increasing responsibility for addressing the needs and concerns of students. Initially, Barbara and the other mentors limited their roles to assisting the four or five graduate students assigned to them. However, several weeks into the course, Barbara noted in her weekly reflections that additional students were stopping by her office for help.

At different points in her weekly reflections, Barbara referred to her need to familiarize herself with specific assessments and other cognitive tools used in The Literacy Center and graduate course to prepare for addressing the inquiries and concerns of students. Barbara observed that those efforts, in turn, deepened her knowledge of the cognitive tools and her facility in using them:

> I think my students found e-mailing me and coming to meet me during my office hours to be of great help to them; however, it was actually me who gained the most from those experiences. I feel much more confident in my knowledge of assessments, strategies, and website activities and in my ability to grow from novice teacher to effective educator one day.

SUSAN. Like Barbara, Susan positioned herself as a guide to those she mentored, but she chose this role based on a different rationale. The members of Susan's group were master's- and doctoral-level students. Based on her students' educational status and in-class performance, Susan inferred a high level of prior knowledge related to tasks associated with The Literacy Center and class, and the inferences she made regarding these students played a key part in shaping her role while mentoring them:

> Since I am working with mainly the doctoral students in this group, I felt comfortable knowing that they were "on the ball" so to speak and probably had thought about what assessments

they will administer this coming week. For this reason, I acted as guide and mentor to this group by giving advice and referencing my personal experiences.

ELLEN. Ellen adopted and discarded roles before finding a mentoring style that felt "just right" in her work with her group of experienced teachers. Initially, Ellen took a perspective similar to that of Barbara, noting the ideal observer during assessment sessions is "a fly on the wall." However, a listserv exchange with the other mentors and course instructor during Week 5 hinted at the tension she experienced in that role.

Three weeks later, Ellen's reflections indicate her ideas had transformed, and while she saw her role as a guide, similar to Barbara and Susan, Ellen's reflections suggest that she felt most comfortable as a participant/observer in the assessment sessions:

> Many things are going well in my field observations. Both the graduate students and Literacy Center children seem comfortable with my observing. In fact, they often invite me to participate or give an opinion on where to go next. I am pleased with this, and prefer it.

In addition to addressing the needs and concerns of a widening circle of individual graduate students in the class and Literacy Center, Ellen's reflections and artifacts suggest a growing sense of responsibility for the group that surfaced in a class seminar that followed The Literacy Center session with children. Class discussion focused on readability formulas and book leveling systems. Two teachers from the same school mentioned a resource sheet they had seen posted in their school containing a table comparing various book leveling systems. In follow-up to the discussion during Week 7, the boundaries between experts and novices blurred, as Ellen asked those teachers to bring the sheet to class the following session.

In addition to broadening her sense of responsibility while growing to recognize the tentative nature of boundaries between experts and novices, over the course of mentoring Ellen noted she deepened her knowledge of assessment tools and content related to The Literacy Center and course in a manner similar to that of Barbara.

An Interpersonal Focus

The data suggest the following four transformative areas related to communicating and coordinating activities:

1. During the early stages of building rapport, each mentor learned to initially restrict and later modify levels of involvement in activities with students as everyone became more familiar with one another.

2. After initial small-group meetings in class, each mentor learned ways to adjust arrangements to extend her availability outside of The Literacy Center and class to answer questions and increase participation.

3. Throughout the semester, although all mentors coordinated efforts to enhance student learning, the ways in which they handled these interactions varied and changed according to mentor and student group, as well as experience level.

4. For all mentors, their increasing mediation of students' understandings of the cognitive tools critical to the course and Literacy Center work with children proved to be valuable opportunities for developing rapport.

A discussion follows of the mentors' transformations in these areas as they apply to each case.

Barbara. *Restricting involvement.* At first, Barbara refrained from taking field notes while observing students in their early sessions with the children. As Barbara explained, "I felt like the graduate students and children were a little uncomfortable with me watching. But for next time, I plan to take field notes."

Adjusting arrangements to extend the opportunities for interpersonal contact. In addition to learning ways to restrict involvement in activities as a means of increasing students' comfort levels during the initial relationship-building period, Barbara discovered the value of making herself available to students outside the center and classroom. In her notes taken during the first meeting with her small group of students, Barbara recorded the personal e-mail addresses of all group members. Most out-of-class inquiries that followed concerned aspects of the case study report sections due weekly and other assignments for the course. In-class debriefing sessions tended to focus on issues related to the assessment sessions with the children. Thus, over time, Barbara increasingly extended her availability outside the classroom and Literacy Center. Her greater presence created more opportunities for mediating students' understandings of the cognitive tools and practices associated with the class and Literacy Center, and these opportunities, in turn, provided additional contexts for building relationships.

> "Keep in mind that I was at the same place you are now this time last year, and I made it! You can, too!"

Coordinating efforts. An examination of the data reveals that, early on, Barbara centered group discussions primarily on her students' needs and concerns, and this focus continued and expanded over the course of the semester. For example, her notes from her initial meeting with the group include the following questions she posed to students, "What should my role be? What would help you most?" After the name of each child tutored by each graduate student, Barbara listed each child's strengths as reported by their tutors (e.g., "very confident"), interests (e.g., "horses!!"), and needs (e.g., "spelling is weak," "pull books!").

Developing rapport. Thus, from an interpersonal perspective, Barbara showed change in a number of ways. She learned ways to restrict and later promote her involvement as everyone became more familiar with one another; created multiple ways to extend her availability to students across a variety of contexts, which was valuable in that different contexts tended to elicit different student concerns; and discovered the value of debriefing discussions centered on her students' agendas. Engaging in these types of interactions not only created more opportunities for assisting students in learning the cognitive tools associated with the center and class; they also provided more ways to build rapport.

Susan. *Restricting involvement.* Similar to Barbara, early in the semester Susan tempered her involvement with her student group until she got to know students better. Susan's weekly reflections suggest she believed that mentoring is a process of knowing when to step in and when to stand back:

> Instead of walking around and doing the "looking over the shoulder" the whole time, I decided to hang back and wait for them to approach me if they needed help. They seem like a group of students who are very willing to seek out help as needed.

Adjusting arrangements to extend the opportunities for interpersonal contact. With in-class debriefing sessions well underway but little out-of-class contact from group members, similar to Barbara, Susan took measures to extend her availability to students, hoping to increase participation levels. During Week 5, Susan sent an e-mail to the four graduate students in her group with her e-mail address, cell phone number, and an attached example of a case study report write-up requested by the graduate students. Along with words of encouragement in her e-mail (i.e., "Keep in mind that I was at the same place you are now this time last year, and I made it! You can, too!"), Susan offered to answer questions and review the final copy of the case study section write-up due the following week. However, only a couple of students responded. Both were novices in terms of prior experience working with elementary-age children. It is also likely both were novices in terms of the assessments and report write-ups required for the course. In both cases, the students asked technical questions about the case study and interpreting assessment data.

Given that all graduate students in Susan's group were experienced classroom teachers, and some were doctoral students, in many respects, these students were "experts" compared with the students in Barbara's group. Perhaps that explains why students did not feel the need for Susan's support to the same degree and why her efforts yielded such limited response. However, it is likely that all of her students were novices in terms of the assessments administered and the assignments (e.g., the case study report) affiliated with The Literacy Center. In fact, their questions to Susan centered on those topics. Group response to Susan's e-mailed offers of help was limited; nevertheless, Susan's assistance did appear to ease anxiety and produced positive responses from those she heard from and responded to.

Shortly after the e-mail offering support, Susan's written reflections note that student questions in class increased and interactions deepened in face-to-face debriefing sessions. As Susan reported:

> I think that it is all coming together for my group now, and since they are into the entire process with both feet, they are able to have more questions and interact on a deeper level during the debriefing sessions. I thoroughly enjoyed these conversations that we had.

Based on these events, it can be surmised that although Susan's e-mailed offers of support never elicited much response electronically for this group of graduate students perhaps her offers fostered greater feelings of camaraderie, and these positive feelings, in turn, contributed to deeper interchanges among group members during face-to-face debriefing sessions in class. It is also quite possible that deeper exchanges evolved from group members' growing familiarity with one another over time.

Coordinating efforts. Compared to Barbara's approach of centering group discussions on her students' needs and concerns, Susan coordinated group sessions somewhat differently. In discussions, Susan addressed her students' needs as they expressed them; however, she also introduced topics emerging out of her own interests and concerns. Her notes from the Week 4 debriefing session with students included specific questions she posed following students' assessment sessions with the children. Similar to Barbara, Susan asked how she could be of help to them. However, she also included probing inquiries about the nature of their assessment sessions: "How did the session go? Are the children comfortable reading? What are your impressions thus far?"

Developing rapport. Given that those in Susan's group were experienced classroom teachers, Susan's transformative changes from the interpersonal perspective looked somewhat different than Barbara's. Although Susan focused some small-group discussions around her students' agendas, she also pushed them to think in new ways. Susan adapted her level of involvement to the capabilities of her students. She extended her availability; however, her students came to the class with a good deal of expertise already, and most likely for that reason the degree to which they took advantage of her offers of assistance was somewhat limited. However, given her offers of support, or possibly due to the rapport that developed over time, group interactions deepened throughout the course of the semester.

> "I sometimes feel that if we hover over them while they have discussions all the time, they will not be comfortable."

ELLEN. *Promoting some types of involvement while restricting others.* Similar to the other mentors, Ellen observed that mentoring involves promoting as well as restricting or delaying involvement initially. For example, early in the semester, Ellen expressed concerns with regard to finding an appropriate level of involvement that was not overbearing during early group discussions. In her weekly reflections she noted, "I sometimes feel that if we hover over them while they have discussions all the time, they will not be comfortable."

Ellen restricted feedback to students following her initial observations of their assessment sessions, but over time, her feedback increased. In her reflections prior to her second observation assessment sessions, Ellen explained how and why she delayed offering her students feedback:

> I didn't think the first observation was either long enough or that it was necessarily appropriate to do this at that time. As my group is now aware of my role, I believe they may be more comfortable receiving feedback, primarily positive, via e-mail.

Adjusting arrangements to extend the opportunities for interpersonal contact. Noting one of her biggest challenges as a mentor, Ellen wrote in her weekly reflections, "It wasn't until Week 5 that I received an e-mail from one of the graduate students in my group, despite prompting for questions. This was a definite challenge for me in the beginning."

In an attempt to elicit more out-of-class interactions with students, Ellen sent an e-mail to all five students in her group, pleading, "I wanted to e-mail and repeat my offer to help with any questions or offer feedback that you may need for the case study background information section.... Again, let me know if you have any questions/comments about the course." Following her note, only one group member responded, twice, with questions. In Ellen's reflections shortly afterwards, she concluded, "E-mail is my best way of communicating with others. One apparent thing, however, is that e-mail is not everyone's favorite form of communication."

Because office visits were not feasible for Ellen, it is difficult to know if extending her availability in other ways would have elicited greater student participation out of class. As with the students in Susan's group, all were experienced classroom teachers. For this reason, all of them were more expert than the students Barbara mentored. As a result, it is possible that they did not feel the need for Ellen's assistance in ways that students in Barbara's group did.

Coordinating efforts. In the early part of the semester, Ellen found it challenging to elicit the active participation of the students she mentored. Reflecting back, Ellen commented, "I think the first few meetings I scared them or something like that because they wouldn't talk."

During Week 5, Ellen experienced a breakthrough. In class, she engaged her students in a collaborative activity to help them with one of the major requirements for the course, the case study write-up. Throughout this workshop, students critiqued and worked collaboratively to improve their write-ups summarizing all the assessment data from a prior session with a Literacy Center student. In her reflections the day following the workshop, Ellen noted:

> I was extremely happy with the "writing workshop" activity that we started within my group last night. This was the first time that my "group" participated as a group, in that everyone participated, and well!

Developing rapport. Similar to Barbara and Susan, Ellen discovered that opportunities to mediate students' understandings of cognitive tools critical to students provided valuable contexts for promoting rapport. They also presented opportunities for leaders, or mentors, to transfer in learning from other contexts and, in the process, enrich the experience. In her reflections, Ellen shared her insights, noting, "The revision session provided a unique opportunity for me to combine my experience from different areas: the Bluegrass Writing Project, previous graduate work, and my own personal teaching."

A Community Focus

The mentors showed two transformative changes in their participation in The Literacy Center and classroom communities: (1) They placed themselves in more active roles, and (2) they made greater intertextual connections as they recognized situations with common purposes or meaning. Specific examples of transformative changes from the community perspective follow.

BARBARA. As noted earlier, Barbara lacked prior classroom teaching experience. Thus, she was unable to draw on that context to assist with her participation in The Literacy Center and classroom communities. However, data collected over the semester indicate that Barbara made several creative and meaningful connections with her graduate course work and experiences working with a mentor back when she was a novice graduate student enrolled in the class and working in The Literacy Center. As Barbara's final reflections indicate, Barbara was able to use her prior learning from these contexts and apply them to enrich her work as a mentor in The Literacy Center community. In her reflections, Barbara explained:

> I took a library science course this semester in which I was introduced to many genres of children's books and learned about so many new, high quality books. All of these things proved to be beneficial for my group of graduate students. I was able to direct them toward books that would be of interest to their clients.

SUSAN. In contrast to Barbara, Susan exhibited a dramatic transformation from the community perspective. In the seminar portion of the class, early in the semester, Susan observed the instructor and noted aspects related to running a graduate class. During Week 6, Susan wrote in her reflections:

> I found it interesting to sit back and observe the way in which the instructor varied the levels of participation as a way of livening up the class. I have never really made detailed observations on how a class is conducted.

In contrast to Barbara, Susan was an experienced, full-time kindergarten classroom teacher and part-time doctoral student. Susan had a number of teaching and graduate course experiences and contexts to draw on to enrich her participation at the community level. Increasingly Susan initiated brief presentations in class on topics of interest to class members. For example, during Week 6, Susan introduced The Literacy Center Education Network's website (www.literacycenter.net) that offers free literacy lessons for young children. Susan explained how she used the website in her own classroom with her kindergarten students and pointed out specific aspects of the site her students particularly enjoyed.

As examples of school-to-university and university-to-school connections made, during Week 12 Susan shared in class one of her favorite strategies used with her kindergartners to develop word-level knowledge, called Making Words. She modeled for the graduate students what they were assigned to do for the following week. The following week in class, in preparation for the final Conclusions and Recommendations section of the case study write-up, the students brought in and demonstrated instructional strategies they used to add to the pool of potential recommendations for struggling readers. At the end of Susan's reflections following class, she commented, "On a personal note, I enjoyed hearing all the strategies from students. It was neat to get a fresh take on old strategies, as well as to learn about brand new ones to use in my classroom and teaching."

"On a personal note, I enjoyed hearing all the strategies from students. It was neat to get a fresh take on old strategies, as well as to learn about brand new ones to use in my classroom and teaching."

Informed by multiple Discourses (Gee, 1996, 1999), such as Discourses related to her graduate course and classroom teaching experiences, Susan became increasingly engaged at the classroom community level over the 15-week semester, initially as observer and later as active participant. Making multiple intertextual connections, Susan shared assessments, strategies, and resources from her classroom, school district, and doctoral work with the classroom community, and took strategies learned from students in class to use with her kindergartners.

ELLEN. Similar to Susan, Ellen increasingly became an active participant at the community level. As a graduate student and full-time language arts teacher at the middle school level, Ellen also had many rich educational experiences to draw on and she made connections across contexts to enrich her participation at the community level. For example, as Ellen illustrates in an e-mail to her instructor, at times she made creative connections from the university classroom to her teaching context:

> I'm going to present on November 7 to the English faculty about "Furthering the KWL" and would love to use your examples in my presentation. I have to present monthly on a differentiation topic for my district, and I'm always looking for ideas!

As with Susan, multiple Discourses (Gee, 1996, 1999) informed Emily's work. Emily transferred experiences and relevant cognitive tools (e.g., strategies, assessments, websites) seamlessly across contexts in all directions. Additionally informed by the Discourse of her professional development workshops in her school district and more recently at professional conferences, Emily made reciprocal connections across The Literacy Center, graduate classroom, school district, and professional conference contexts.

In her final reflections, Ellen noted additional areas of growth that she associated with her participation in the community-of-practice reading center and course:

> My new role as mentor forced my leadership skills to adapt and grow. With the close of this class, I am now comfortable with my speaking abilities, comfortable with establishing rapport in a leadership role, and comfortable providing effective and constructive feedback to adults. All of the challenges were necessary for me to develop as a leader in my profession, and I believe I have grown from the experience. I enjoy teaching adults, and this opportunity has given me a unique opportunity to discover that fact.

Implications

The major focus of this study was on the professional development of mentors, advanced graduate students working with adults for the first time within the context of a literacy center designed around a sociocultural framework. Clearly, the mentors transformed in a number of positive ways. Frequently, learning occurred bidirectionally, and the boundaries between experts and novices were not always distinct. The study extends the work of Richards (2006), who found the framework beneficial in supporting the professional development of preservice teachers working in a summer literacy camp with struggling readers. In Richards's investigation, the framework provided a supportive learning context for the tutors and children attending the camp.

The findings are also relevant to the limited body of research on literacy coaching. The Literacy Center's sociocultural framework fostered the development of traits identified as important to successful coaching (Bean, Swan, & Knaub, 2003; Fisher, n.d.; Rainville, 2007). The results also lend support to Rainville's (2007) conclusions that literacy coaching is "situated" in a particular context. Despite similar training, Barbara, Susan, and Ellen defined their mentoring roles in different ways, shaped in part by variations in the prior knowledge and previous teaching experiences of those they mentored. Methods effective in establishing rapport worked somewhat differently across contexts; however, all mentors found the mediation of cognitive tools critical to The Literacy Center and the university classroom provided rich opportunities for building relationships. The findings also suggest that the larger a mentor's Discourse map (e.g., Discourses from classroom teaching experience, graduate course work, education-related workshops; Gee, 1999), the greater the opportunities are for making intertextual connections associated with enriched learning experiences.

The sociocultural framework of The Literacy Center offers a supportive learning environment of potential interest to others who direct extended learning literacy programs. In addition to The Literacy Center, the framework created an effective learning context for different participants in a summer literacy camp involving preservice teachers, graduate students, and young struggling readers (Richards, 2006). In other literacy programs structured around a sociocultural framework, participants may vary and include literacy program directors, parents or guardians, volunteer college students, or retirees, among other participants.

The mentors who worked in The Literacy Center gained insights that differed, in part, from those of the preservice teachers who participated in the summer literacy camp (Richards, 2006). Yet all the mentors experienced professional growth related to their personal, interpersonal, and community participation in their respective literacy programs. Rogoff's (1995) three planes of analysis provide a useful way to approach the collection of data and help illuminate the various transformative changes that otherwise may be overlooked.

The Functional Pattern Analysis method (Rogoff & Topping, 2002) used in conjunction with Rogoff's (1995, 1997, 2003) three planes of analysis is a useful method for reducing extraneous details from multiple cases so that patterns in the data become more apparent and generalizations made are grounded in the individual cases. These methods have relevance for other researchers conducting similar types of studies.

It should be noted that although the framework implemented provided a valuable initial mentoring experience for graduate students, there is still a need for coaching initiatives to move beyond the college or university classroom to begin to make an impact in schools. In fact, coaching experiences in authentic school contexts are required for graduate literacy programs to attain National Recognition from the International Reading Association and the National Council for Accreditation of Teacher Education.

Words of Advice

- For those interested in creating an extended learning literacy program, a community-of-practice model provides a supportive framework for a range of participants.
- For educators in graduate literacy programs, consider a university-based or off-campus community-of-practice, extended learning literacy program as a context for graduate students' initial mentoring experiences, particularly for those who have never worked with adults before. Mentoring tutors in a program of this type provided a supportive learning environment for the graduate students in the study. The experience also fostered some of the traits (e.g., leadership, communication skills) considered essential to effective mentoring (Bean et al., 2003; Fisher, n.d.).
- Allow time for positive relationships among group members in a community-of-practice, extended learning literacy program to flourish, and experiment with varying the levels of involvement among group members as everyone becomes more comfortable with one another. Increasing the availability of mentors outside the tutoring program and mediating tutors' understandings of the instruments and tools essential to their work promoted rapport. Providing mentors for tutors who

engage in similar practices may foster positive relationships among group members in other extended learning literacy programs, as well.

- Researchers interested in examining transformative changes across multiple cases will find the Functional Pattern Analysis method (Rogoff & Topping, 2002) used in conjunction with Rogoff's (1995) three planes of analysis to be useful for reducing extraneous details across cases and capturing aspects of change that otherwise maybe overlooked.

REFERENCES

Bean, R.M., Swan, A.L., & Knaub, R. (2003). Reading specialists in schools with exemplary reading programs: Functional, versatile, and prepared. *The Reading Teacher, 56*(5), 446–455.

Fisher, D. (n.d.). *Coaching considerations: FAQs useful in the development of literacy coaching.* Retrieved October 20, 2007, from www.literacycoachingonline.org/briefs/Coaching ConsiderationsFinal020707

Gall, M.D., Gall, J.P., & Borg, W.R. (2007). *Educational research: An introduction* (8th ed.). New York: Pearson.

Gee, J.P. (1996). *Social linguistics and literacies: Ideology in discourse* (2nd ed.). New York: Falmer.

Gee, J.P. (1999). *An introduction to discourse analysis: Theory and method.* London: Routledge.

Gray, J.H., & Tatar, D. (2004). Sociocultural analysis of online professional development: A case study of personal, interpersonal, community, and technical aspects. In S.A. Barab, R. Kling, & J.H. Gray (Eds.), *Designing for virtual communities in the service of learning* (pp. 404–436). New York: Cambridge University Press.

International Reading Association. (2004a). *The role and qualifications of the reading coach in the United States.* Newark, DE: Author.

International Reading Association. (2004b). *Standards for reading professionals—revised 2003.* Newark, DE: Author.

Lave, J., & Wenger, E. (1991). *Situated learning: Legitimate peripheral participation.* New York: Cambridge University Press.

Merriam, S.B. (1998). *Qualitative research and case study applications in education.* San Francisco: Jossey-Bass.

Rainville, K.N. (2007). Situated identities, power, and positioning: Inside the practices of three literacy coaches in New Jersey. *Dissertation Abstracts International, 68*(6), 259. (UMI 3269108)

Richards, J.C. (2006). Preservice teachers' professional development in a community of practice summer literacy camp for children at-risk: A sociocultural perspective. *The*

Qualitative Report, 11(4), 771–794. Retrieved October 20, 2007, from www.nova.edu/ssss/QR/QR11-4/richards.pdf

Rogoff, B. (1990). *Apprenticeship in thinking: Cognitive development in social context.* New York: Oxford University Press.

Rogoff, B. (1995). Observing sociocultural activity on three planes: Participatory, appropriation, guided participation, and apprenticeship. In J.V. Wertsch, P. Del Rio, & A. Alvarez (Eds.), *Sociocultural studies of mind* (pp. 139–164). New York: Cambridge University Press.

Rogoff, B. (1997). Evaluating development in the process of participation: Theory, methods, and practice building on each other. In E. Amsel & K.A. Renninger (Eds.), *Change and development: Issues of theory, method, and application* (pp. 265–285). Mahwah, NJ: Erlbaum.

Rogoff, B. (2003). *The cultural nature of human development.* New York: Oxford University Press.

Rogoff, B., Baker-Sennett, J., Lacasa, P., & Goldsmith, D. (1995). Development through participation in sociocultural activity. In J.J. Goodnow, P.J. Miller, & F. Kessel (Eds.), *Cultural practice as contexts for development* (pp. 45–65). San Francisco: Jossey-Bass.

Rogoff, B., & Topping, K. (2002). Mutual contributions of individuals, partners, and institutions: Planning to remember in Girl Scout cookie sales. *Social Development, 11*(2), 266–289. doi:10.1111/1467-9507.00198

Toll, C.A. (2005). *The literacy coach's survival guide: Essential questions and practical answers.* Newark, DE: International Reading Association.

Vygotsky, L. (1978). *Mind in society: The development of higher psychological processes* (M. Cole, V. John-Steiner, S. Scribner, & E. Souberman, Eds. & Trans.). Cambridge, MA: Harvard University Press.

ABOUT THE CONTRIBUTOR

Nina L. Nilsson *is an assistant professor who teaches graduate and undergraduate literacy-related courses in the Department of Education at Saint Joseph's University, Philadelphia, Pennsylvania, USA. Throughout her career in higher education, she has worked closely with university-based, after-school extended learning programs geared toward supporting and advancing struggling readers. A former elementary school teacher and reading specialist, she focuses her research on issues related to the reading development of diverse and challenged learners. Her work also encompasses the professional development of preservice and inservice teachers in areas related to the literacy instruction of struggling readers. E-mail: nnilsson@sju.edu*

SECTION III

Summer Literacy Programs

Allington and McGill-Franzen (2003) caution that

> Summer setback affects children from families of different socioeconomic groups differently. Available research indicates that the reading achievement of poor children, as a group, typically declines during the summer vacation period, while the reading achievement of children from more economically advantaged families holds steady or increases modestly. (p. 69)

Schools and community programs have heeded this warning by initiating effective summer programs that provide rich literacy experiences to children at risk across the nation. By providing materials, instruction, and motivation to children, tutors have helped enhance students' reading development in varied types of summer programs. Section III presents examples of these diverse summer tutoring initiatives.

John S. Burgin, Patricia E. Bandré, and Gail D. Hughes describe in Chapter 13 a quality summer program for children in kindergarten through grade 4 who live in a high-poverty neighborhood. The program not only provides literacy experiences for elementary students, but also it prepares education students from the University of Arkansas in Little Rock to teach reading and provides professional development for novice classroom teachers. This chapter examines whether Literacy Camp participants became knowledgeable about reading strategies and if children's abilities to talk about reading strategies they have learned related to improved reading comprehension.

Erin K. Jurand writes about another effective literacy camp in Chapter 14. The study of students' progress during this three-and-a-half-week writing program focused on how embedding visualization strategies in the writing process influenced students' individual writing scores according to the 6-Trait Analytical Model. Working with 19 students in kindergarten through grade 4, she found students learned to view and use their visual environment as a tool to help them write.

Chapter 15 takes us to Let's Make Movies Camp, where the campers learn filmmaking by making their own films. James L. Welsh, Deborah A. Kozdras, James R. King, and Jenifer Schneider propose, however, the campers are not just having fun;

they are "braiding" literacy and video experiences in ways that require students to compose and make meaning, participate in active learning, collaborate with others, and problem solve.

Joyce C. Fine and Lynne D. Miller's Chapter 16 details a community literacy club that presents structured, targeted instruction around informational books. The authors look particularly at how students' comprehension and fluency were influenced by their program.

The programs described in Section III demonstrate that even short summer efforts, when focused, can stop students from sliding backward in their literacy progress over the months when regular school is out of session. All of the contributors to this section offer evidence-based information that illuminates how and why their summer literacy programs work, and they provide details you can use to launch successful summer reading programs, as well.

REFERENCE

Allington, R., & McGill-Franzen, A. (2003). The impact of summer reading setbacks and the reading achievement gap. *Phi Delta Kappan, 85*(1), 68–75.

CHAPTER 13

Literacy Camp: An Effective Summer Intervention

John S. Burgin, Patricia E. Bandré, and Gail D. Hughes

Literacy interview question #1: How do you decide if you want to read a book? When you get a new book, what do you do or think about before you read it?

I get a little scared. I take a deep breath.

Open the book?

Say the first word.

Get happy!

Get a hot dog!

Get a drink of water.

Say thank you mom, but that's too much books!

Clean up. We're not supposed to read it when we get back from lunch.

Ask the teacher if I know how to read it.

Read the title. Keep it safe from people that try to hurt it.

I think about what if the book tears up so I'll put it back if it's loose.

Ask what the title is. Do a picture walk. See if something surprising happened.

These examples of children's answers to our first literacy interview question illustrate some of the more humorous ways in which children in Literacy Camp thought about literacy at the beginning of the program. We started Literacy Camp five years ago to create opportunities for the following:

- A quality summer program for children in kindergarten through grade 4 who live in a high-poverty neighborhood

- A practicum experience for graduate students in reading at the University of Arkansas at Little Rock (UALR)

- Professional development for new classroom teachers from the schools that host our program

- A research project to generate data that could be used to inform instruction

Two schools served as a site for Literacy Camp. Each agreed to help collect assessment

Literacy Tutoring That Works: A Look at Successful In-School, After-School, and Summer Programs, edited by Janet C. Richards and Cynthia A. Lassonde. © 2009 International Reading Association.

data and to use Title I funds to hire five classroom teachers. Literacy Camp consisted of two one-month-long sessions with approximately 60 children in kindergarten through grade 4 who participated in each session. Children attended Monday through Friday from 8:00 A.M. until 11:30 A.M. Breakfast was served. Each classroom was staffed with a graduate student paired with a classroom teacher. Teachers ate lunch together and met until 1:30 P.M. to problem solve and plan the next day of instruction. Maximum class size was 15, but the average class was about 10 children. We assigned children to classes based on their reading level rather than their grade. The curriculum was based on Dorn and Soffos's (2001) comprehensive literacy approach and Clay's (1993b) conception of a Reading Recovery lesson.

Following is a generic schedule for the program, but teachers were free to rearrange the elements:

- Breakfast (20 minutes): Teachers eat with the children much like a family meal.
- Familiar Reading (20 minutes): Children quietly read several of their favorite books. Teachers administer informal reading assessments with individual children.
- Shared Reading and Interactive Read-Aloud (45 minutes): Whole groups chorally read fun texts and anchor charts. The teacher reads aloud to the class books by an author the class has chosen to study. Teachers and children cooperatively construct anchor charts comparing and contrasting the author's books.
- Guided Reading (45 minutes): Small groups read texts at the appropriate level. Books are purchased with grant funds and sent home with the children as gifts.
- Writer's Workshop (1 hour): Whole-group strategy minilesson is followed by individual conferences in small groups. Minilesson topics often include writing conventions, procedures for publication, and writer's checklists. By the end of the program, each class publishes a classroom newspaper of student work.
- Interactive Read-Aloud and Writer's Share Time (20 minutes): Books are introduced and discussed much like a new book for a guided reading lesson. Teachers model making text-to-text, text-to-self, and text-to-world connections as they read. Share time emphasizes children reading their texts from writer's workshop.

Several aspects of the curriculum and format were key to the program's success. First, there were two teachers in each classroom and the teacher–student ratio was low. This enabled teachers to provide individual attention in small groups during guided reading and writer's workshop. Rather than teach spelling as a whole-group activity with the same words for all the children, teachers had the time to take advantage of teachable moments. In other words, when a child did not know how to spell a particular word, teachers modeled problem-solving strategies and did word work with the child within the context of what the child was reading or writing at the time.

Also central to the program's success was daily rather than weekly planning and the direct relationship between the assessments we administered and the plans teachers collaboratively created each afternoon. In addition to the running records, observation notes, and writing samples collected each day, the results of a literacy interview we administered individually at the beginning of the program helped determine the scope and sequence of the summer program.

We created a literacy interview to narrow the focus of instruction and build children's awareness of their cognitive processes. Much like Reading Recovery sessions (Clay, 1993b), instruction progressed from modeling a new strategy, to prompting for strategies, then to holding the child accountable for orally articulating problem-solving strategies. Teachers used the results of the preprogram literacy interview to systematically build developmentally appropriate checklists one item at a time before the author study and read-aloud, writer's workshop, and guided reading.

Once a majority of children demonstrated the ability to use an item on the anchor chart, teachers added another item. Anchor chart topics included how to figure out a word you don't know, how to skim a new book, how to plan what you are going to write, how to revise and edit, and how to spell an unknown word. The results from the preprogram interview were used to plan instruction, and the results from the postprogram interview provided data for evaluation. In this way, we aligned our curriculum, instruction, assessment, and evaluation.

Questions Guiding the Research

The overarching research question for our study was straightforward: Does Literacy Camp make any difference in children's literacy achievement? More specifically we wanted to know the following:

- Will Literacy Camp positively affect children's ability to articulate problem-solving strategies?
- Does the ability to articulate problem-solving strategies correlate with children's increased reading and writing ability?

After the first year of Literacy Camp, teachers believed children's writing abilities improved substantially, but they did *not* believe that a comparison of Developmental Reading Assessment (DRA, 1997) scores before and after camp would document significant gains in reading level. Regardless of reading level increases, teachers believed that children's reading strategies at point of difficulty improved.

During the second and third year of the program, we collected writing samples before (pre) and after (post) the program for 140 summer school children who had attended camp at least 70% of the time and compared them to a matched control group of children who did not attend. We matched children by reading score, writing score, gender, school and grade, and primary language. The results suggest that kindergarten, third-, and fourth-grade children experienced significant growth in writing ability as a result of the summer program. Although first- and second-grade children's gains were not significant, their peers in the control group experienced a significant "summer loss" (Burgin & Hughes, in press) because their writing scores in the fall were lower than their spring scores.

> We still had no way to measure children's improved strategic reading ability other than using preprogram and postprogram [data].

Our intuition that children's writing abilities improved was validated, but we still had no way to measure children's improved strategic reading ability other than using preprogram and postprogram DRA (1997) levels. During the third and fourth years of the program, we created the literacy interview and collected preprogram and postprogram data to measure children's abilities to articulate problem-solving strategies. Then, during the fifth year of the program, we administered a revised version of the interview and collected a parallel set of preprogram and postprogram running records (Clay, 1993a) and scored writing samples to estimate the construct validity of the interview.

Theoretical Background and Perspectives

Different types of reading and writing surveys and interviews are common in the literature (Atwell, 1998; Au, Mason, & Scheu, 1995; Gambrell, Palmer, Codling, & Mazzoni, 1996; Kear, Coffman, McKenna, & Ambrosio, 2000; Messina & Baker, 2003). Originally developed in the late 1960s, the Burke Reading Interview (Goodman, Watson, & Burke, 1987) is one of the earliest and perhaps the most influential, and the Garfield Reading Attitude Survey is probably the most well known (McKenna & Kear, 1990).

The surveys and interviews available in the literature had several drawbacks for the purposes of our research:

- The majority of instruments focused on intermediate-age children.

- Many surveys used a multiple-choice format inappropriate for primary-age children.

- The purposes of the instruments were to assess attitude, confidence, motivation, or interests rather than knowledge and understanding of reading and writing strategies.

- Although several instruments vaguely referred to tracking changes over time, the stated purpose of the instruments was to plan instruction and choose texts of interest.

- With the exception of the Garfield Reading Attitude Survey (McKenna & Kear, 1990) and DRA grades 4–8 (2003), instruments offered no scoring system or rubric to evaluate responses, but even these had very limited utility. The Garfield Reading Attitude Survey offers percentile ranks to compare individual scores by grade level to a national sample, while the DRA grades 4–8 uses students' written responses concerning "wide reading" and "self-assessment and goal setting" as a very small part of the scoring rubric to determine the students' instructional reading level.

For the purposes of this study, the Burke Reading Interview (Goodman et al., 1987) was the best match. The interview generates strategic rather than strictly attitudinal information, it is appropriate for primary-age children, and it is designed to be a one-on-one interview rather than a written survey. Although a scoring system was once developed, its expressed purpose was to "help teachers understand the wide variety of possible student responses to each question" (J.C. Harste, 2006, personal communication). The scoring system was never widely published, nor was it ever used to document changes over time in reading behaviors. Regardless of its strengths and weaknesses, the Burke Reading Interview's reading-strategies questions served as a model for the instrument used in this study. We created parallel-writing questions.

Methodology

Participants

Three faculty members developed the questions, agreed on prompts and probes, and administered the literacy interviews. All children (92% free or reduced-cost lunch; 83% African American, 15% Latino, 2% Other) in grades K–4 were interviewed during the first (preprogram interview) and last two days of each session (postprogram interview). Prompting or probing was especially important with the younger children in this study because they seemed satisfied to answer with only a nod of their head or a word or two in response. The entire interview was structured, rather than informal, to facilitate the comparison of pre and post responses. University of Arkansas at Little Rock (UALR) faculty interviewed children in the hallway outside their classroom for the first two years of the study.

Data Sources

Our data are divided into two sets. Data Set 1 comprises 94 of the 140 children who attended 70% of a session during the third and fourth years of the program. Lack of attendance at the very beginning or end of a session and our decision not to interview children with a DRA level of less than 3 reduced our sample size substantially. (Responses of children with a DRA level less than 3 tended to be off topic because the questions were developmentally inappropriate.)

During the fifth year of the program, we created Data Set 2 with 68 children. This data set was compiled separately because we learned from our past experience and improved the data collection protocol. Improvements included the following:

- A substantial revision of the interview
- The decision to have the classroom teachers conduct the interviews
- The decision to sort the data by the reading level ranges associated with kindergarten through grade 4 rather than their actual age and grade level
- Our exclusion of children from the total N who had a perfect score on any question during the preprogram interview
- The collection of parallel sets of pre- and postprogram scored writing samples and running records

During the first summer we used the interview, we piloted the instrument to test the questions. We eliminated some of the questions after the first and second years because younger children generated off-topic responses, or because other questions better addressed the topic. We retained two yes/no questions as a warm-up: Are you a good reader? Are you a good writer? Two questions provided a context and scenario for prompts and probes: What is your favorite book? What do you like to write about? By far, the most important revision came from refining our prompts and probes for common answers.

During the pilot of the literacy interview, we identified four core questions that seemed to consistently resonate with children. These questions were common to the revised interview and the pilot. Core questions are italicized in the following numbered list of revised literacy interview questions. In the results section of this chapter, the four core questions are referred to in figures as Q1 Book, Q2 Word, Q3 Spell, and Q4 Edit. Our standardized prompts to common answers are in parentheses:

> "Help teachers understand the wide variety of possible student responses to each question."

1. Do you ever read for fun? What is your favorite book?

2. Do you think you are a good reader? What makes you a good reader?

3. *How do you decide if you want to read a book? When you get a new book, what do you do or think about before you read it? (How do you do a picture walk? How do you skim a new book?) Anything else?* (Q1 Book)

4. *When you are reading, what do you do when you get stuck or come to a word you don't know? (What does "sound it out" or "skip it" mean? What do you do?)* (Q2 Word)

5. Do you think you are a good writer? What do you like to write about?

6. When you write a new story, what do you think about before you start writing?

How do you plan what you want to say? What do you do?

7. *What do you do when you don't know how to spell a word? (What does "sound it out" mean? What does "write it down" mean? What do you do?)* (Q3 Spell)

8. *When you are finished writing down everything you want to say (sloppy copy or first draft), what do you do next? (Revise or edit? What do you look for?)* (Q4 Edit)

Certainly the literacy interview is a credible means of planning and focusing instruction, but using a comparison of the results from the preprogram interviews to the postprogram interviews to document the success of the program requires a higher standard—construct validity. We needed reliable reading and writing scores to address our second research question, Does the ability to articulate problem-solving strategies correlate with increased performance in reading and writing ability? Developing a rubric to sort responses from the literacy interview was a straightforward process, but the collection of reliable reading and writing scores presented several challenges.

Data Analysis

READING ASSESSMENT. Schools provided spring DRA (1997) scores that we used to form reading groups for the summer, but fall scores were not available because the district used spring scores to create fall reading groups. Administering over 200 DRA tests ourselves in a timely manner was simply too large a task and would have taken too much time away from instruction over the short summer session.

During the first few years of the program, we thought the running records (Clay, 1993a) we generated were not formal enough to be credible for research purposes. In later years, we realized our running records were more reliable than the DRA (1997) scores provided to us by the schools because the reading levels assigned to children were based on reading multiple texts over the first few days of Literacy Camp, not just one running record or DRA administration. Likewise, the postprogram reading levels were based on the teacher's experience with the child in guided reading groups rather than any one administration of an informal assessment. We decided the running record scores were reliable enough to be used as preprogram and postprogram data for this study.

WRITING ASSESSMENT. The results of our previous efforts to use scored writing samples to evaluate the summer program (Burgin & Hughes, in press b) were also limited by the quality of the data we collected from the local schools. The quality of the scoring rubrics the local school district provided varied widely. The rubrics used for kindergarten, first and second grades, and third and fourth grades differed substantially. The kindergarten instrument was a holistic rubric with anchor papers, and the third- and fourth-grade analytic rubric was excellent. However, the instrument used for the first and second grades was really a checklist in which the checks were added up to calculate the 1 through 4 scoring range. Consequently, the interrater reliability estimates for the spring scores in grades 1 and 2 were not acceptable.

We addressed these limitations by having the two participating schools trade papers. Teachers scored the samples a second time and averaged the two scores. We further examined the reliability of the writing scores using generalizability theory (Crocker & Algina, 1986) to estimate the amount of benefit a second scoring added to measures of reliability (Burgin & Hughes, in press a). This analysis demonstrated that averaging the two writing scores did indeed produce numbers reliable enough to be used for research purposes.

Consequently, we decided that the writing samples we collected for our new data set needed to be scored twice using the same rubric for all the samples for kindergarten through grade 4. We chose the primary version of the 6-Trait Analysis (2005) as a model because the range of behaviors it described was appropriate for both our primary-aged children and the third- and fourth-grade children in our study. Although the rubric was not designed for intermediate-aged children, our intuition was validated when only one of the children topped out on the scale on the preprogram test.

The writing samples we used for preprogram analysis were collected by the local schools at the end of the school year. All the samples were written in one sitting in response to the district's grade-level prompts. The postprogram writing samples were collected during the last two days of Literacy Camp, in one sitting, in response to prompts that were similar to the district's grade-level prompts. Prior to scoring the writing samples, we scored several papers together and created concrete examples to help us agree on the meaning of the descriptors within the 6-Trait primary rubric (2005). After each of us had scored the papers using a 5-point scale across the traits (ideas, organization, voice, word choice, sentence fluency, and conventions), we averaged the trait scores to create a single writing score.

LITERACY INTERVIEW. We transcribed children's responses to interview questions and sorted them by core question number, preprogram interview, postprogram interview, and session attended. We then listed the responses in rank order by DRA (1997) scores from lowest to highest. One person read the responses in order, noting commonalities, and roughly ranking statements on a three-point scale. The same person then repeated the process using the newly revised descriptors and a 4-point scale. Repeating the process again finally generated a 5-point rubric for each core question (see Table 13.1). A second person then scored the children's responses using that rubric. Rather than averaging scores, we met to discuss the differences in our scoring, reached a consensus, and improved the rubric further.

> Rather than averaging scores, we met to discuss the differences in our scoring, reached a consensus, and improved the rubric further.

Limitations

The ability to articulate spelling and revising strategies is not the same thing as being able to write better stories, and tables of percentage increases from preprogram to postprogram *cannot* establish "construct validity" for the literacy interview questions. One hundred and sixty-two children's responses to four questions are an inadequate sample, and quantifying literacy is *not* that simple. Nonetheless, this study represents our efforts to reflect on the way we organized Literacy Camp. Ideally, the lessons we learned will help us to do a better job next year, and our experience will help others start their own programs.

Pragmatically, only two questions matter:

1. Did holding children accountable for articulating problem-solving strategies help them write better stories and read books more fluently?

2. Did interviewing children and constructing anchor charts help focus instruction during the short summer session?

Table 13.1 Literacy Interview Scoring Rubrics for Four Core Questions

Question	Response-Scoring Guide
Q1 Book: How do you pick a book? What do you do before you read a new book?	1. Off topic or "Don't know," i.e., "Get a hot dog!" 2. One strategy without explanation of use, i.e., "Look at pictures" or "Read the title" 3. Two or more strategies without explanation of use 4. At least one strategy with explanation of use, i.e., "Look at the back cover to see if it sounds interesting" or "Read the title and make predictions about what it will be about" 5. Multiple strategies with at least one explanation of use
Q2 Word: What do you do when you come to a word that you do not know?	1. Passive, i.e., "Look, "Ask," or "Don't know" 2. One strategy without explanation of use, i.e., "Sound it out," "Skip it," or "Dictionary" 3. Two strategies without explanation of use 4. One strategy with an explanation of use, i.e., "Break apart the word and look for parts I know" or "Skip it and reread the sentence" 5. Multiple cuing systems (auditory and visual) with at least one explanation of use, i.e., "Break apart the word and look for parts I know" and "Skip it"
Q3 Spell: What do you do when you don't know how to spell a word?	1. Passive, i.e., "Ask my teacher" 2. One strategy without explanation of use, i.e., "Sound it out" or "Look in the dictionary" 3. Two strategies without explanation of use 4. One strategy with an explanation of use, i.e., "Think of a rhyming word I can spell," "Say it slowly and write what I hear," or "Write it down to see if it looks right" 5. Two or more strategies that refer to visual and auditory cues with at least one explanation of use
Q4 Edit: When you read over your work, what do you look for?	1. No response or response that does not refer to revise/edit, i.e., "Name and date" 2. Reference to mechanics (spell, caps, periods) only or reference to "make sense" only 3. Mechanics and "make sense" 4. Mechanics or word choice (verbs, adjectives) and "make sense" with explanation of use 5. Mechanics or word choice and "make sense" and revise content (opening, sequence, ending)

We think so, but it is the reader of this chapter who ultimately must decide if the data support our conclusions.

Results

Data Set 1: Two Years of Data

In Table 13.2, the percentages of all children demonstrating a gain are disaggregated by grade level and question number. A one-sample z-test for proportions revealed that we could expect to see a difference in at least 70% of the population ($z = 2.32$, $p < 0.05$, one-tailed) if the program was replicated with another group.

In response to Q1 Book: What do you do before you read a new book? 81% of the children (76/94) learned to preview a text to gather information before they began reading. A one-sample z-test for proportions suggests we could expect to see a difference in at least 50% of a

Table 13.2 Data Set 1: Percentage of Participants With Gains by Grade Level and Question

Data Set 1	Kindergarten (n = 9)*	First (n = 28)	Second (n = 27)	Third/Fourth (n = 27)	All Children (N = 94)
Q1 Book	67	57	63	67	59/94 = 63
Q2 Word	78	71	89	81	76/94 = 81
Q3 Spell	56	71	52	52	55/94 = 59
Q4 Edit	44	54	44	52	46/94 = 49

Note. Children with a DRA (1997) score of less than 3 were excluded from the study.

comparable population that attended Literacy Camp ($z = 5.96$, $p < 0.05$, one-tailed). Furthermore, 53/76 or 70% of the children experiencing growth had gains of more than 1 point on the 5-point scale. Theoretically, these strategies help children better use meaning as a cuing system to problem solve, improve their comprehension, and help them make better book choices.

Sixty-three percent of children (59/94) increased the number of strategies they were able to articulate when faced with an unknown word in a text (Q2 Word). A one-sample z-test for proportions suggests that we could expect to see a difference in at least 50% of another similar group ($z = 2.46$, $p < 0.05$, one-tailed). Additionally, 29/59 or 49% of the children made gains of more than 1 point. A majority of children developed several strategies to handle unknown words. Consequently, they should be able to quickly cross-check and use multiple cuing systems to problem solve.

In response to Q3 Spell: What do you do when you do not know how to spell a word? 59% of the children (55/94) moved beyond passive spelling strategies or were able to articulate multiple strategies for spelling unknown words. A one-sample z-test for proportions predicts similar gains for at least 50% of children from another population ($z = 1.83$, $p < 0.05$, one-

tailed). Moreover, 30/55 or 55% exhibited gains of more than 1 point. As a result, younger children should become able to write more independently, focus more on the message and less on the challenges of transcription, and require less teacher support.

When asked Q4 Edit (When you read over your work, what do you look for?) the responses demonstrate that children became better at revising and editing their work. Forty-nine percent (46/94) were able to articulate multiple strategies. Most gains were of only 1 point on the scale; yet, on this particular scale, 1 point represents a huge cognitive shift. Obviously, the younger children (kindergarten and grade 1) were not developmentally ready for behaviors at the top of the scale. Instead they tended to move from passive to active strategies rather than up the scale to more sophisticated strategies like writing a good lead. Regardless of age, very few children were able to articulate strategies at the top of the scale.

Data Set 2: Revised Survey Results

Regardless of the differences between the pilot and revised literacy interview, Table 13.3 documents similar percentages of children with gains for both Data Set 1 and Data Set 2. The effects of excluding children who scored a 5 on the pre-program interview can clearly be seen for Q1

Table 13.3 Data Set 2: Children With Gains Compared With Data Set 1

N = 68	First grade DRA 3–16	Second grade DRA 18–28	Third grade DRA 30–38	Fourth grade DRA 40+	Total Set 2	Total Set 1
Q1 Book	20(1)*	18(5)	7(6)	3(5)	44/51 = 86%	81%
Q2 Word	14(0)	12(0)	10(2)	8(1)	44/65 = 68%	62%
Q3 Spell	11(1)	10(2)	6(1)	7(1)	33/63 = 52%	59%
Q4 Edit	13(0)	5(0)	8(0)	3(0)	27/68 = 40%	49%

Note. Numbers in parentheses indicate children who had the highest possible score on the preprogram DRA and were excluded from the total.

Book. In Data Set 2, 86% of children experienced gains, but in Data Set 1 only 81% of children gained. Seventeen children were excluded from the total for Q1 Book because they could already articulate strategies to preview a book before the Camp started. Conversely, no student was awarded a perfect score on the preprogram interview for Q4 Edit. Although children in Data Set 2 scored higher on average in response to Q1 Book and Q2 Word, children in Data Set 1 scored higher on Q3 Spell and Q4 Edit. Nonetheless, the similarities between Data Sets 1 and 2 address a serious limitation of Data Set 2—sample size. The total N for both studies was 162. The consistency of the results was remarkable and builds credibility for the results of both data sets.

Table 13.4 represents the number of children who scored higher on the postprogram interview, the postprogram running records, or both. Overall, 81% of children had a higher postprogram score on running records or the literacy interview. Sixty percent of children gained on both running records and at least one question from the literacy interview. Thirty-seven percent of children scored higher on running records and both reading interview questions. As expected, the lack of gains for children who read above a DRA (1997) level 40 depressed the overall percentage of student gains. The percentage that improved on both the reading test and on

the interview was much higher in the DRA range of 3 to 38.

Unexpectedly, three children's running record scores went up, but their scores on Q1 Book and Q2 Word did not. Seventy-five percent of children with higher running records scores also improved on the reading interview questions. Overall, the interview questions seemed to be a reliable predictor of higher running record scores at the end of the program. The results for children with higher postprogram writing scores were equally encouraging (see Table 13.5).

Overall, 71% of the children's postprogram writing scores increased. Eighty-two percent of children scored higher on the 6-Trait Analysis (2005) of their postprogram writing sample or on the literacy interview rubric, but only 49% scored higher on both measures. Surprisingly, 22% of the children scored higher on the writing sample, but their responses to literacy interview questions Q3 Spell and Q4 Edit did not improve. These results suggest that the construct validity of the writing interview questions was lower than for the reading questions. More importantly, these results highlight the limitations of this study.

Implications

Certainly, we do not think that articulating problem-solving strategies causes higher read-

Table 13.4 Children With Reading Gains on Running Records or Interview Responses

N = 68	1st DRA 3–16	2nd 18–28	3rd 30–38	4th 40+*	Total
Read gain only	3	0	0	0	3/68 = 4%
Q1 & Q2 Only	3	2	3	3	11/68 = 16%
Q1 or Q2 + Read	9	5	1	1	16/68 = 24%
Q1 + Q2 + Read	7	8	9	1	25/68 = 37%
Total Read Gain	22/26 = 85%	15/19 = 79%	13/13 = 100%	4/10 = 40%	55/68 = 81%
Total Gain Q + R	16/26 = 62%	13/19 = 68%	10/13 = 77%	2/10 = 20%	41/68 = 60%

Note. Children with a DRA of 40+ were least likely to make gains in a short period; their inclusion depressed overall scores.

Table 13.5 Children With Writing Gains on 6-Trait Analysis (2005) or Interview Responses

N = 61*	1st DRA 3–16	2nd 18–28	3rd 30–38	4th 40+	Total
Write gain only	8	3	1	1	13/61 = 21%
Q3 & Q4 Only	3	1	1	2	7/61 = 11%
Q3 or Q4 + Write	4	9	3	2	18/61 = 30%
Q3 + Q4 + Write	5	2	3	2	12/61 = 20%
Total Write Gain	20/25 = 80%	15/17 = 89%	8/9 = 89%	7/10 = 70%	50/61 = 82%
Total Q + Write	9/25 = 36%	11/17 = 65%	6/9 = 67%	4/10 = 40%	30/61 = 49%

Note. Seven writing samples were compromised due to human error; consequently, we excluded the children's interview scores.

ing scores, but the results of this study suggest that it helps. The results lend credibility to the practice of prompting children to articulate strategies, and building anchor charts was a good way to teach children to articulate strategies before shared reading, guided reading, and writer's workshop. Certainly, asking children about what they think or like is an important part of providing effective instruction that builds on children's background experiences and connects their experiences to new ideas and texts.

Words of Advice

The literacy interview was an important tool during Literacy Camp, but other factors were more significant contributors to the successes of our summer program. Having two teachers in each classroom, reducing class sizes, and grouping children by DRA level had powerful effects. Equally important were affective issues that should not be underestimated. Simple things often affected the participants' attitudes about the summer program, such as the following

- It is important to relieve teachers of the burden of teaching multiple subject areas. Teachers should be able to focus on doing one thing well. Give them the luxury of time to plan daily, so if something doesn't work, they can simply change it without affecting the rest of the schedules they have to follow during the regular school year. Time to experiment can help them work through new ideas and become more efficient when they are pressed for time in the fall.

- Literacy Camp teachers reported that the most important part of the summer program for them was the bonds that they formed with their coteachers, and the professional development that took place during their informal conversations.

- Labels matter. For example, the term *summer school* often has negative connotations because it is associated with failing. During our first year of the program, we found that some of the parents and children objected to the insinuation that they had not done well in school the previous year, so we started calling the summer program Literacy Camp.

- Mixing age groups can be empowering to both older and younger learners. Even children reading at or above their grade level are at risk in a high-poverty neighborhood, so our population was not limited to children who struggled during the regular school year, and classroom rolls were not restricted by age. Forming classes around DRA (1997) scores allows for mixed age groups—older children with DRA levels lower than their grade level, and younger children with higher DRA levels. This allows the older children to be the experts in the top group in their classroom, and younger children get to hang out with older children.

- Attitudes affected the curriculum as well. Establish a routine, focus the curriculum, and build a team as quickly as possible. It was also important to us that we not teach isolated skills. In an effort to address both concerns, we used themes like the author study to make the curriculum meaningful. Articulating problem-solving strategies was briefly the focus of instruction at the beginning of group activities, but the overall focus was determined by content of the books we read, the texts we wrote, and the connections we made.

- Publishing our own classroom newspapers narrowed the focus further, generated a theme, and provided a common purpose for the class. Children took pride in the final document. Likewise, the 10 or more books each child took home were gifts that kept on giving.

To make a long story short, no one thing mattered most. It was the little things that added up to a sum greater than its parts. We hope our experiences will give our audience ideas. Ultimately, replication is the only test of significance that matters.

REFERENCES

Atwell, N. (1998). *In the middle: New understandings about writing, reading, and learning* (2nd ed.). Portsmouth, NH: Boynton/Cook.

Au, K.H., Mason, J.M., & Scheu, J.A. (1995). *Literacy instruction for today.* New York: HarperCollins College.

Burgin, J.S. , & Hughes, G.D. (in press a). Credibly assessing reading and writing abilities for both student and program assessment. *Assessing Writing: An International Journal 14(1).*

Burgin, J.S., & Hughes, G.D. (in press b). Using writing samples to measure the effects of a summer literacy program for low SES elementary children. *Research in the Schools.*

Clay, M. (1993a). *An observational survey of early literacy achievement.* Portsmouth, NH: Heinemann.

Clay, M. (1993b). *Reading Recovery: A guidebook for teachers in training.* Portsmouth, NH: Heinemann.

Crocker, L., & Algina, J. (1986). *Introduction to classical and modern test theory.* Fort Worth, TX: Harcourt Brace College.

Dorn, L., & Soffos, C. (2001). *Shaping literate minds: Developing self-regulated learners.* Portland, ME: Stenhouse.

Gambrell, L.B., Palmer, B.M., Codling, R.M., & Mazzoni, S.A. (1996). Assessing motivation to read. *The Reading Teacher, 49(7),* 518–533. doi:10.1598/RT.49.7.2

Goodman, Y.M., Watson, D.J., & Burke, C.L. (1987). *Reading miscue inventory: Alternative procedures.* New York: Richard C. Owen.

Kear, D.J., Coffman, G.A., McKenna, M.C., & Ambrosio, A.L. (2000). Measuring attitude toward writing: A new tool for teachers. *The Reading Teacher, 54(1),* 10–23.

McKenna, M.C., & Kear, D.J. (1990). Measuring attitude toward reading: A new tool for teachers. *The Reading Teacher*, 43(8), 626–639. doi:10.1598/RT.43.8.3

Messina, L., & Baker, E. (2003). Awaking the reader within. In A. Fielding, R. Schoenbach, & M. Jordan (Eds.), *Building academic literacy: Lessons from reading apprenticeship classrooms grades 6–12* (pp. 47–90). San Francisco: Jossey-Bass.

ABOUT THE CONTRIBUTORS

John S. Burgin *is an associate professor in the Early Childhood Education and Reading department at the University of Arkansas at Little Rock. In addition to his teaching responsibilities, he has been the director of a summer literacy program for children in the high-poverty area surrounding the university for six years. Previous to his tenure at UALR, he served as a kindergarten teacher, Title I Reading Specialist, and Reading Recovery Teacher in the Little Rock Public Schools for 20 years. E-mail: jsburgin@ualr.edu*

Patricia E. Bandré *is an assistant professor of reading education at the University of Arkansas at Little Rock. She holds a doctorate degree in children's literature and reading education from The Ohio State University. Her research interests focus on the acquisition and use of read-alouds in the classroom and student response to read-alouds. Prior to completing her doctoral studies, she taught intermediate grade students in rural Kansas. E-mail: pebandre@ualr.edu*

Gail D. Hughes *is an associate professor of educational foundations at the University of Arkansas at Little Rock where she focuses on graduate courses in research and statistics. She also serves as a coeditor for the* Journal of Educational Research, *copy editor for* Research in the Schools, *and is a member of the editorial board for* Educational Technology, Research, and Development. *E-mail: gdhughes@ualr.edu*

CHAPTER 14

Camp Imagination:
A Summer Writing Tutoring Program for Students at Risk

Erin K. Jurand

Mrs. Yost: [teacher and tutor] I have a story to tell. You know you cannot put a big, fat, heavy worm on your hook so I pulled it apart and all this red gunky stuff flew on me and my hands. I decided not to look at it and just pull. I had to put him on the hook and sometimes you have to double the worm up. If I had to write a story today, I would have to write about the long, thick worm. I am not an artist, but I will try to draw my storyline. I will use brown to draw a long, fat worm. Maybe, I will draw what he looked like after I pulled him apart. He did not look the same—separated with red yuckies coming out. Maybe, I should draw the hook. Remember the hook had that little snag on it so the worm does not slide off. Then, I will draw a worm on the hook.

Beyonce: [fourth grader who attends Camp Imagination] Oh, you could put it in order. You could put the whole worm first, then him pulled apart, and then put the worm on the hook.

Mrs. Yost: What is that called?

Beyonce: Organizing.

Mrs. Yost: [nodding] Good—and also sequencing. If you were going to visualize and write about fishing you could do this.

The incorporation of visualization in the writing process is the main focus of Camp Imagination, a summer tutoring program. Students from different schools within a district are bussed to one elementary school located near a military installation in the midwestern United States for writing instruction. The sum-mer tutoring program takes place from 8:30 to 11:30 A.M. every day for 3½ weeks and is separated into two instructional groups: primary (kindergarten and grade 1) and intermediate (grades 2 through 4).

I proposed the idea of a summer tutoring program based on the success I experienced

Literacy Tutoring That Works: A Look at Successful In-School, After-School, and Summer Programs, edited by Janet C. Richards and Cynthia A. Lassonde. © 2009 International Reading Association.

with my pilot exploration, the Flint Hills Youth Writing Camp at Kansas State University. I showed a video that documented the camp to my school district, and the district summer school committee decided a writing camp would be one of the four summer camps offered to students in the district. The district's summer camp adopted many of the recommendations I made to create the summer tutoring program for writers.

Questions Guiding the Research

My overarching question for the study described here was the following:

- How does visualization embedded in the writing process influence potential effects in the students' individual writing scores according to the 6-Trait Analytical Model (Spandel, 2004)?

My subquestions were as follows:

- What types of instructional methods, activities, and techniques engage struggling writers in visualization during the writer's workshop?
- What activities in a nontraditional summer school approach motivate students who struggle with writing?

Theoretical Background and Perspectives

Piaget's (Piaget & Inhelder, 2000) theory of cognitive development served as the main theoretical framework for the inquiry because elementary-age students are the focus of the study. Piaget noted four general stages of development that contribute to a child's cognitive ability: sensorimotor, preoperational, concrete-operational, and formal-operational. The preoperational and concrete-operational stages of development are of most importance to this study because of the students' ages, grade levels, and writing abilities. Piaget's theory advocates the use of concrete examples in the classroom to increase students' abilities to construct meaning.

A second framework comes from Vygotsky (1978), who theorized that language is developed through social interactions. He believed children's thinking develops in the context of actions in which the child engages and is internalized in social and cultural settings (Efland, 2002). The writing workshop encourages writers to interact with other writers to create social interaction and literacy practices.

> Visual literacy is "the ability to understand (read) and use (write) images and to think and learn in terms of images."

Visual literacy is also important to this study. Visual literacy is "the ability to understand (read) and use (write) images and to think and learn in terms of images, i.e., to think visually" (Hortin, 1983, p. 99). If visualization helps students' reading comprehension, it is plausible that visualization may help with writing.

An additional perspective comes from Graves (2003) who altered teachers' understanding of writing in the classroom when he coined the term *writing workshop*. Writing workshop consists of an uninterrupted block of time devoted to students' writing, sharing, and conferring with one another and their teacher (Atwell, 1987). The writing workshop allows students to develop writing in a safe, comfortable learning environment where students keep journals or notebooks and live "the writerly life" (Calkins, 1994) by taking daily notes on observations, feelings, or stories. Understanding how visualization in the writing process influences struggling learners requires understanding of the theories, research, and practices presented.

Methodology

Participants

Thirty-two students attended the first summer tutoring program. I selected 19 students in grades K–4 (4 kindergarteners, 6 first graders, 3 second graders, 2 third graders, and 4 fourth graders) to represent the range in developmental levels using the maximum variation sampling (Patton, 1990) technique. I chose this type of purposeful sampling to enable common patterns to emerge distributed across gender, race, and grade. Racial demographics of students I selected included 50% Caucasian, 28% African American, 11% Hispanic, and 2% biracial. I chose these particular students because they attended 17 of the 18 days of summer camp and showed an ability to be social and extroverted. A child's high attendance rate in the summer camp meant he or she participated in most of the visualization techniques. Social students spoke more in-depth and comfortably about how these techniques may contribute to their growth as writers.

The district's Curriculum and Instruction Department assigned five female certified classroom teachers to the summer writing camp. Each teacher had requested to teach summer school, and they had varying degrees of teaching experience. Three teachers taught the primary summer tutoring program of 15 students, and 2 teachers taught the intermediate summer tutoring program of 17 students to provide a low student–teacher ratio. The district Curriculum and Instruction Department paid their salaries.

INSTRUCTIONAL DESIGN. The summer tutoring program's main design incorporated visualiza- tion techniques to assist students through the writing processes. Students participated in four field experiences:

1. Fishing at the neighborhood pond
2. Hiking on the prairie
3. Visiting a local nature center
4. Touring the city fire department

Teachers chose field experiences to provide motivation for students to write because these real-world events gave students purpose and audience for their writing. The students recorded their immediate responses to the field experiences in their art/writing journals. After each field experience, both classes brainstormed ideas through discussion and review of digital photographs the teachers took. Once students determined a topic, they created an artistic representation of the subject using a variety of media that included markers, crayons, pencils, clay, and watercolors. For each writing project, students and teachers referred to the students' artwork.

The Picture-Writing strategy teachers used to integrate visual art as part of the prewriting process (Andrzejczak, Trainin, & Poldberg, 2005) served as the primary activity to incorporate visualization and the writing process. Each day of the summer tutoring program looked different, but Graves's (2003) writing workshop contributed daily to the tutoring framework. The day usually began with a minilesson inspired by Calkins (1994), consisting of a 10- to 20-minute block of instruction on topics such as choosing words, learning and practicing writing conventions, selecting writing topics, and using art to stimulate students' understanding of details. Students also learned how to write descriptive narratives, personal memoirs, and informational technical pieces. Teachers selected quality literature that served as touchstone literary pieces

(Nia, 1999) for the minilessons. These books illustrated different literary styles and provided schema prior to the field experiences.

Students drafted, revised, and edited ideas by sketching first and then writing in their art/writing journals similar to Olbrych's (2001) artists-writers workshop. During the revising and editing stages, students collaborated with one another. They traded papers and read their writing aloud to help them further develop details, increase word choice, and correct standard conventions to written language. Teacher–student conferring was an integral part of the summer tutoring program. Through conferences teachers counseled students on how to reread to ensure sentence fluency, stretch out sounds in words, and remain on topic.

Teachers modeled the writing process for the primary students. The teachers showed how to use the field experiences and the photographs to brainstorm ideas about which to draw, and then they modeled using the drawings to generate ideas about which to write. The revision techniques included how to read the writing aloud to oneself and to a partner to check for clarity and accuracy. During the revision process students reviewed their pictures and writing to ensure the two corresponded.

Students conferred with teachers before proceeding to the editing phase of writing. The conferences focused on using digital photographs and student-created artwork to add detail to writing. During the editing process teachers modeled counting the number of sounds they heard to help spell unfamiliar words, adding punctuation, and correcting capital letters. Students shared the final writing and art pieces during author's chair.

During revision, the intermediate group focused on increasing the level of detail. This group used techniques and tools, such as zooming in on an idea to narrow a writing topic and using a sentence-amplifier wheel to aid students with adding details in their work. Zooming in is a revising technique in which students use successively more detailed drawings of their storyline. In the editing process, intermediate students focused on writing conventions such as paragraph structure and format, spelling, and punctuation. The intermediate teachers modeled revising and editing techniques to the students. Then the students applied these techniques through self-revising and editing and peer revising and editing.

> Teacher–student conferring was an integral part of the summer tutoring program.

Camp culminated after three weeks of field experiences and writing. As a closing activity, the students chose their favorite experience and continued to develop the piece using the complete writing process. Each child then showcased his or her piece at the high school during an end-of-summer-school exhibition. One primary teacher, one intermediate teacher, and I evaluated all final pieces using the 6-Trait Analytic Model (Spandel, 2004).

EXPLICIT EXAMPLES OF INSTRUCTION. After hiking at the local prairie conservation area, the students reviewed the digital photographs taken of their experience. To begin, Mrs. Pullman (all names are pseudonyms), a primary teacher, had the primary students close their eyes and remember what they saw. She conducted a think-aloud and said, "I remember walking over the bridge, and it was going up and down a little. I remember when we were walking in the squishy mud. I remember trees." Students closed their eyes and Mrs. Pullman asked them to make a "mind movie," a term the students were familiar with from reading, to help them visualize. She told the students they were going to draw their favorite scene or memory from their hike the previous day. The students were instructed to refer to the digital photographs to recall events and inspire drawings. After drawing their favorite scene from the prairie, the primary teachers taped large charts which resembled eyes, a nose, a mouth, an ear, or a hand on the bulletin board. The teachers called on students to help them write describing words to match each sense by using their experiences from the prairie. Students shared ideas such as, "Tree was hard," "The sky was blue and gray," and "There were birds chirping." Once the charts were filled with descriptive words, teachers gave students the opportunity to write a descriptive poem reflecting their drawings. Students completed the poetry assignment using the word wall. The students shared their pictures and writings of their favorite part of the field trip to the prairie with one another.

> I kept all researcher notes in a daily journal in which I reflected on the day's lessons, activities, and observations.

The day after the field trip to the prairie reserve, the intermediate students talked with table partners about what they saw. The topic of the day's minilesson was comparing two objects to create a simile. The intermediate teacher, Mrs. Yost, modeled how she observed a 150-year-old tree during the field experience. She then found a digital photograph of the tree. While thinking aloud she thought of other objects that she had seen that looked similar to the tree. She compared the brown bark to dead grass. After writing the simile, students shared what they saw during their field experience with a partner and tried to create similes. Then the students completed their art/writing journal entry with a drawing and a description of the drawing comparing it to another object.

Data Sources

I collected data through extensive field observations of students and teachers. Data were videotaped sessions of the writer's workshop, student and teacher interviews, and student artwork and writing pieces. Additionally, I kept all researcher notes in a daily journal in which I reflected on the day's lessons, activities, and observations. This list is consistent with the types of data Yin (1989) suggests to collect when conducting qualitative research.

FIELD NOTES. I recorded observational field notes in chronological order and created a written account of what I heard, saw, experienced, and thought while collecting and analyzing information (Bogdan & Biklen, 2003). With Institutional Review Board approval, I was able to closely observe the students as they drew and wrote. I also was able to record student and teacher conversations.

STUDENT INTERVIEWS. I conducted individual and small-group interviews with the 19 selected students. To reduce noise and confusion between speakers, I also either individually interviewed students or paired students based on age, ability levels, and their demonstrated willingness to work together. I reworded and condensed interview questions as Davidson (1996) suggests to create less-confusing questions.

TEACHER INTERVIEWS. I interviewed teachers using purposeful conversations (Morgan, 1997) to obtain a deep understanding of the lessons during the summer tutoring program. I scheduled the teacher interviews toward the end of camp to provide more time for teacher reflections after using different visualization techniques. I documented informal interviews or conversations in the observational field notes.

ARTIFACTS. I duplicated or digitally photographed all student-created documents as they emerged to preserve the writing and drawing during the different stages of the writing process. I collected the baseline district criterion-referenced test scores and the final art/writing samples for all 19 students in both the primary and intermediate camps. Artifacts included student art/writing journals, artwork, and writing samples.

Data Analysis

INITIAL CODING. I reduced and organized the data (LeCompte & Schensul, 1999) to provide insight on how visualization embedded in the writing process might help struggling learners increase their 6-Trait scores. I evaluated the final writing pieces using the 6-Trait Analytical Model (Spandel, 2004) and coded them to determine the writing level of each piece. I used Spandel's Young Writer's Rubric to assess the primary camp students' writings because it addressed the K–1 students' writing levels and abilities clearly. I employed the Northwest Regional Educational Laboratory (NWREL)'s 6+1 Trait Rubric (NWREL, 2004) to assess the intermediate camp students' writings, because the Young Writer's Rubric (Spandel, 2004) does not address the level and abilities of students in the upper intermediate grades.

Although all of the 6 Traits are included in Spandel's (2004) model, the district evaluated certain traits at identified grade levels. I evaluated kindergarten and first-grade students' writing for the Ideas, Word Choice, and Conventions traits to maintain consistency with current district assessment standards. I assessed second-grade students' writing for the Ideas, Organization, Word Choice, and Conventions traits. I evaluated third- and fourth-grade students' writing on all 6 Traits: Ideas, Organiza-

tion, Voice, Word Choice, Sentence Fluency, and Conventions.

For the purposes of this study, I used the NWREL (2004) writing level names for the levels because of their correspondence to a 1 through 5 number scale described further here. Also, NWREL states it is possible for students in all grades to receive high scores for their writing. If a score fell between two whole numbers, I rounded it up to the nearest whole number (i.e., 2.5 = 3). With the individual trait scores assigned (1, the lowest, through 5, the highest), I averaged all scores and rounded the average score to the nearest whole number and matched the scores with a writing level. These levels are Not Yet (1), Emerging (2), Developing (3), Effective (4), and Strong (5). This method of assessing individual trait scores, determining their averages and corresponding writing levels is consistent with NWREL's and the district's methods of evaluation.

FOCUSED CODING. After initial coding of student writing samples, I began to focus code the field notes and interviews using categorical aggregation (Stake, 1995) to search for meaning in the data. The field notes, read and analyzed in chronological order, revealed certain repeated words and phrases. I identified the code of motivation, or the source that motivated students to write and to learn to see their visual environment through pictures, graphic organizers, and charts. The students used visual tools to help reinforce visualization embedded in the writing process. The code motivation and learning to see assisted in answering the subquestions of the case study.

Limitations

The context and timeframe of the case study do not mirror the traditional duration of the school year. Although students accomplished a lot in the

3½-week summer tutoring period, their ability to continue to develop the concepts and repeated visualization–writing links appears limited in the regular classroom. Due to the study's narrow time span, any changes to the students' writing levels may not be representative of any changes that may occur using the same techniques over the traditional school year.

Additionally, the study participants' sample size is small although the 19 students selected for analysis offered diversity in demographics. Furthermore, teachers selected the students to attend the camp because of their academic needs. As a result, those selected to attend summer school were categorized as struggling learners and were not representative of an entire population of students in a classroom.

Results and Discussion

I identified the spring 2007 district writing criterion-referenced test (CRT) for students in first through fifth grades as a baseline writing level for selected summer participants. Kindergarten students do not take the CRT. Therefore, I assessed each kindergartener's first journal entry according to the 6-Trait Analytical Model (Spandel, 2004) criteria for the traits of Ideas, Organization, and Conventions. Kindergarten teachers usually assess these traits at the end of the school year. I averaged the 6-Trait scores from the baseline to determine the overall score and corresponding writing level of Not Yet (1), Emerging (2), Developing (3), Effective (4), and Strong (5; NWREL, 2004). I assessed the writing piece from the end of the summer tutoring camp in the same manner as the baseline.

A holistic analysis of the 10 primary students' 6-Trait scores for Ideas, Organization, and Conventions revealed an increase from the baseline to the final writing. The Ideas and Conventions traits showed the most improvement.

Some students assessed below a 3 in the baseline assessments; however, by the final piece, all primary students scored a 3 or higher on grade-level appropriate traits.

The intermediate camp consisted of 9 second-, third-, and fourth-grade students. Scores in the traits of Ideas, Voice, and Conventions increased from the baseline to the final writing. The overall scores for Word Choice and Sentence Fluency remained the same for the duration of the summer tutoring program.

Writing Level

The baseline writing level was taken from the district's spring 2007 CRT writing scores. Classroom teachers assessed the students' CRT using the 6-Trait Analytical Model (Spandel, 2004). The traits analyzed at each grade level for the baseline writing assessment corresponded with the traits assessed for the final writing piece. To replicate the same procedure for determining the writing level, I averaged the traits to the nearest whole number.

For the baseline, one student was assessed as Not Yet, two students were assessed as Emerging, eight students were assessed as Developing, and eight students were assessed as Effective. The final writing levels for the 19 participants fell into two categories: Developing and Effective. Three of the four kindergarten students increased their writing level. Four first-grade students increased their writing level from Developing to Effective. Two first-grade students remained at the Effective level.

The results for the intermediate writing camp differ considerably from the primary writing camp. More of the primary camp students increased their assessed writing levels. In the primary camp, 7 of 10 students increased at least one writing level. Of the remaining 3 primary students, 2 students did not change writing levels and 1 student decreased by one level.

In the intermediate group of students only 2 of 9 students increased writing levels while 5 of 9 did not change. The remaining 2 of 9 intermediate students actually decreased by one level each in the baseline versus final writing piece comparison. Overall, 9 of the 19 students increased from their baseline to final writing level, 7 students did not change, and 3 students decreased from their baseline writing level to their final writing level.

Motivation

Motivation appeared in 259 instances of my field notes and interviews describing how the actual experience provided an idea for writing. Teachers commented how the field experiences gave students a better idea of what to write because they provided real-world experiences that gave students the details and schema needed to write an exemplary piece. For example, a second-grade boy commented how he stared at the turkey vulture at the nature center for a long time because he knew he wanted to draw and write about it because he had never seen one before. Similarly, a fourth-grade girl recounted an experience where she learned about the parts of a catfish that gave her an idea to draw and then write about a fish. Most of the students reported they got their ideas to write from the field experiences. This is indicative of the scores for the Ideas trait in both the primary and intermediate writing camp.

Learning to See

Through minilessons offered by teachers, students learned to see their visual environment as a tool to help them write. Students looked at word wall charts, digital photographs, and their own art and writing. The strategies students used to observe their environments differed as much as their abilities. A first-grade boy provided two examples of his learning to see during an interview. The first example referred to a minilesson to help students with spelling. The second example described how a visual tool in the room gave him an idea to draw. He was not the only student who expressed how looking around the room helped him brainstorm ideas about which to write. A third-grade girl discussed how her visual environment inspired her when she gets stuck. She said, "I just look at the picture for 10, 20 seconds and I just figure it out." A fourth-grade girl commented how looking at digital photographs helped her remember information to give her "ideas and creations."

> "I just look at the picture for 10, 20 seconds and I just figure it out."

How Visualization Helped

The 6-Trait scores and writing levels of the primary students experienced a more positive increase than the scores and writing levels of the intermediate students. Perhaps students in the intermediate camp thought drawing was not suited to their developmental stage because in intermediate classrooms the predominant way to communicate is through language. Even though students in the intermediate writing camp could draw detailed pictures, further study is needed to explore why intermediate writers did not experience as high of an increase on the 6 Traits as the primary students. Observations concluded the primary students used the drawings created in the writing process as a way to scaffold their learning and become more independent writers.

Visualization embedded in the writing process encouraged drawing as a form of brainstorming. Students drew, colored, painted, and used clay to make visual representations of their ideas. The students, excited about their visual creations, wanted to share their work. These visual representations evolved into writings.

Students commented that their motivation to write stemmed from their use of imagination and art, as well as the freedom to choose what to write. The teachers believed the minilessons taught the students to observe their visual environment. This included how to read and use a word wall, which contributed to the students' growth in word choice. An intermediate teacher commented that to know what to write, students had to learn how to refer back to the details they incorporated in their drawings. Once students accomplished this task, students who revised their writing also wanted to revise their drawings so they corresponded. When students are actively engaged and using different parts of their brain and multiple senses, they are motivated to share their art and writing samples.

Implications

It appears visual activities as precursors to writing have the potential to enhance students' writing abilities in a number of ways. Therefore, primary and elementary teachers might consider adding these types of visualization in the writing process during the standard 10-month school year. Visual activities include word walls, book illustrations, field experiences, digital photographs, and drawing or modeling.

The instructional time period during summer school was three hours a day, which provided an uninterrupted amount of time to focus on writing. Graves (2003) suggests a writing block should be at least 45 minutes a day three days a week. But teachers face increasingly demanding schedules and often do not have time to devote to a writing block of 45 minutes every day. Perhaps school districts might consider scheduling longer blocks of time for writing instruction.

If teachers cannot take students on out-of-school field trips that provide stimulation for writing, they might consider inviting guest speakers to their classrooms, such as community service professionals or animal experts. In addition, teachers might write grant proposals that could provide money to purchase digital cameras and enhance printing capabilities to enable students to see and recall vivid details about their surroundings and experiences.

Words of Advice

- The success of the program depends on the knowledge of the teachers. Teachers need to be trained before summer school begins. Teachers should be informed of their expectations before agreeing to teach.

- Lessons should be planned before the program begins and lessons should have clear, measurable objectives.

- Teachers should be open to innovative instruction during summer school instead of using a prescribed program. They should feel comfortable developing creative lessons and expect to be engaged in teaching. If teachers are expected to coteach during summer school, they need time to get to know their partner's teaching style and personality before summer session begins.

- Classrooms should maintain a low student–teacher ratio. Small class sizes provide time for teachers to assist students frequently and to provide direct instruction. Teachers should implement visualization embedded in the writing process slowly through modeling. Minilessons provide the direct instruction students need to learn techniques to help them write. The summer tutoring program teachers believed minilessons influenced the observed increase in the 6-Trait scores.

- Be consistent with implementation of visualization embedded in the writing process to provide a routine and structure that helps students succeed. Atwell (1987) asserts that predictable routines make it easy for students to write. Visualization embedded in the writing process is important for every writing assignment, not just for the district test at the end of the year.

- Results of summer school final assessments should be shared with the school district to help with the design of future summer programs. Ultimately, the participating teachers should share techniques used in the summer school program with other teachers during the school year to implement learned strategies.

REFERENCES

Andrzejczak, N., Trainin, G., & Poldberg, M. (2005). From image to text: Using images in the writing process. *International Journal of Education & the Arts, 6*(12), 1–17.

Atwell, N. (1987). *In the middle: Writing, reading, and learning with adolescents.* Portsmouth, NH: Boyton/Cook.

Bogdan, R., & Biklen, S.K. (2003). *Qualitative research for education: An introduction to theory and methods* (4th ed.). New York: Allyn & Bacon.

Calkins, L.M. (1994). *The art of teaching writing* (2nd ed.). Portsmouth, NH: Heinemann.

Davidson, J.L. (1996). *My block and beyond: A documentation of how drawing in conjunction with writing contributes to the thinking process.* Unpublished document. (ERIC Document Reproduction Service No. ED 406300)

Efland, A.D. (2002). *Art and cognition: Integrating the visual arts in the curriculum.* New York: Teachers College Press.

Graves, D.H. (2003). *Writing: Teachers & children at work* (20th anniv. ed.). Portsmouth, NH: Heinemann.

Hortin, J. (1983). Visual literacy and visual thinking. In L. Burbank & D. Pett (Eds.), *Contributions to the study of visual literacy* (pp. 92–106). Blacksburg, VA: International Visual Literacy Association.

LeCompte, M.D., & Schensul, J.J. (1999). *Analyzing and interpreting ethnographic data.* Walnut Creek, CA: Altamira.

Morgan, D.L. (1997). *Focus groups as qualitative research* (2nd ed.). Thousand Oaks, CA: Sage.

Nia, I. (1999). Units of study in the writing workshop. *Primary Voices, 8*(1), 3–11.

Northwest Regional Educational Laboratory. (2004). *6+1 Trait writing.* Retrieved April 12, 2007, from www.nwrel.org/assessment/about.php?odelay=1&d=1

Olbrych, E. (2001). Revising teaching: Drawings, writing, and learning with my students. *Primary Voices, 10*(2), 10–18.

Patton, M.Q. (1990). *Qualitative evaluation and research methods* (2nd ed.). Newbury Park, CA: Sage.

Piaget, J., & Inhelder, B. (2000). *The psychology of the child* (2nd ed.). New York: Basic.

Spandel, V. (2004). *Creating writers through 6-trait writing: Assessment and instruction* (4th ed.). Boston: Pearson.

Stake, R. (1995). *The art of case study research.* Thousand Oaks, CA: Sage.

Vygotsky, L.S. (1978). *Mind in society: The development of higher psychological processes* (M. Cole, V. John-Steiner, S. Scribner, & E. Souberman, Eds. & Trans). Cambridge, MA: Harvard University Press.

Yin, R. (1989). *Case study research: Design and methods* (Rev. ed.). Newbury Park, CA: Sage.

ABOUT THE CONTRIBUTOR

Erin K. Jurand *is a National Board Certified teacher with a Generalist/Middle Childhood certification and seven years of elementary classroom experience. She completed her Ph.D. at Kansas State University, Manhattan, Kansas, USA, in 2008, and is an adjunct professor at American University, Washington, DC, USA. Her research focuses on how to embed visualization in the writing process, and her dissertation was selected to present at Topeka's Capitol Research Summit. She received the International Reading Association 2007 Eleanor M. Johnson Outstanding Literacy Classroom Teacher award. Other awards include the Kansas State University 2005 and 2008 Outstanding Graduate Student in Education Award. She is also a member of the National Writing Project, after attending the Flint Hills Summer Institute in 2005. E-mail: jurand@ american.edu*

CHAPTER 15

Media Literacy Summer Camp: What Works and Why

*James L. Welsh, Deborah A. Kozdras, James R. King,
and Jenifer Schneider*

We're in Dressing Room 2 in the basement of the historic Tampa Theatre, a grand 1920s movie palace. Although the Tampa Theatre has always been primarily a movie palace, since opening day in 1927 live performers have also graced its stage, so this room has hosted thousands of performers over the years—from silent film stars to crooners to rock bands. On this day, though, Dressing Room 2 hosts four 9-year-old filmmakers putting the finishing touches on their very first film. Alan, Chad, Craig, and Joseph (pseudonyms) have turned the dressing room into an editing suite for their movie. Over the preceding four days, they've each played a part—multiple parts, actually—in the creation of their masterpiece. From brainstorming to scripting to storyboarding to videotaping, these boys have done it all. Now they are editing their movie with the guidance of their camp counselor. At this point in the process, their counselor has decided to take on the role of editor, with hands on the computer controls, but still leaving all editing decisions to the young filmmakers. Earlier, the counselor had each of the boys experience what it is like to be in the editor's chair, listening carefully to input from collaborators and assembling the raw footage. With the premiere less than an hour away, the counselor has decided to take over the controls to make sure the boys meet their deadline. At each decision point, he asks the boys what they want to do, executes their decisions quickly, and directs them to the next choice.

The teaching decision (to operate the computer and execute the boys' decisions) is one of hundreds each of the five counselors at this moviemaking camp has had to make over the course of the weeklong experience. The counselors know that the young filmmakers learn the most by making the decisions and experiencing the filmmaking process directly. The counselors also know that product is important to everyone, these boys included. The boys, as well as those in other groups in the camp, must have a product for the premiere, and the fastest way to make that happen is for the counselor to take the reins. This situation exemplifies the decision structures that teachers must navigate to facilitate the successful completion of digital video products in small groups.

Literacy Tutoring That Works: A Look at Successful In-School, After-School, and Summer Programs, edited by Janet C. Richards and Cynthia A. Lassonde. © 2009 International Reading Association.

On the surface, this camp is about kids making movies. But, underneath this surface, there is literacy work going on. Like their counselor, these boys also made hundreds of decisions over the course of the week. They chose one camera angle over another because they learned that different shots are used to communicate different types of information. They made compositional choices about the actions and dialog of their characters in scriptwriting because they wanted their film to reflect their beliefs about fairness, determination, and cooperation. They carefully chose music, sound effects, and visual effects based on what they were trying to achieve with their audience. On the surface, they made a movie about characters from a video game. Beneath the surface, they wrote a story for an authentic audience; they selected elements from a variety of semiotic systems; and they constructed a genre-specific, multifaceted narrative film. They also recognized the similarity between what they had done and what countless professional filmmakers do when they create film adaptations of characters from other media. The camp is a literacy camp because of what happens underneath. When the camp is over, the kids are able to strategically deploy the video text making techniques that they learned in camp. They can communicate with an audience through film more effectively than they could before the camp.

"Let's Make Movies" began in the summer of 2004 as "Kids Make Movies," a collaboration of the Tampa Theatre and the Florida Center for Instructional Technology (FCIT), a center at the University of South Florida College of Education. In 2004, FCIT's director took a few members of his staff into the Tampa Theatre for two weeks as an experiment. FCIT staffers were accustomed to training preservice and inservice teachers in many different types of software and instructional strategies, including digital video. FCIT had the expertise and the equipment. Tampa Theatre had an amazing space, a dynamic community relations director, and extensive contacts within the community. For two weeks, the trainers, most of whom had experience as K–12 teachers, were camp counselors. Each summer since, the camp has grown and changed, adding both instructional elements and traditions, as FCIT staff and Tampa Theatre staff learned. During the summer of 2007, the camp's current lead instructor

(a doctoral student in Literacy Studies and the lead author of this chapter) invited a research team to observe the camp. The researchers soon realized that the campers were engaged in high-level literacy activities. Since that summer, the data from the camp has been continuously reviewed, yielding a number of interesting findings, some of which are presented here.

In 2008 we offered four one-week movie-making camps at the Tampa Theatre. A total of five USF College of Education students and graduates collaborated with the camp director (Welsh, the lead author) and acted as camp counselors. Participants (students between the ages of 9 and 16) created stop-motion animation and short films in small collaborative groups over the course of each one-week session and presented their creations on Friday of each week in a film festival format. The lead instructor, along with two other members of the research team, observed the process and the products of the camp. The goals of the research were to document the use of literacy skills among participants engaged in creating digital media and to study the interaction between students and counselors in new literacy settings to inform teacher training and teacher preparation.

The campers learn filmmaking by making films. Individual literacy constructs of film are transferred to the campers by teaching practices that labeled the constructs during their uses in production. For instance, many scenes in films and television shows begin with an "establishing shot"—an exterior shot showing the place where the action of the following scene will occur. Nearly every episode of the television series *The Brady Bunch* started with an exterior shot of the Brady house. This shot tells you where we are and may carry other information, like the time of day. At the camp, the students are shown examples of this type of shot. It is labeled as an establishing shot, its purpose is described, and then the students shoot establishing shots. Subsequent to the camp, when watching television, they will always recognize the establishing shots within a show. Did they need to know the name and function of this shot to understand its use as a consumer? No, but now that it is known to them, they can strategically deploy this literacy construct within their own media production and in their critical consumption of others' media products. Labeling the filmic and cinematic elements (Metz, 1974) makes those elements portable and gives these young filmmakers power.

The most important work of the camp is literacy work. Campers and counselors learn about communication, collaboration, and compromise over the course of the week. This important work depends upon certain essential conditions. Some relate to pedagogy, but others relate to seemingly mundane choices, such as software and equipment. Although these elements are incidental to the intellectual work of the camp, they are no less essential to the success of the camp than the instructional approach of the counselors. The conditions present at the camp are described in this section for the benefit of others who may wish to create a similar environment. The choices of equipment and instructional logistics represent the lessons learned over four summers of camp.

We believe that having professional educators as camp counselors makes a tremendous difference in the quality of the camp experience. The counselors take an active role within each group. In some ways, this camp resembles an apprentice model and one therefore might expect the counselors to have professional expertise in film production, but this is not the case. Professional filmmakers do not necessarily have the ability or the desire to transfer skills to novices, nor would they necessarily know how if they wanted to do so. Instead, these teacher/counselors understand how to teach communication, and communication is at the heart of filmmaking.

In addition, this camp depends upon having a lead instructor with some knowledge and experience of filmmaking. This experience base includes the technical operation of the equipment and a general knowledge of how visual storytelling is traditionally executed in film and television. The lead instructor also functions as technical support for the equipment and trains the campers and the counselors in its proper operation. These three functions—lead teacher, filming technician, and visual storyteller—are fulfilled by one person at our camp, but could be addressed by different people.

Vital to the functioning of the camp is the support staff within the theatre. First and foremost among these is the theatre's public relations manager, who tirelessly promotes the project, handles all registrations, and manages the day-to-day logistics of drop-offs and pick-ups. She also interacts with local media for news coverage of the camp.

The camp employs a utilitarian approach to equipment and software (see Table 15.1). Consumer-grade materials allow for a moderate technology learning curve, so that instructional time can focus on learning techniques and literacy strategies. Although the equipment is simple, the techniques are professional and effective. For a detailed description of the equipment and software used at the camp and the philosophy used to select it, please visit the summer camp website, fcit.usf.edu/lmm.

In the first few years of the camp, editing and instruction took place in the main auditorium of the theatre at long tables set up to skirt the stage. While the ambiance of a 1927 movie palace simply cannot be matched, that arrangement required setting up and tearing down all of the tables, chairs, and computers every day due to the nightly use of the theatre to screen movies. Instruction and editing now take place primarily in the recently created green room—a

small lounge for performers just off of the main auditorium.

Instructional Sequence and Patterns of the Camp

Each week of the camp has a morning session from 9 A.M. to noon and an afternoon session from 1 P.M. to 4 P.M. Each session starts with a gathering of the whole camp where we briefly discuss the day's agenda. About halfway through each daily session, the camp gathers again in the main auditorium for a popcorn break. During the popcorn break, the campers watch short films, music videos, and excerpts of feature films and discuss the ways that filmmakers present their ideas. (Examples of these discussions can be found in the Results section.)

Learning the Tools of Visual Literacy

On the first two days of the camp, the campers are assigned to different small groups for each activity. Instructional activities and minilessons cover the operation of the camera, basic editing, lighting, recording sound, simple special effects, acting, scriptwriting, and storyboarding. That's a lot of ground to cover in a short amount of time, but at least half of the participants in any session are returning campers. Because all of the films are group projects, no one person needs to master all aspects of the filmmaking process. Informal peer teaching occurs throughout the camp.

Brainstorming Ideas

During one of the second-day activities, each camper writes treatments (brief descriptions) for three different movie ideas. This is an individual activity and it is one of the quietest

Table 15.1 Materials Needed for Camp	
Equipment	Laptop computers
	Video cameras
	Tripods
	Microphones
	Work (clamp) lights
	Extension cords
Software	iMovie
	iStopMotion
	Garageband
	Celtx
Consumables	Paper
	Videotapes
	Storyboard blanks
	Project planning sheets

moments of the entire week. Most of the campers have been thinking of topics for their final movie at least since the camp began, but some quieter campers may not find it easy to tell others about their ideas. This activity helps generate many different ideas and it helps get everyone's ideas on the table. Next, in small groups the campers share the ideas they have written. After that, all of the campers reassemble in the main auditorium and they are asked to share a movie idea that they really liked from the small-group setting that was not their own. Finally, thoroughly stimulated and having heard many different ideas for movies, the campers are advised that all filmmaking is about compromise and that they will need to be willing to adapt their vision for a film to the other people in their final group.

The campers are asked to get up, move around, and sit with the group with whom they would like to work. The counselors monitor the forming groups and mediate any issues that emerge. The process is typically quick and free from controversy, although it can appear momentarily chaotic. In some cases, the counselors resemble stock traders, calling out things like, "I've got two for a ghost story here. Anyone else for a ghost story? Looking for two more...." The campers are steered toward groups of three to five. Although the procedure works well, counselors are prepared to resolve a number of issues, including groups that are too small (1 or 2), groups that are too large (6 or 7), individuals who are unwilling to compromise, and campers unable to decide which group to join. Because they have been grouped differently for each activity up to that point, even campers who arrived at the camp without knowing anyone have had multiple interactions with others by the time they are asked to choose groups. Often students who came in knowing what movie they wanted to make or with whom they wanted to

work change their minds during the activities of the first few days. While the groups are forming, each counselor chooses the group with which he or she will work. By the end of day two, campers have formed a group around a movie concept and have learned basic strategies of filmmaking.

Developing Ideas and Organizing

After the groups are formed, each group starts writing a project description—a brief synopsis of the film they will make, including identification of audience and purpose. Next, the group starts writing their script and creating storyboards. The filmmakers are guided in this process to rely on a three-act story structure commonly used in professional screenwriting. The writing is collaborative, often with the counselor acting as scribe while the young filmmakers walk, talk, and barter through the composition process. This process continues into day three.

Revising for Voice, Word Choice, and Audience

When scripts and storyboards are ready, filming begins. During the process of filming, important aspects of composition continue. Script revisions happen spontaneously as students respond to the creative and technical needs of the production (i.e., How do we show the audience that someone falls from a balcony? How can we strengthen the genre elements within our movie?). Most groups begin filming on day three, begin editing on day four, and finish their movie on day five, sometimes within minutes of the big-screen premiere. On day five, families are invited one hour before the end of the session and the whole camp gathers to watch the first screenings of the films, in the main auditorium of historic movie palace that has hosted premieres for over eight decades.

Questions Guiding the Research

This study is part of a larger ethnographic research project that investigated a moviemaking summer camp over two summers.

- What are the moviemaking strategies used by student filmmakers? How can these strategies and the participants' perspectives be useful to classroom teachers?
- What is the teaching approach used by the camp counselors?

To investigate our research questions, we used a variety of participant-observation methods (Patton, 2002), including visual ethnography (Pink, 2002), that resulted in our data.

Theoretical Background and Perspectives

Teaching media literacy through digital videos is a well-practiced approach. Although media literacy has been a part of learning standards in countries such as Canada, England, and Australia for as long as 20 years, these standards have not gained cultural capital amid the accountability and testing furor in the United States. In light of current capabilities of video-editing software (such as Windows MovieMaker and iMovie) and websites that enable easy distribution of video (such as YouTube), it is easier than ever to create and distribute professional-looking short movies, complete with titles and special effects. Screen activity is a central part of life for American children and teens. A recent survey by the Kaiser Family Foundation (2001) found that children ages 8 to 18 spend almost eight hours per day using media

(television, movies, video games, books, recorded music, Internet, magazines, newspapers). Many literacy educators recognize the need to respond to what have been called the new literacies (New London Group, 1996) in order to make education more relevant (Hobbs, 2006).

Methodology

Our researcher perspective is informed by hermeneutics in that our interpretations of meaning relied on "the cultural context in which it was originally created as well as the cultural context within which it is subsequently interpreted" (Patton, 2002, p. 113). Patton further notes that hermeneutics offers an interpretive perspective for texts (broadly construed here to include video) that is dependent on intended meanings and cultural contexts. From these perspectives, interpretations can never be absolute. Within a hermeneutic approach, a researcher constructs reality with the help of the participants. Our variation of hermeneutics was communitarian grounded theory (Kozdras, Welsh, & King, 2008).

> Interpretations of meaning relied on "the cultural context in which it was originally created as well as the cultural context within which it is subsequently interpreted."

Participants

During the summer of this study, the participants included four counselors who were recent graduates of the University of South Florida and one counselor who was a preservice teacher. Each camp included 20 young filmmakers, in 8 sessions, for a total of 160 students. The students were grouped by grade level (grades 3 through 5, 6 through 8, and 9 through 12) and included a balanced mix of males and females.

Data Sources

Data cited in the study come from an ongoing ethnography of the Let's Make Movies Digital Video summer camp. Excerpts are referenced for the month and year in which they were collected.

Data were collected across the four one-week sessions of the camp. The data set included 41 short films made by the campers, observational field notes, audiotaped interviews, videotaped interviews, and video recordings of the processes (composition process videos).

Data Analysis

As a community of researchers informed through a hermeneutic approach, we participated in a process we call a communitarian grounded theory modeling (Kozdras et al., 2008), which we offer as an extension of a traditional grounded theory (Glaser, 2001; Strauss & Corbin, 1998) approach to inductive data analysis. In our communitarian approach, we work as a research team in a continuous reiterative process of intertextual interpretation.

Using communitarian methods in this study, we interpreted the results, reconnected with observational and interview data, subjected findings to intertextual elaborations and extensions, and attempted to connect the ideas of all researchers to the products and to the data collected, through our reiterative interpretation. First, we searched for students' deployment of literacy strategies through the processes. We mined the data sources and participated in communitarian discussions to collaboratively locate these instances of strategy use. Then we searched for teacher strategies deployed during these literacy activities that served to guide, build, or otherwise encourage student motivation and success with the use of their chosen strategy. Through a communitarian grounded theory approach to analysis, we considered a multiplicity of perspectives in a reiterative interpretive process.

> Today, students are taught the language of the traits so they can consciously attend to these key features as they write.

Limitations

This study is a description of a particular movie camp, and is not intended to be generalized. Most of the participants were white and paid tuition to attend the camp. Furthermore, the study is situationally specific. We also recognize that the digital media literacy and popular culture inclusion that were enacted at the camp may not be considered sufficiently studious in other educational settings, such as schools. These limits, however, do not preclude others from using the model and the methods that we report here.

Results

Looking for Literacy: 6+1 Traits of Writing

In analyzing the students' moviemaking processes, we found that their behaviors were easily categorized according to the 6+1 Traits writing model. Based on the work of Diederich (1974), the 6+1 model was originally developed to provide teachers with a common language to use in the assessment of student writing (e.g., ideas, organization, voice, word choice, sentence fluency, conventions, and presentation). However, through efforts of the Northwest Regional Educational Laboratory (NWREL), this writing model has evolved into a method of *teaching* writing (Arter, Spandel, Culham, & Pollard, 1994). Today, students are taught the language of the traits so they can consciously attend to these key features as they write (Culham, 2003, 2005; Spandel, 2005).

We used our familiarity with the traits to create a strand of analysis of the students' literacy behaviors that was based on the 6+1 Traits model of composing, in this case, digital videos. Student filmmakers brainstormed themes and developed *ideas*. They *organized* their ideas into narrative story structures and inserted authorial *voice* by adapting a certain tone or perspective (e.g., scary, sarcastic, funny). They made specific *word choices* to convey meaning and reworked sentences so that their writing could be read *fluently and for aural prosody*. Although the script wasn't edited for *conventions* such as spelling, capital letters and punctuation, the textual features of the final products (e.g., titles, credits) were reviewed for mechanical correctness. The final product was submitted for *publication* as a movie and shown to family, friends, and theater guests. These elements of the 6+1 Traits model transferred to video composing.

Although the application of writing traits to the scriptwriting processes within moviemaking may seem seductively obvious, we suggest that the 6+1 Traits model more productively maps onto the whole of the digital video production, when that production is understood as the composition of a media text. Therefore, we applied the traits to filmmaking as an entire composition process. Although writing a script can be interpreted as analogous to writing a story, we broaden the analogy to say that creating a movie is analogous to writing a story. Some *ideas* occur during the scriptwriting process, but many others occur later in filmmaking, often while developing creative solutions to problems during production. The *organization* of the movie, which finds its final form at the end of the filmmaking process during video editing, roughly parallels the organizational plan developed during scriptwriting, and in this way

scriptwriting parallels the prewriting process in textual storytelling. The *voice* of the filmmaker is evident in choices of camera angles, lighting, and sound effects, as well as the tone of the script used. *Word choice* applies to words spoken by the actors or text that appears on the screen, but can also be interpreted more broadly to include nontextual signifiers (such as the hat a character wears, background music, or a particular camera angle) chosen for inclusion in the movie to convey a piece of information. *Sentence fluency* applies to the flow and pace of the movie. The filmmaker's choices regarding the length of each shot, the number and type of shots in a sequence, and the transitions between the shots establish the "shot and scene fluency" of the movie. *Conventions* of filmmaking involve the expectations of film viewers with regard to the presentation of elements in a film. Conventions help viewers understand the information presented. The *publication* trait involves exporting a final movie for screening at the theatre and inclusion on a DVD of the campers' movies.

Interactions Between Students and Counselors: Describing Camp Counselor Strategies

Several themes emerged from our observations of the interactions between participants in the camp. We believe that these themes have implications for classroom instruction and can point the way toward more successful integration of digital video and other new media literacies in the classroom. Further, we believe that these themes represent essential conditions for the success of this ongoing camp.

VALUING PARTICIPANT IDEAS. Young filmmakers' ideas were valued. All campers were encouraged to create new ideas for movies. The campers wrote the scripts, shot the video, edited the final movies, and made creative decisions throughout the process about their work. The primary job of the counselors was to help the campers realize their own goals for their films, not to control content.

COMPOSITION AND MEANING MAKING. During the creation of products, the counselors employed instructional strategies for writing to support the students' meaning making in digital video. The counselors were trained writing teachers. They supported the campers throughout the process of generating and articulating ideas, creating project descriptions, writing scripts, and composing storyboards.

An example was found during a daily popcorn break. Halfway through each daily session, the camp met as a group in the main auditorium to watch short films, music videos, and clips from feature films and discuss film techniques and visual storytelling. The lead instructor would typically show a short clip and guide a discussion about the clip. For example, in one clip a boy looks across a crowd and sees a girl in whom he is romantically interested. After showing the clip, the following conversation between instructor and students took place (instructor's words are in italics):

> *How do you think the boy felt about the girl?*
> He liked her.
> *How did the filmmaker tell you that? How did you know?*
> When he looked at her, the romantic music started.
> *Okay, so, one way the filmmaker told us was with music. What else did you notice?*
> It went to slow motion.

> *Aha, the shot of her was in slow motion. Anything else?*
> The look on his face when it cut back to him.
> *Right. So the filmmaker used the different shots to show that the boy was looking at the girl, and then music and slow motion and the boy's acting helped us know how he felt. Can you think of other ways music can be used to tell us what is happening?* (Researcher notes, July 2007)

SCAFFOLDING. In addition to the use of teaching strategies for composition, the counselors also demonstrated a systematic approach to learning that involved scaffolding. In another example, the campers watched a humorous short film in which a piano falls on a character from high in the air, in the style of an old cartoon. The lead instructor's words appear in italics in the resulting conversation.

> *What happened there?*
> A piano fell on him.
> *How do you think they got that shot? The one where we see him standing there and we see the piano fall on him?*
> Maybe with computers.
> *It could be computers. They do a lot of special effects with computers. How else could the director have gotten that shot?*
> With a green screen?
> *Sure, that could be it. Let's take another look at that shot in slow motion. What do we actually see?*
> It doesn't really look like it's hitting him.... Maybe it didn't really fall where he was! Maybe he was standing behind where it fell so that it would look like it fell on him from where the camera was!

Wow. You're right. The director could have gotten that shot just by lining things up so that they looked like they overlapped. Those are all good ideas. So, there are lots of ways you could make it look like something is happening that didn't really happen. (Researcher notes, July 2007)

This interaction highlights the students as the generators of solutions to the posed problem of representation. The counselor consistently honors the partial correct responses and then probes for additional solutions to the problem. We see this strategic form of interaction as a powerful and professional discourse that leads students to more sophisticated acts of meaning making.

ACTIVE LEARNING. Throughout the camp, the lead instructor and the counselors used minilessons to introduce the campers to a variety of filmic and cinematic concepts in which they could use their projects. Directly following these minilessons, the students were able to try out these concepts. The students' trials occurred in a low stakes, supportive environment where the students explored the concepts, skills, and strategies in an authentic setting.

Discussion

In this camp, the students began the moviemaking process by generating ideas and brainstorming and recording possible topics. This initial brainstorm included consideration of character, setting, dialogue, and plot (typical of classroom writing). However, during this initial brainstorming, the students also discussed stage directions, filmic and cinematic elements, character movement/action, props, and sound effects. In this respect, we find that the act of composing movies extends students' traditional composing

strategies by creating the need for students to write and think, not only with words, but also with sound, movement, music, dialogue, and images. Moviemaking is a tool that has the potential to change students' cognition while allowing students to simultaneously fulfill an important component of the learning process—personal entertainment and anticipated audience reaction. Creative freedom was the essence of the moviemaking camp, and the counselors' understanding of multimedia literacy processes and the director's careful attention to the camp culture and pedagogy achieved it.

> The content of the films reflected the interests and opinions of the filmmakers and not the goals, no matter how beneficent, of the camp staff.

The knowledge, values, attitudes, and behaviors that are characteristic of the camp are the result of intersecting discourses, including filmic, youth culture, pop culture, teacher culture, and performance discourses. Camp isn't school. With that in mind, the camp staff seeks to create an atmosphere where the young filmmakers can express their visions without imposing an adult agenda. The content of the films reflected the interests and opinions of the filmmakers and not the goals, no matter how beneficent, of the camp staff.

That being said, the camp staff does have an agenda and does have goals. Acknowledging that fact is important in protecting the expression of the campers. As adults associated with the theater (a nonprofit cultural organization), and the university (a public institution of higher learning), we would be thrilled to see movies where young people express a love of learning and culture—"serious" content that would indicate that the camp is doing "important things." In contrast to our bourgeois desires, the topics more commonly chosen by young filmmakers include horror movies, teen comedies, superhero movies, and parodies of any film or television show released in the preceding six months. The adults can suggest, but the campers choose. The camp staff imposed some limitations on the amount of violence that can be shown during the films, on the use of copyrighted material, and on the use of last names. Otherwise, the choices are the campers'. If it were any other way, the campers would lose ownership of the creative process, and they wouldn't come to camp.

The main mechanism of control of content is the promotion of campers' audience awareness. Counselors ask questions such as the following:

> You will be sitting next to your mother on Friday while she watches this film. What do you want to include? There are a lot of younger kids that will be watching this movie. What do you think is appropriate for them? (Researcher notes, July 2007)

Although awareness of audience can be used to limit objectionable content, the primary use is to promote good filmmaking and good storytelling. The counselors must continually interrogate the process so that the filmmakers' vision can be successfully communicated to the audience. Counselors ask questions such as the following: "Does this shot tell the viewers everything they need to know to follow what is going on? Will the audience get this joke? Is this line of dialogue clear enough to convey your message?" (Researcher notes, July 2007)

Active engagement is a key element of camp culture. The counselors are not babysitters, making sure the kids are entertained until their families return. The counselors are professional educators and the lead teacher counts on them to bring many elements of their teaching with them into their roles at the camp. Although the adults do not control the content of the movies, neither do they sit back and leave the campers to fend for themselves. Counselors are cheerleaders, coaches, referees, mentors, and advocates. They make sure that all of the members of a group are heard in the process of filmmaking and they keep the groups focused.

Traditional literacy skills are situated in a multimedia context at the camp. The process of generating ideas, writing a script, and creating storyboards incorporates writing and reading as part of a meaningful undertaking. Scripts and storyboards are not graded. Counselors insist that campers create them, but they do so as knowledgeable mentors, guiding the students toward their own goals of self-expression through filmmaking. This is how films are made. Students used traditional literacies extensively in the preparation of their digital media products. Yet, the use of traditional literacies, like reading and writing storyboards, disappears inside the final product. This means that when viewers see the final product, it is unlikely that they will intuit the reading and writing that contributed to its creation.

The braiding of literacy and video tasks in the digital video opened unique teaching and learning complexities. The campers saw many examples of short films and segments from feature films throughout the week. The examples served as students' learning occasions. The counselors also saw these examples with the students, and understood the literacy learning potentials within the example films. Because the counselors were experienced in teaching reading and writing, the films were viewed as instances of literacy teaching opportunities. For example, these counselors used the concepts of story structure to guide the campers. In fact, we saw the counselors effectively balancing many, often oppositional, agendas. This is why it was important to have trained educators as counselors. We maintain that these teachers were uniquely able to balance their appreciation of their students' moviemaking desires with the educative demands of "getting the movie done."

Camp organizers must be well prepared and provide a wide variety of meaning-making examples and options, but also give the students creative control of their projects. This balance is vital to ensuring engagement and personal investment on the part of the students. Learning happens when students must make difficult content decisions based on the perceived needs of the intended audience. When content and creative decisions are made by teachers on behalf of the students, the learning potential of the activity may be limited. Teachers' navigation of these complex, situated problems requires a tightly organized superstructure. The structural elements of the camp must be in place long before any kids show up to become campers.

Implications

During the 2007 camp, Steve Persall, a reporter from the *St. Petersburg Times*, spent one morning observing and interviewing many of the students and counselors. In the subsequent newspaper article, Persall (2007) notes that counselors in the camp incorporate reading and writing strategies with strategies to teach digital video production. "Components designed to build reading skills have a few words changed to suit another medium. They [counselors, camp director, researchers] use words like 'transmediation' and 'culture convergence' when children aren't listening, like cagey parents hiding broccoli under pudding" (¶ 14). We feel this "broccoli under pudding" approach is what makes the camp a place to which the young filmmakers willingly return every year. As researchers, we feel the pudding comes from honoring the filmmakers' ideas and helping them to achieve their goals.

We do this by using good teaching strategies, not an artificially manufactured set of skills. Learning appeared in a real literacy context— filmmakers used traditional storytelling strategies, film language, and digital technology skills to achieve their ultimate goal of communicating an idea to an audience. Counselors (in the roles of writing teachers) used well-established instructional approaches that helped their fledgling writers generate interesting texts for real audiences.

Future Directions for Research

The students' appropriation of popular culture content suggests a careful reexamination of schools' reluctance to embrace popular media. Furthermore, the affordances for teaching that are part of digital video production must be considered seriously by educators for the teaching opportunity structures that they provide. In attempts to sanitize classrooms, or to adhere to canonical, "high culture" texts, schools may also be prohibiting productive, effective affordances for the creation of powerful literacies. What is missing from the current study, and remains to be investigated, is the interplay of teacher-as-authority identities, grading requirements, and curriculum pressures, to name a few of the situated variables that will affect students' creation of digital literacies when they are imported into classrooms.

Recently, Bruce (2008) has recommended studying "the compositional aspects of multimedia through the lens of video" (p. 13). In the current study, we took an analytic look and found that digital video composition strategies emerged as similar to those employed during

> We feel the pudding comes from honoring the filmmakers' ideas and helping them to achieve their goals.

composition of traditional written texts. We continue to investigate the parallels between the processes of digital video composition and traditional writing, and we continue to work on understanding the unique approaches that teachers can expect to use when they engage with digital literacies in their classrooms.

Further, although we identified teacher actions that supported successful composition, these results cannot be generalized to other settings. What remains to be studied is how to capture the pudding of the camp experience and apply it to the broccoli of a school setting. We are addressing this transfer in a series of reports on what we call fast literacy (King, Schneider, Kozdras, Minick, & Welsh, 2007), which is the purposeful grafting of media literacy practices into classroom contexts.

Words of Advice

To conduct a similar camp experience, we suggest that the counselors should be elementary or secondary educators. Counselors who have taught in classrooms are more likely to understand ways to teach both literacy and filmmaking while allowing students to maintain ownership of their movies. We suggest the following guidelines in selecting counselors:

- Educators should serve as counselors.
- Counselors should emphasize filmmaking as a mode of communication.
- Education counselors must value student ownership and control of filmmaking.
- Effective counselors teach hands-on skills, in context, at the point of need.

NOTE

For more information about this project, visit the University of South Florida Contemporary Literacies Collaborative at www.fcit.usf.edu/clc/.

REFERENCES

Arter, J., Spandel, V., Culhan, R., & Pollard, J. (1994, April). *The impact of training students to be self-assessors of writing.* Paper presented at the annual meeting of the American Educational Research Association, New Orleans, LA.

Bruce, D.L. (2008). Multimedia production as composition. In J. Flood, S.B. Heath, & D. Lapp (Eds.), *Handbook of research on teaching literacy through the communicative and visual arts* (Vol. 2, pp. 13–18). Newark. DE: International Reading Association; Mahwah, NJ: Erlbaum.

Culham, R. (2003). *The 6+1 traits of writing: The complete guide grades 3 and up: Everything you need to teach and assess student writing with this powerful model.* New York: Scholastic.

Culham, R. (2005). *The 6+1 traits of writing: The complete guide for the primary grades.* New York: Scholastic.

Diederich, P.B. (1974). *Measuring growth in English.* Urbana, IL: National Council of Teachers of English.

Glaser, B.G. (2001). Doing grounded theory. *Grounded Theory Review, 1*(1), 1–18.

Hobbs, R. (2006). Multiple visions of multimedia literacy: Emerging areas of synthesis. In M.C. McKenna, L.D. Labbo, R.D. Kieffer, & D. Reinking (Eds.), *International handbook of literacy and technology* (Vol. 2, pp. 15–28). Mahwah, NJ: Erlbaum.

Kaiser Family Foundation. (2001). *Kids and media @ the new millennium.* Retrieved November 29, 2007, from www.kff.org/entmedia/1535-index.cfm

King, J.R., Schneider, J.J., Kozdras, D., Minick, V., & Welsh, J. (2007, April). *Transforming literacies into designs: Fast literacies, faster pedagogies.* Paper presented at the annual meeting of the American Educational Research Association, Chicago, IL.

Kozdras, D., Welsh, J., & King, J.R. (April, 2008). *Kids make movies: Investigating media literacies in action through rhizomatic and memetic analyses.* Paper presented at the annual meeting of the American Educational Research Association, New York City.

Metz, C. (1974). *Film language: A semiotics of the cinema* (M. Taylor, Trans.). Chicago: The University of Chicago Press.

New London Group (1996). A pedagogy of multiliteracies: Designing social futures. *Harvard Educational Review, 66*(1), 60–92.

Patton, M.Q. (2002). *Qualitative research and evaluation methods* (3rd ed.). Thousand Oaks, CA: Sage.

Persall, S. (2007, July 20). Movie moguls in the making. *St. Petersburg Times.* Retrieved November 29, 2007, from www.sptimes.com/2007/07/20/Features/Movie_moguls_in_the_m.shtml

Pink, S. (2002). *Doing visual ethnography.* London: Sage.

Spandel, V. (2005). *Creating writers through 6-Trait writing assessment and instruction* (4th ed.). Boston: Allyn & Bacon.

Strauss, A.L. & Corbin, J.M. (1998). *Basics of qualitative research: Techniques and procedures for developing grounded theory* (2nd ed.). Thousand Oaks, CA: Sage.

ABOUT THE CONTRIBUTORS

James L. Welsh *is a graduate student at the University of South Florida College of Education, Tampa, Florida, USA. He is also the director of Contemporary Literacies Integration for the Florida Center for Instructional Technology (FCIT). As part of his duties for FCIT, he works with undergraduates and faculty on effective technology integration, and he directs a digital video summer camp series. Formerly, he taught third and fourth grades. E-mail: jlwelsh@coedu.usf.edu*

Deborah A. Kozdras *is a graduate student at the University of South Florida College of Education, Tampa, Florida, USA. She is currently working on her dissertation, focusing on the multimedia composition process. She has written a number of lesson plans for ReadWriteThink.org that involve digital media literacy. Formerly, she taught elementary school in Canada. E-mail: demikoz@aol.com*

James R. King *is a professor of Literacy Studies at the University of South Florida, Tampa, Florida, USA, where he teaches graduate and undergraduate courses in literacy. His research foci include early literacy intervention, media literacies, social justice, and service learning. E-mail: king@tempest.coedu.usf.edu*

Jenifer Schneider *is an associate professor in Literacy Studies at the University of South Florida, Tampa, Florida, USA, where she teaches graduate and undergraduate courses in literacy. Her research interests include writing, workplace literacy, and new media literacies. E-mail: jschneid@tempest.coedu.usf.edu*

CHAPTER 16

The Community Literacy Club: Engaging and Having Impact on Communities of Teachers and Learners

Joyce C. Fine and Lynne D. Miller

It's Friday of week three, Museum Day, and it's also the end of a three-week summer tutoring program. We're all tired—tutors, professors, and students alike—from the intensity, but our adrenalin is pumping. The students come out of their classrooms with their tutors and wait eagerly with mounting excitement for their families to arrive. They are ready to share their original, informational books with their families and their community.

Families arrive and the students escort them to their rooms and seat them in a semicircle before taking their places next to their tutors. The families, too, feel a sense of tension and some anxiety. They all wonder if their children, struggling readers, will be able to stand in front of a group and read the books they have created.

The pairs of tutors and students share their topics: passions they explored, researched, and then wrote about in informational books. Students know it is their choice whether to read their book aloud with everyone's attention focused on them.

As each child has his or her turn, families empathize with their children. When it comes to Nick's turn, his dad holds his breath as Nick proclaims, "I want to read my book." As he reads, his dad takes deep breaths. Nick reads well, with expression. When he comes to the end, a tear flows down his dad's smiling face and he mouths "You did it!" to Nick.

The joy of shared literacy and a sense of accomplishment within a community of students, families, and teachers comes after much dedicated effort and from many years of planning and refining all the details for the Diagnosis and Remediation courses mandated by the state of Florida for Master's of Science in Reading Education programs. These refinements have resulted in an integrated set of courses delivered as an intensive summer experience and known as the Community Literacy Club (CLC). This name is an extension of Smith's (1988) concept of the literate world of people who regard themselves as readers and who thoughtfully read to become knowledgeable and to gain pleasure.

Literacy Tutoring That Works: A Look at Successful In-School, After-School, and Summer Programs, edited by Janet C. Richards and Cynthia A. Lassonde. © 2009 International Reading Association.

Typically, master's candidates enroll in the Diagnosis and Remediation classes and become part of the CLC experience after taking approximately half of the other required courses in the program. The candidates already hold teacher certification at the elementary or secondary levels. As experienced teachers, the candidates bring vast amounts of knowledge and skills to the clinical setting. The CLC experiences provide an opportunity for candidates to integrate what they already know about teaching and learning with what they are learning in depth about literacy development.

We, the authors of this chapter, initiated integration of courses when we recognized candidates in our program needed to learn more about how to support "the whole child" rather than just how to "test and teach," which is typical of the outdated medical model of diagnosis and remediation. We wanted candidates to experience different types of assessment, build relationships with struggling literacy learners, and understand the many ways students make gains with strategically planned authentic literacy lessons.

The CLC reflects collaboration between the university and a local public school. The university is located in a large, diverse, urban area of the United States, an excellent laboratory for educating candidates to teach diverse populations. We wanted this clinical practicum to be on site, where our teacher candidates would be situated in the context of the challenges of working with students who are low-performing, English-language learners (ELLs) from low socioeconomic status families who have few resources to support their children's literacy learning.

The school provides classroom space for tutoring and whole-group sessions, access to some materials and library books, the use of their laminating machine and materials, janitorial or custodial services, and access to computers, internet, and printers. Most important, the school supplies students by actively recruiting them to participate. School personnel often stay on site to supervise students after tutoring until they are picked up by their families.

The university supplies the tutors, who are candidates in the Master's in Reading program. Many of the tutors are second-language learners themselves. After having passed a program-required benchmark assessment of their knowledge of content and pedagogy in reading, candidates are allowed to participate in the CLC. There are a few resources supplied by the university such as book-binding combs and name tags that amount to under US$100. The university also supplies a classroom for four class sessions on campus prior to the start of tutoring.

The tutors provide their own school supplies. They purchase a trifold board for creating a literacy niche (a place to celebrate the different literacy accomplishments of the students), and they construct an assessment toolkit (a plastic file box containing copies of assessments in organized hanging file folders). Tutors also supply paper, pencils, crayons, and a variety of magazines for sources of information and pictures.

We meet with the tutors for four night classes prior to beginning the CLC. During these four sessions, we help the tutors make connections between theory and practice related to assessment and instruction. At the last of these night classes, families and students come to meet the tutors. The tutors are as anxious to meet the students as the students are to meet their tutors. The tutors interview the families and collect important background information about the students' physical development, family life, and instructional history. During these interviews, the students participate in a group activity. If time permits, the tutor may begin assessment of his or her student.

Once the daytime tutoring sessions begin, tutors meet from 9 A.M. to 1:30 P.M. every day for three weeks, Monday through Friday. One-on-one tutoring sessions with the students occur between 10:00 A.M. and 12:00 P.M. daily. Tutors receive university class instruction before and after tutoring sessions—9 A.M. to 10 A.M. and 12:00 P.M. to 1:30 P.M. While tutors work with their respective students one-on-one, tutor–student pairs are clustered in small communities in different classrooms. During the two-hour block of tutoring, there is a shift of focus each hour (see Table 16.1).

During Part I, the first week, the tutoring time is divided into an hour in which tutors assess students using a variety of specific informal instruments to develop a multidimensional profile of students' literacy development. This is followed by an hour of diagnostic teaching, a time of instruction in which tutors carefully observe students' behaviors to gain insight on the processes each uses as he or she tackles literacy tasks. As part of diagnostic teaching, each tutor works with his or her student to construct a personalized literacy niche. The niche is centered within an open trifold board that contains sam-

ples of the student's work and other types of text used to support literacy instruction.

During Part II, the next two weeks of the practicum, the first hour consists of instruction targeted to address specific areas of need identified from the assessments. This targeted instruction is based on reflection using a Decision Chart (see Figure 16.1). The tutors use various text genres to teach targeted areas for growth. They use many informational books so students will become familiar with this genre, in particular, for as Duke (2000) notes, informational text builds prior knowledge necessary for content area reading.

The second hour's activities center on mentoring literacy. For this hour's focus, the tutor acts more as a caring big sister or big brother rather than a teacher. This change in instructional approach requires the tutor–student pair to find common bonds based on interests and passions. Using a Venn diagram, they write what they really like to do and would want to do if they could do anything. They explore their passions to identify some aspect that is meaningful to both. This might be an admiration of animals, a favorite music genre, or a particular sport. When tutors and students have identified a shared passion, they think about what information they might each need if they were to make their own informational book about their interests or goals. The bookmaking process in-

Table 16.1 Split Focus for the Different Parts of Tutoring

Part I. Assessment (Week 1)		Part II. Intervention (Weeks 2 and 3)	
10:00–11:00	Diagnosis (using a variety of assessment tools)	10:00–11:00	Intervention (using instruction targeted to address identified needs)
11:00–12:00	Diagnostic Teaching (using teaching activities and observing students' responses)	11:00–12:00	Mentoring Literacy (using literacy to explore a mutually identified interest)

Figure 16.1 Decision Chart for Diagnosing Reading Difficulties

Purposes:
- To reflect on student's ability to use the components in fluent reading
- To support the assessment of individual students and determine the proficiencies and difficulties for appropriate services
- To communicate assessment information to various audiences for both accountability and instructional purposes
- To participate in a study group to identify, plan, and be able to implement professional development to ensure the teaching of the needed components

Process:
1. List the data/facts/insights from the interviews, assessments, observations, or your reflections in the first column. Use as many rows as needed.
2. Identify the areas for growth/needs from each in the second column. Some sources will reveal the same needs as other sources. Look at which areas emerge from several sources. Which ones are the most critical? Which ones will contribute to the most significant gains if addressed in the time you have to tutor?
3. Select the appropriate materials—resources, processes, strategies, and activities for targeted instruction that will help the student the most in the time you have to tutor.
4. Write the rationale for targeting these areas of growth for your student.
5. Be ready to communicate the areas for growth/needs and the plan for intervention with your colleagues and other stakeholders.
6. Write how to explain, demonstrate, and use guided practice for at least three of the strategies.
7. Be ready to support other tutors to find appropriate materials or to read further on the identified areas for growth/needs.

Examiner's Name _____ Student's Name _____

Sources (interviews, IRI, assessments, observations, reflections)	What was indicated as an area for growth or a need?	Which areas for growth/needs will I target? Which resources, processes, strategies, or activities will help?

cludes using print and nonprint technology to research information. Students use the information to write about their passion by creating an original informational book while tutors write about their passion in their own informational book. As we saw in the opening vignette, they share these books on Museum Day.

Museum Day begins with a 15-minute, student-led conference in which students share with a family member or caregiver what they accomplished during the tutoring sessions. Items displayed on the literacy niche often become prompts for what students elect to share. Families or caregivers may then ask questions. Finally, tutors provide other information about each student's literacy development, including specific recommendations for continued literacy support at home. Following the conferences, the small communities of tutors, their students, and the visitors gather together to appreciate their books and artifacts from the Community Literacy Club. Students may just show and tell about their book or read it to the group.

Questions Guiding the Research

Our specific questions for this study were the following:

- What is the impact of the CLC experience on the comprehension development of elementary school struggling readers?
- What is the impact of the CLC experience on the fluency development of elementary school struggling readers?

Theoretical Background and Perspectives

The Community Literacy Club is based on social interactionist theoretical perspectives (Cox, 2002), which posit that multiple factors influence students' literacy development and must be considered during assessment. Therefore, we bear in mind a physical, sociocultural, emotional, and psycholinguistic framework and assess each of these areas to determine the extent to which they support or hinder students' literacy achievements.

The physical aspect includes general state of health, including chronic situations and temporary ones. Chronic conditions may involve hearing or vision conditions while temporary ones may be ear or eye infections, lack of sleep, or inadequate nutrition. If chronic or temporary conditions are neglected, they may interfere with the ability of students to focus on learning. Sociocultural aspects have to do with the context for engaging in literacy, students' educa-

tional history, and the degree to which families support and value literacy. The social context is important because many students will engage in literacy activities if they feel challenged, but not pressured. Some will be more engaged if the literacy activities occur outside of school rather than in school. The description of students' educational history is critical to determine whether they have participated in consistent, high-quality instruction or if they have experienced adverse academic effects from situations such as frequent mobility (Smith, Fien, & Paine, 2008). The third sociocultural aspect, degree of family support, includes the value placed upon the acts of reading and writing, whether students are encouraged to read and write at home, or if literacy activities are looked upon as a waste of time.

Emotional influences include students' attitudes toward reading, interests in reading, and motivation to read, as well as their perceptions of themselves as readers. Do students enjoy reading and listening to stories? Are students willing to take risks to develop as readers? The emotional filters through which students approach literacy learning influence greatly their intention to read, their engagement in wide reading, and, ultimately, their decisions to be readers. These social-emotional filters are often rooted in cultural identities (Gee, 2001).

In this framework, psychological aspects include students' experiences and background knowledge in general and with language specifically. Students' experiences and knowledge directly affect their ability to construct meaning, to develop requisite vocabulary, and to comprehend. The extent of their previous interactions with text also plays a significant role in students' abilities to use this literacy knowledge as they seek to gain meaning from more and more complex levels of text.

In addition, we assess students' phonemic awareness, phonics skill, fluency, comprehension, and vocabulary. Because of the emphasis placed on these five components of reading by the Report of the National Reading Panel (National Institute of Child Health and Human Development [NICHD], 2000), tutors employ a variety of informal assessments to determine what students already know and what students need to learn next. Instruction follows that integrates the physical-social-emotional-psycholinguistic framework with the effective instruction of these five areas.

There are other theoretical perspectives that have contributed to our decisions about choices of materials and activities other than assessment and intervention. One important consideration is introducing informational books (Duke & Bennett-Armistead, 2003). These books address students' interests, enhance their vocabularies, expand their knowledge of the natural and social world, and are a key to later success because they provide a bridge to reading textbooks in the content fields. Another major theoretical contribution is the importance of students having positive interactions with adults in learning language and literacy (Vygotsky, 1934/1986). When interactions are developmentally appropriate, beginning where students are and leading them forward with the aid of more knowledgeable adults (Vygotsky, 1934/1986), these interactions have the potential to lead students to higher levels of functioning (Karpov, 2003).

Because many of the students who participate in the CLC are stalled at the emergent or beginning stage of reading, we wanted to look at the interaction of fluency and comprehension. We knew a proficient reader is usually a fluent reader and a fluent reader has more cognitive energy to focus on meaning.

In *What Really Matters for Struggling Readers*, Allington (2001) relates the classic study on fluency by Clay and Imlach (1971) in which they noted how beginning readers who made the greatest progress were able to read in five- to seven-word phrases with appropriate intonation and with four to five times as many spontaneous self-corrections as the students who made the least progress, who were reading in only one- to two-word segments. Allington continues with several hypotheses for why some students who can read accurately still do not read with phrasing and intonation. One of these hypotheses is the result of contextual factors such as the increased number of times disfluent readers are interrupted and the resulting trained behaviors to wait for confirmation from a teacher or tutor after each word.

> Students with access to appropriate levels of text and uninterrupted reading settings gain greater fluency.

According to Allington (2001), students with access to appropriate levels of text and uninterrupted reading settings gain greater fluency. Another hypothesis is a developmental lag in students who read accurately but not fluently. These students, whom Valencia and Buly (2004) describe as Slow Comprehenders, may have a lack of automaticity and a slow reading rate. They do not choose to spend time reading and because of the lack of volume in reading, they do not develop phrasing and intonation, falling further and further behind their peers. A third hypothesis is that some students have limited experiences with being read to and hearing fluent readers. Allington relates research by Dowhower (1987) and Rasinski (1990) who write about the importance of providing models of fluent readers. These studies have used repeated readings either assisted by a teacher or with students rereading text multiple times. Either way, repeated reading has a positive effect on students' fluency.

More recent neurological research states there is much known about the difference between the kind of fluency that is a goal for students as they begin to read and fluency at the later stages (Wolf, 2007). In the beginning stages, there is a focus on gaining automaticity to call words and to understand them in context. Following that stage, the more traditional type of fluency—including accuracy, rate, and prosody—is possible (Wolf, 2007). This latter type of fluency is most often what is considered necessary for reading comprehension.

Methodology

Our study involves one summer's 26 tutor–student pairs in the CLC. We employed a pre- and poststudy assessment design. Because the focus of this study was to document the overall impact of the CLC on participating students' literacy development in the areas of comprehension and fluency, we did not use a control group.

Participants

The 26 students in this study were all identified as struggling readers by their schools' teachers. Many were second, third, or fourth graders who had been retained at least once. Most were ELLs. In addition to having difficulty in developing literacy abilities, several of the students had other issues such as autism, abandonment, adoption, attention-deficit hyperactivity disorder, or an array of learning disabilities.

Data Sources

Within the first three days of the CLC, tutors assessed students' comprehension using the Beginning Reading Inventory: Pre-Primer Through Grade Twelve and Early Literacy Assessment (BRI, 2005) and students' fluency by using procedures in *Fluency: Strategies and*

Assessments (Johns & Berglund, 2005). Tutors reassessed students' comprehension and fluency within the last three days of the CLC, using the same instruments, but selected alternative passages as prescribed in the procedures, given students' developing literacy abilities.

Data Analysis

Each tutor first analyzed data from the assessment instruments. Because of the structure of the Master's in Reading program, most tutors had previously received intensive, explicit instruction in the use of the assessment instruments and in the analysis and interpretation of results in other classes. As part of the CLC course work for tutors, they received additional explicit training with the instruments prior to use with their respective students. We carefully supervised data collection and reviewed tutors' analyses and interpretation for completeness and accuracy.

Limitations

The CLC approach is particular to our intensive summer literacy program through a university–school collaboration. Because of the unique structure of this experience, a limitation of this study is that there was no control or comparison group. Other limitations are that some parents decide to take family vacations so that some students are not able to complete the program, or sometimes behavioral issues preclude poststudy testing.

Results and Discussion

As measured by the BRI (2005), results indicated the comprehension of 53% of the students increased between one and three reading levels in a three-week time span (see Table 16.2). The comprehension of 19% of the students remained

Table 16.2 BRI Results (*N* = 26)

Pre-Post Increase in Reading Levels (*BRI*)	Number of Students	Percent of Students
1 reading level	11	42
2 reading levels	7	7
3 reading levels	1	4
Remained at same reading level	5	19
Insufficient data*	2	8

*Missing postassessment data.

Table 16.3 Fluency Results (*N* = 26)

Pre-Post Reading Level for Fluency Assessment	Number of Students	Percent of Students	Increase in WCPM
Increased 1 level	13	50	Range: 12 to 68 1 student > 60 3 students > 50 4 students > 30 2 students > 20 3 students > 10
Increased 2 levels	2	8	Range: 9 to 21 1 student > 20 1 student > 1
Remained at same assessment reading level	10	38	Range: 7 to 62 1 student > 60 1 student > 50 2 students > 30 2 students > 20 2 students > 10 2 students > 1
Insufficient data*	1	4	

*Results indicated that the CLC experience had an overall positive impact on students' comprehension and fluency development.

at the same overall reading level. Two of the students in this study completed the prestudy assessments but were not able to complete the poststudy assessments. One of these students was noncompliant, refusing to complete the assessments, and the family of the other student took him on vacation before the CLC ended. There was insufficient data to assess how the CLC experience affected the reading comprehension of these two students.

As measured by fluency procedures described in Johns and Berglund (2005), results indicated that 96% of the students increased their fluency (see Table 16.3). There was insufficient poststudy assessment data for the remaining 4% of the students. Fifty-eight percent of the students not only increased in their words-correct-per-minute (WCPM) scores but also were reading instructional-level material more fluently at one to two grade levels higher on the poststudy assessment than on the prestudy assessment. Although 38% of the students' BRI reading levels remained the same from the beginning to the end of the CLC, all of these students increased in their WCPM scores for the fluency assessments, several by more than 50 WCPM, meaning that they are, perhaps, moving to the second stage of fluency in which students are able to focus on overall meaning.

Implications

It is notable that 19 students gained in comprehension and 25 students gained in fluency while participating in the CLC for a relatively short period of time, three weeks total. Because the treatment incorporated many aspects to support students, one might say that the improvements stemmed from the interaction of the overall CLC experience. One of the criticisms of the National Reading Panel Report (NICHD, 2000) is the omission of research that looks at the interaction of different aspects of reading such as fluency with comprehension or between instruction and various personal and social-contextual factors (Braunger & Lewis, 2006). The CLC creates an environment in which students experience the interaction of different aspects of reading. The different aspects combine to create a nurturing community, one in which the whole is greater than the sum of its parts. A challenge to the field remains the dilemma of conducting experimental research to provide evidence of the value of this multidimensional type of intervention.

We designed the CLC based on an evolving integration of research and best practice.

> The different aspects combine to create a nurturing community, one in which the whole is greater than the sum of its parts.

The following reflect some of the quality multidimensional aspects of this experience:

- Tutors and students worked in small communities that gave students a sense of security and the courage to contribute to a community.

- An assessment battery combined with diagnostic teaching provided data to drive instruction.

- A Decision Chart, a graphic organizer for synthesizing all assessment results, linked assessment to intervention.

- Tutors were able to increase their abilities to use evidence from assessment data to systematically and effectively address the learning needs of each student.

- Integration of intervention and the mentoring literacy events expanded students' perceptions of the uses of literacy.

- ELLs can build literacy through these intense learning experiences.

- Mentoring has the potential to meet students on mutual interest levels and associate literacy with pleasure and fun.

- Use of informational literature from multiple sources, including technology, for reading and bookmaking led students to higher levels of literacy performance.

- Creating a literacy niche personalized students' own print-rich environment, encouraged engagement with literacy and learning processes, and provided tangible, positive social feedback.

- The culminating event, Museum Day, celebrated students' work without distracting from the focus of instruction and gave an authentic purpose for creating informational books.

Words of Advice

The following practical ideas contributed to the overall success of the CLC for students and tutors:

- Letters of invitation for students to join the CLC must stress to families the need for them to bring their children for the duration of tutoring for the *entire* three-week CLC experience. Some families will look at a free clinic as babysitting until they are ready to leave for vacation. This kind of noncommittal thinking causes problems for the students and the tutors.

- Take names of students who return their permission slips in the order in which they are returned to the school. Maintain a waiting list of those who would be willing to come if some students drop out of the tutoring program.

- The success of quality tutoring programs is directly linked to supervision by literacy professors who are experts in the field and who can give immediate counsel and corrective feedback to tutors who are emerging literacy professionals.

NOTE

The authors wish to thank the administrators at the school, the families who brought their students regularly, the tutors who worked so diligently to make a difference to the students, and the students who worked so earnestly to learn to read and who, subsequently, learned to love reading.

REFERENCES

Allington, R.L. (2001). *What really matters for struggling readers: Designing research-based programs*. New York: Longman.

Braunger, J., & Lewis, J.P. (2006). *Building a knowledge base in reading* (2nd ed.). Newark, DE: International Reading Association; Urbana, IL: National Council of Teachers of English.

Clay, M.M., & Imlach, R.H. (1971). Juncture, pitch, and stress as reading behavior variables. *Journal of Verbal Learning and Verbal Behavior, 10,* 133–139. doi:10.1016/S0022-5371(71)80004-X

Cox, C. (2002). *Teaching language arts: A student- and response-centered classroom* (4th ed.). Boston: Allyn & Bacon.

Dowhower, S.L. (1987). Effects of repeated reading on second-grade transitional readers' fluency and comprehension. *Reading Research Quarterly, 22*(4), 389–406.

Duke, N.K. (2000). 3–5 minutes per day: The scarcity of informational texts in first grade. *Reading Research Quarterly, 35*(2), 202–224. doi:10.1598/RRQ.35.2.1

Duke, N.K., & Bennett-Armistead, V.S. (2003). *Reading & writing informational text in the primary grades: Research-based practices*. New York: Scholastic.

Gee, J.P. (2001). Reading as situated language: A sociocognitive perspective. *Journal of Adolescent & Adult Literacy, 44*(8), 714–725. doi:10.1598/JAAL.44.8.3

Johns, J.L., & Berglund, R.L. (2005). *Fluency: Strategies and assessments* (2nd ed.). Dubuque, IA: Kendall/Hunt.

Karpov, Y.V. (2003). Development through the lifespan: A neo-Vygotskyian perspective. In A. Kozulin, B. Gindis, V.S. Ageyer, & S. Miller (Eds.), *Vygotsky's educational theory in cultural context* (pp. 138–155). New York: Cambridge University Press.

National Institute of Child Health and Human Development. (2000). *Report of the National Reading Panel. Teaching children to read: An evidence-based assessment of the scientific research literature on reading and its implications for reading instruction* (NIH Publication No. 00-4769). Washington, DC: U.S. Government Printing Office.

Rasinski, T.V. (1990). Effects of repeated readings and listening-while-reading on reading fluency. *The Journal of Educational Research, 83*(3), 147–150.

Smith, F. (1988). *Joining the literacy club*. Portsmouth, NH: Heinemann.

Smith, J.L.M., Fien, H., & Paine, S.C. (2008). When mobility disrupts learning. *Educational Leadership, 65*(7), 59–63.

Valencia, S.W., & Buly, M.R. (2004). Behind test scores: What struggling readers *really* need. *The Reading Teacher, 57,* 520–531.

Vygotsky, L.S. (1986). *Thought and language* (A. Kozulin, Trans.). Cambridge, MA: MIT Press. (Original work published 1934)

Wolf, M. (2007). *Proust and the squid: The story and science of the reading brain*. New York: HarperCollins.

ABOUT THE CONTRIBUTORS

Joyce C. Fine *is an associate professor and the program leader for Reading Education at Florida International University, Miami, Florida, USA. She has designed and taught on-site, in-school, after-school, and summer practicum courses focused on*

elementary and adolescent learners, for undergraduate and graduate candidates. She was a member of the National Commission on Excellence in Elementary Teacher Preparation sponsored by the International Reading Association and a member of the Reading First Teacher Education Network. E-mail: Joyce.Fine@fiu.edu

Lynne D. Miller *is an associate professor and the program leader for Elementary Education at Florida International University, Miami, Florida, USA. Her research interests revolve around the toe-to-toe teaching of reading to individuals of all ages who struggle in their development of literacy skills and abilities. She has designed and delivered in-school and summer practicum experiences to support the literacy development of students and to facilitate the professional development of undergraduate and graduate candidates in the area of Reading Education. E-mail: Lynne.Miller@fiu.edu*

APPENDIX

An Annotated Bibliography
Relevant to Literacy Tutoring Programs

Compiled by Susan Bennett

Allor, J., & McCathren, R. (2004). The efficacy of an early literacy tutoring program implemented by college students. *Learning Disabilities Research and Practice, 19*(2), 116–129.

> Allor and McCathren examined the effectiveness of a structured tutoring program over a two-year period. Education majors volunteered to tutor reading to at-risk first graders in an urban school. The noncertified tutors received minimal training. However, the authors provided scripted, integrated plans and found one-to-one instruction can be effective.

Anderson, D. (2002). Interfacing email tutoring: Shaping an emergent literate practice. *Computers and Composition, 19*(1), 71–87.

> Anderson examined e-mail tutoring interfaces and analyzed the collaboration in online writing labs to identify literacy techniques that were similar to those used in face-to face-tutoring. Similar to other literacy approaches, e-mail tutoring faces the issue of how to keep the student motivated and engaged.

Cohen, P.A., Kulik, J.A., & Kulik, C.L.C. (1982). Educational outcomes of tutoring: A meta-analysis of findings. *American Educational Research Journal, 19*(2), 237–248.

> Cohen, Kulik, and Kulik conducted a metaanalysis of educational literature on the effects of tutoring. They analyzed 65 tutoring programs with diverse variables and settings. The results confirm that tutoring programs have an affirmative effect on tutors and the students they tutor. Students develop positive attitudes toward the subject matter and improve academically as well.

D'Agostino, J.V., & Murphy, J.A. (2004). A meta-analysis of Reading Recovery in United States schools. *Educational Evaluation and Policy Analysis, 26*(1), 23–38.

> D'Agostino and Murphy coded and analyzed 36 studies that examined Reading Recovery, a literacy intervention. The article demonstrated that some research lacks rigor and possesses methodological limitations that leave inconclusive results as to the effectiveness of Reading Recovery. However, results indicated positive effects on standardized assessments for discontinued and continued students.

Davenport, S.V., Arnold, M., & Lassmann, M.E. (2004). The impact of cross-age tutoring on reading attitudes and reading achievement. *Reading Improvement, 41*(1), 3–12.

> In this study, 10 fifth-grade students with learning disabilities tutored kindergarten students two times a week for 30–40 minutes. The researchers examined the effect of cross-age tutoring on reading attitudes and achievement for both fifth-grade and kindergarten students. The researchers contend the fifth-grade students made progress in achievement and developed more awareness as readers. Davenport, Arnold, and Lassmann state that without a control group, evidence is inconclusive in regard to positive attitudes toward reading.

Devin-Sheehan, L., Feldman, R.S., & Allen, V.L. (1976). Research on children tutoring children:

A critical review. *Review of Educational Research*, *46*(3), 355–385.

> Devin-Sheehan, Feldman, and Allen examined research about tutoring, focusing particularly on the findings and variables that affect the outcome of the tutoring. Examples of these variables include race, socioeconomic factors, sex, and age. Results indicated that tutoring is valuable to diverse populations. However, according to the authors, tutoring research lacks rigor and theoretical foundations.

Elbaum, B., Vaughn, S., Hughes, M.T., & Moody, S.W. (2000). How effective are one-to-one tutoring programs in reading for elementary students at-risk for reading failure? A meta-analysis of the intervention research. *Journal of Educational Psychology, 92*(4), 605–619.

> The authors conducted a meta-analysis on 29 studies that examined one-to-one reading interventions. The findings do not support evidence of significant benefits of Reading Recovery when compared to other one-to-one interventions. The results suggested that one-to-one tutoring with trained tutors facilitates positive gains in reading achievement for elementary students at risk of failure. Two studies demonstrated no significant difference between the benefits of small-group and one-to-one instruction.

Ellson, D.G., Barber, L., & Harris, P. (1968). A field test of programmed and directed tutoring. *Reading Research Quarterly, 3*(3), 307–367.

> Female high school graduates received seven 3-hour training sessions in order to participate in this study. The researchers compared programmed tutoring with direct tutoring. The programmed tutoring provides control of the tutor's behavior, and the direct tutoring follows the classroom teacher's reading instruction. The results suggest tutoring programs provide significant improvement for reading achievement when they supplement classroom instruction. According to Ellson, Barber, and Harris, the programmed tutoring was more effective than direct tutoring.

Fitzgerald, J. (2001). Can minimally trained college student volunteers help young at-risk children to read better? *Reading Research Quarterly, 36*(1), 28–46.

> First and second graders identified as at risk of failure in school participated in this study. Thirty-nine college students with diverse backgrounds volunteered and received minimal training to tutor the students from four different elementary schools. The tutoring sessions followed Reading Recovery instructional plans and met twice a week for 40 minutes. Overall, students made improvement on reading achievement, and the tutors and supervisors thought the tutoring was beneficial.

Friedland, E.S., & Truscott, D.M. (2005). Building awareness and commitment of middle school students through literacy tutoring. *Journal of Adolescent & Adult Literacy, 48*(7), 550–562.

> Preservice teachers enrolled in a literacy course tutored seventh and eighth graders who were at least two grade levels behind in reading. Data included tutors' daily reflections, surveys of students' reactions, and interviews with the students. The reflections revealed preservice teachers benefited from the literacy course. In addition, the students developed an awareness of their literacy development through choice and relationship building.

Hart, S.M., & King, J.R. (2007). Service learning and literacy tutoring: Academic impact on preservice teachers. *Teaching and Teacher Education, 23*(4), 323–338.

> Hart and King investigated the impact of service learning on content acquisition. The participants were preservice teachers enrolled in a Linking Literacy to Assessment course. Two sections of preservice teachers tutored at a community center as a service learning experience. The other two sections tutored independently in the field for one hour a week. The researchers suggest the service learning experiences facilitated increased academic achievement as well as motivation to learn course content.

Hock, M.F., Pulvers, K.A., Deshler, D.D., & Schumaker, J.B. (2001). The effects of an after-school tutoring program on the academic performance of at-risk students and students with LD. *Remedial and Special Education, 22*(3), 172–186.

> In this article, the researchers reported results of two studies to investigate after-school tutoring programs. Participants included university students and the junior high students they tutored. The re-

searchers found that the tutors taught strategies successfully through the junior high students' assignments. The results indicated that the junior high students improved on quizzes and tests. In addition, these students continued to thrive after completion of the tutoring program.

Houge, T.T., Peyton, D., Geier, C., & Petrie, B. (2007). Adolescent literacy tutoring: Face-to-face and via webcam technology. *Reading Psychology*, 28(3), 283–300.

> Houge, Peyton, Geir, and Petrie investigated the literacy growth of 25 middle and high school students tutored by secondary education majors. These students were delayed readers and writers who struggled with content texts. One group of students received face-to-face tutoring and the other group received tutoring through webcam technology. The researchers confirmed their hypothesis that students experience success whether tutoring is one-to-one or via webcam.

Jacobson, J., Thorpe, L., Fisher, D., Lapp, D., Frey, N., & Flood, J. (2001). Cross-age tutoring: A literacy improvement approach for struggling adolescent readers. *Journal of Adolescent & Adult Literacy*, 44(6), 528–536.

> In this study, 21 seventh-grade students tutored 4 third-grade students for eight months. These seventh graders were more than four grade levels behind in reading and from a low socioeconomic status area; in addition, their first language was not English. The tutors received training for a Strategic Reading plan that incorporated intrinsic engagement with instructional methods. According to the authors, students made improvement in fluency and attitudes, although they were not confident the effect was a result of just the cross-age tutoring. They do believe accountability and the Strategic Reading played a key role in success.

Juel, C. (1996). What makes literacy tutoring effective? *Reading Research Quarterly, 31*(3), 268–289.

> Juel examined 30 tutoring dyads that were tape recorded and videotaped over an academic year. A weak college reader tutored a struggling first- or second-grade reader. Both college and elementary students made significant literacy improvement. Juel identified the success of the first and second graders

as dependent on modeling and scaffolding on the right level. The college students succeeded through self-selected readings, journal entries, tutoring, and the writing of children's books.

Kourea, L., Cartledge, G., & Musti-Rao, S. (2007). Improving the reading skills of urban elementary students through total class peer tutoring. *Remedial and Special Education, 28*(2), 95–107.

> In this article, the researchers used a multiple baseline design to examine the effects of total class tutoring, a peer-mediated intervention, on six at-risk students. Results indicated five of the six students demonstrated significant improvement in sight-word acquisition. Students demonstrated gains in comprehension and fluency in paragraphs with sight words they had learned; however, more research should be conducted. Parents, teachers, and students participated in a survey that revealed they considered the intervention to have had positive effects.

Leal, D., Johanson, G., Toth, A., & Huang, C. (2004). Increasing at-risk students' literacy skills: Fostering success for children and their preservice reading endorsement tutor. *Reading Improvement, 41*(4), 51–72.

> Leal, Johanson, Toth, and Huang conducted this six-year study with six different groups to investigate the effects of preservice tutors' attainment of a reading endorsement, to consider demographic differences, and to identify successful reading strategies. Each student authored a book that the tutors used for reading and writing instruction. The results suggested reciprocal learning for the preservice teachers and students. Both oral reading and listening comprehension increased after the tutoring was completed.

Marious, S.E., Jr. (2000). Mix and match: The effects of cross-age tutoring on literacy. *Reading Improvement, 37*(3), 126–130.

> Marious briefly examined cross-age tutoring studies and found three components for successful programs: training, planning, and techniques. In addition, the author revealed that tutors and students alike made gains in reading strategies and skills; therefore the program was beneficial to all.

Paterson, P.O., & Elliot, L.N. (2006). Struggling reader to struggling reader: High school students' responses to a cross-age tutoring program. *Journal of Adolescent & Adult Literacy*, 49(5), 378–389.

> This article focused on the perceptions and responses of ninth-grade students who tutored second- or third-grade students for an academic year. These participants were struggling readers of diverse ethnicity and low socioeconomic status. The high school students received training and instruction from their teacher and reading specialist on literacy instruction that included different aspects of reading. Paterson and Elliot conducted a constant-comparative analysis of journals, photographs, presentations, and interviews. The study demonstrates the significant role and impact that social constructivism has on reading. The high school students shared similar experiences with the elementary students and improved in their reading knowledge.

Pullen, P.C., Lane, H.B., & Monaghan, M.C. (2004). Effects of a volunteer tutoring model on the early literacy development of struggling first grade students. *Reading Research and Instruction*, 43(4), 21–40.

> University students who were predominately education majors tutored first-grade students who attended 10 different schools. Both control and treatment groups received regular classroom instruction. Additionally, the treatment group received 40 tutoring sessions for 15 minutes over 12 weeks. The tutor used a three-step lesson during each session: rereading with an emphasis on strategies, a running record, and reading a new book. The treatment group demonstrated significant improvement in phonological awareness and decoding skills.

Rush, L.S. (2004). First steps toward a full and flexible literacy: Case studies of the four resources model. *Reading Research and Instruction*, 43(3), 37–55.

> Rush conducted this qualitative, interpretive case study and tutored the participants, two female middle school students and one male. The tutoring program emphasized improvement in reading comprehension and critical thinking. The study suggested the validity of the use of the four resources model as a framework for instruction in the classroom.

Shanahan, T. (1998). On the effectiveness and limitations of tutoring in reading. *Review of Research in Education*, 23(1), 217–234.

> Shanahan reviewed empirical research on various aspects of tutoring in reading. He contended that tutoring facilitates achievement growth and is an effective strategy. However, solid instruction is essential as a basis before tutoring can be effective. According to Shanahan, future research should emphasize a more theoretical approach and focus on the social dimensions of tutoring.

Wasik, B.A. (1998). Volunteer tutoring programs in reading: A review. *Reading Research Quarterly*, 33(3), 266–291.

> Wasik reviewed 17 empirical studies about volunteer tutoring. The three criteria for the selection of the studies were use of adult volunteers, a focus on reading, and implementation with students in kindergarten to third grade. A deficiency exists in volunteer tutoring research due to limited studies with comparison groups. The results show that successful volunteers received training on reading instruction.

Wasik, B.A., & Slavin, R.E. (1993). Preventing early reading failure with one-to-one tutoring: A review of five programs. *Reading Research Quarterly*, 28(2), 178–200.

> Wasik and Slavin reviewed research in order to understand the effectiveness of five reading improvement tutoring programs, such as Reading Recovery and Success for All. They only included 16 studies that compared traditional tutoring to one-to-one instruction by adults of students learning to read in first grade. The most successful programs included instruction by certified teachers and a comprehensive approach to reading instruction.

Wheldall, K., Colmar, S., Wenban-Smith, J., Morgan, A., & Quance, B. (1995). Teacher-child oral reading interactions: How do teachers typically tutor? *Educational Psychology*, 12(3&4), 177–194.

> These authors reported the results of three studies that focused on teachers' or tutors' behaviors while listening to students read. In each study, students' ages ranged from 4–16 and students were low- to average-skilled readers. Overall, findings revealed that most teachers selected books that were below or

above students' instructional level. In addition, the results suggested the majority of teachers were quick to respond to errors, particularly to those of the low-skilled readers, which limited opportunities for students to self-correct. Finally, the authors contended that teachers provided little praise.

ABOUT THE CONTRIBUTOR

Susan Bennett *is a doctoral candidate and teaches undergraduate literacy courses at the University of South Florida, Tampa, Florida, USA.*

She is comanaging editor of the Journal of Reading Education. *Bennett's past experiences as an elementary teacher for six years—including on a Navajo reservation—and as a musician contribute to her research interests, which include culturally relevant pedagogy and creative arts. She is currently in the early stages of her dissertation, which focuses on preservice teachers' perceptions of culturally relevant pedagogy and writing within the community. E-mail: siouxsan99@yahoo.com*

AUTHOR INDEX

Hock, M.F., 208–209
Hoein, T., 36
Hoffman, J.V., 10
Hoover-Dempsey, K.V., 86
Hortin, J., 173
Houge, T.T., 209
Huang, C., 209
Hughes, G.D., 161, 164
Hughes, M.T., 1, 63, 86, 208
Hunt, L.C., Jr., 74
Hyde, A., 24

I

Imlach, R.H., 201
Inhelder, B., 173
Institute of Education Sciences, 63
International Reading Association, 11, 62, 135,
    139, 142, 143, 144
Invernizzi, M., 37, 86, 120, 125
Irvin, J.L., 47
Iversen, S., 63

J

Jacobson, J., 209
Jaggar, A., 98
Jayroe, T.B., 86
Jenkins, J.R., 86
Johanson, G., 209
Johns, J.L., 202, 203
Johnson, R.B., 37
Johnson, T., 29
Johnston, F., 120, 125
Johnston, P.H., 16, 120, 124, 125, 129
Juel, C., 11, 37, 86, 209
Justice-Swanson, K., 24

K

Kaiser Family Foundation, 187
Karpov, Y.V., 201
Kear, D.J., 99, 100, 101, 162
Keehn, S., 11
Kelly, P.R., 42
Kemmins, S., 75
Kerlinger, F.N., 40
Kiger, N.D., 71
King, J.R., 187, 194, 208
Kinzer, C., 11
Klemp, R.M., 47

Klingner, J.K., 49
Knaub, R., 142, 153
Kourea, L., 209
Kozdras, D., 187, 188, 194
Kress, J.E., 60, 61
Krippendorff, K., 122
Kuhn, M.R., 16, 52
Kulik, C.L.C., 86, 207
Kulik, J.A., 86, 207

L

Labbo, L.D., 11
Lacasa, P., 143
Lane, H.B., 210
Lapp, D., 72, 139, 209
Larkin, E., 22, 27, 31
Lassmann, M.E., 207
Lave, J., 142, 144
Leal, D., 209
LeCompte, M.D., 177
Lenters, K., 47
Leu, D.J., Jr., 11
Lewis, J.P., 114, 204
Lipson, M.Y., 100
Liston, D.P., 121
Livingston, A., 62
Lougee, A., 99
Lyons, C.A., 135

M

Mahiri, J., 49
Mahler, J., 22
Marious, S.E., Jr., 209
Martinez, M., 11
Maryland State Department of Education, 70, 74
Mason, J.M., 162
May, J.P., 27
Mazzoni, S.A., 162
McAndrew, D.A., 135
McCathren, R., 207
McGee, P., 11
McGill-Franzen, A., 1, 157
McGlinn, J., 28
McKenna, M.C., 99, 100, 101, 162
McLurkin, D.L., 87
McTaggert, R., 75
Mello, R., 111
Merriam, S.B., 144, 145

Wixson, K.K., 100
Wolf, M., 202

Y
Yin, R., 176
Young, J.P., 53

Z
Zeece, P.D., 28
Zeichner, K.M., 121
Zemelman, S., 24
Zeni, J., 98

SUBJECT INDEX

Note. Page numbers followed by *f* or *t* indicate figures or tables, respectively.